A Chanticleer Press Edition

Taylor's Guide to Ground Covers, Vines & Grasses

Houghton Mifflin Company Boston 1987

Library of Congress
Cataloging-in-Publication Data
Taylor's guide to ground covers, vines & grasses.
(Taylor's guides to gardening)
Based on: Taylor's encyclopedia of gardening.
4th ed. 1961.
Includes index.
1. Ground cover plants.   2. Ornamental
climbing plants.   3. Ornamental grasses.
4. Ground cover plants—Dictionaries.
5. Ornamental climbing plants—Dictionaries.
6. Ornamental grasses—Dictionaries.
7. Lawns. 8. Landscape gardening. I. Taylor's
encyclopedia of gardening.   II. Title: Guide
to ground covers, vines & grasses.   III. Series.
SB432.T38   1987   635.9′64   86-20022
ISBN 0-395-43094-1 (pbk.)

Prepared and produced by Chanticleer Press,
Inc., New York

Designed by Massimo Vignelli

Color reproductions made in Italy
Printed and bound in Japan

First Edition.

DNP   10   9   8   7   6   5   4   3   2   1

Contents

Contributors

Gordon P. DeWolf, Jr., Ph.D.
Coordinator of the Horticulture Program at Massachusetts Bay
Community College in Wellesley Hills, Massachusetts, Gordon P.
DeWolf revised and edited the fifth edition of *Taylor's Encyclopedia
of Gardening,* upon which this guide is based. DeWolf previously
served as Horticulturist at the Arnold Arboretum at Harvard
University and is a frequent contributor to *Horticulture* magazine.

Mary Ann McGourty
Editor of the plant descriptions in this guide and author of most of
the gardening essays, Mary Ann McGourty is the proprietor of
Hillside Gardens, a nursery in Norfolk, Connecticut, that specializes
in uncommon perennials and perennial-garden design and
installation. She and her husband, Fred, grow some 700 kinds of
perennials in their garden.

Frederick McGourty
General consultant for this book, Fred McGourty was editor of the
Brooklyn Botanic Garden handbooks for 18 years and is co-author of
Perennials: How to Select, Grow & Enjoy, published by HPBooks. He
now manages Hillside Gardens with his wife, Mary Ann.

Winton (Woody) Frey
The West Coast consultant for this book, Woody Frey is a professor
of ornamental horticulture at California Polytechnic State University
in San Luis Obispo, California.

Pamela Harper
The principal photographer for this book, Pamela Harper is a
well-known horticultural writer, photographer, and lecturer. Her
articles have appeared in such magazines as *Flower and Garden,
American Horticulturist,* and *Pacific Horticulture.* Harper has also
taken more than 80,000 photographs of plants and gardens.

Gary Koller
Author of the essay on garden design, Gary Koller is Managing
Horticulturist at the Arnold Arboretum in Boston, Massachusetts,
and lectures in landscape architecture at Harvard University.

Katharine D. Widin
Author of the essay on pests and diseases, Katharine Widin holds an
M.S. and Ph.D. in plant pathology. Currently she operates a private
consulting firm, Plant Health Associates, in Stillwater, Minnesota.

Preface

Existing in wonderful variety, ground covers, vines, and ornamental grasses are versatile plants that offer countless possibilities for the landscape. Think of a cool, dark green carpet of periwinkle beneath a tree, a brightly flowered clematis gracing a trellis on a summer's day, or a majestic stand of rushes whispering in the breeze at pondside. These and hundreds more plants are featured in this guide, along with expert advice on how to grow, care for, and use them to create a beautiful and enjoyable environment.

Ground covers are a diverse group of low-growing shrubs, perennials, and even some annuals. An important part of any garden, they link a house with its surroundings and ensure the success of a design scheme by unifying all of the elements—trees, shrubs, walkways, patios, and lawns. Carefully chosen and creatively used, these practical plants can add considerable interest to your home setting.

No one type of plant can fill every need, but many choices exist. There are evergreen ground covers and deciduous ones; some for sun and some for shade; plants with extensive, tenacious roots that help prevent erosion on steep banks; and others suited for areas where rocks or roots make mowing difficult. There are even plants rugged enough to thrive in poor soil or in low light conditions where a lawn might be desirable but cannot be maintained. Large expanses of lawn can be monotonous and the upkeep costly; ground covers are a practical alternative. The economy-minded and creative homeowner can opt for a smaller lawn integrated with other, easy-to-care-for ground covers and have the bonus of various leaf colors, textures, shapes, and even showy flowers from plants that all the while do the job of suppressing weeds.

Even though ground covers are low-maintenance plants, they still require some care and attention. This guide will provide you with all the information you need to have ground covers performing at their best.

Vines and ornamental grasses are also wonderful plants to round out a garden design. A flowering vine clambering over a stone wall or a clump of ornamental grass planted next to a pond can add interest to an area that might otherwise seem dull and ordinary. Vines give a vertical dimension most gardens lack. One vine with handsome foliage can hide an ugly masonry wall, while another on a trellis can take your breath away with the beauty of its flowers. The grasses, long overlooked in this country but now gaining attention, offer an array of new and different textures and forms to traditional border settings. Many are admired for their lovely flowers and seed heads and are exceptionally striking as accent plants.

Whatever your landscape needs, this book will introduce you to a wide range of beautiful plants that in both practical and unusual ways can enhance your surroundings.

Preface

Acknowledgments
Mary Ann McGourty, editor of the plant descriptions and garden essays, gives special thanks to her husband, Frederick McGourty, for his wise counsel, encouragement, and good humor under fire in connection with this project. Many thanks also go to Pamela Harper and to Woody Frey for their advice, and to Marian Appellof at Chanticleer Press for guiding the work along and assembling all the pieces with skill and grace.
Dolores R. Santoliquido and Robin A. Jess executed the plant drawings that appear next to the encyclopedia descriptions. Dolores Santoliquido also illustrated the garden design essay; Mary Jane Spring illustrated the section on pests and diseases; and Alan D. Singer provided the drawings that accompany the other gardening essays. The title page drawing was contributed by Sarah Pletts, and the zone map by Paul Singer.

Introduction

Ground covers are both decorative and problem solvers—some thriving in the shade of trees or where lawns won't grow, others ideal for planting on a bank to prevent soil erosion. Vines trained up an arbor or porch create natural screens and add vertical interest; trimmed down to size, some can be used as ground covers, too. Many ornamental grasses are suited to naturalized plantings or make excellent screens; others are good in borders.

There is no mystery to growing any of these versatile plants—all that you need to know can be found in this guide. Designed for both amateurs and seasoned gardeners, this book makes it easy to cultivate a garden that suits your individual tastes and needs. It can also help you identify plants that you see when you visit gardens and nurseries.

If you have never planted a garden or landscaped your property before, you will find practical tips that will get you started and keep you going. If you have been gardening for years but want to reduce the size of your lawn or perk up your surroundings, you will discover new plants and fresh ways to use old favorites.

How to Use This Guide

This guide contains three types of material: color plates, plant descriptions, and expert articles that guide you through every aspect of growing ground covers, vines, and grasses.

The Color Plates and Visual Key

More than 300 of the most popular and interesting ground covers, vines, and ornamental grasses in cultivation today are illustrated, many with a detail showing seasonal variations such as fall foliage color or ornamental fruit. The color plates are divided into four groups: ground covers that are grown primarily for their foliage; ground covers that are grown for their flowers; vines; and grasses. Within these groups the illustrations are arranged by color and shape to help you select the right plants for the visual effect you want to achieve.

Visual Key

The color section begins with the Visual Key, which shows how the photographs are arranged and gives an overview of the various plant, leaf, and flower shapes.

Captions

The captions that accompany the color plates provide essential information: the seasons during which a plant is most effective in your garden, the soil and sunlight conditions it can tolerate, and the zone to which it is hardy. The captions also give the scientific and common name of the plant and its height. A page reference directs you to the description of your plant in the Encyclopedia of Ground Covers, Vines, and Grasses.

Encyclopedia of Ground Covers, Vines, and Grasses
Here you will find a full description of each plant featured in the
color plates. These descriptions are based on the authoritative
Taylor's Encyclopedia of Gardening, revised and updated for this guide.
Divided into three distinct groups—ground covers, vines, and
grasses—the descriptions within each category are arranged
alphabetically by genus and cross-referenced by page number to the
color plates. Each description begins with a heading indicating the
genus name, followed by the common and scientific family names.
Pronunciation of the scientific name precedes a brief overview of
the genus.

Genus
This section presents the general characteristics of the garden plants
in the genus; the How to Grow section outlines broad growing
requirements for the genus.

Species, Hybrids, and Cultivars
After the genus description, you will find detailed information on
the plants included in the color plates and additional information
about popular cultivars. Each species description includes the zone to
which the plant is hardy. A black-and-white illustration next to a
species description depicts the mature plant, and is representative of
other plants in the genus.

Gardening Articles
Written by experts, these articles explain every aspect of gardening
with ground covers, vines, and grasses—how to prepare the soil,
when to plant, and other important cultivation information, as well
as tips on designing your garden and caring for a lawn. The zone
map on page 22 tells you the zone in which you live so you can
select plants that are hardy in your particular location.
The section on botany explains the distinctive characteristics of each
plant group, how plants spread, how to identify the parts of a
flower, and the importance of scientific names. The article on
keeping records offers practical advice on keeping track of what you
plant, when you plant it, and seasonal weather variations, while the
gardening calendar provides a schedule for seasonal maintenance
activities. Should you run into difficulty, the pest and disease chart
will help you identify your problem, then cure it. Commonsense
advice on buying plants includes a list of major nurseries and seed
suppliers. All the technical terms are defined in the glossary.

The Plant Chart
Designed to help you select plants and solve gardening problems,
the special plant chart provides basic information at a glance about
each plant's hardiness zone, whether it has significant flowers, its
growth rate, effective season, and potential uses in the landscape.

The chart is divided into three groups, and within each group, the plants are arranged alphabetically by scientific name.

Using the plant chart is simple. Suppose you live in Connecticut (zone 6) and a large portion of your front yard is a steep bank in the shade of a big oak tree, where a lawn is nearly impossible to maintain easily. You want a ground cover that will spread reasonably quickly and remain effective throughout the year, but flowers are not a priority. Scan the chart for plants that are good for banks and slopes, then for those that are useful year-round. Make sure these plants are hardy in your zone. *Asarum caudatum, Berberis verruculosa,* and *Gaultheria shallon* are possible choices.

Perhaps you would like a fast-growing flowering vine to brighten up a wall with blooms in summer and fall; *Clematis paniculata* may be just the answer. Do you want an ornamental grass that will add interest to a flower bed or border and be beautiful to look at even in the dead of winter? *Acorus gramineus* or *Carex morrowii* 'Aureo-variegata' are good possibilities. Once you have determined which plants may suit your purpose, turn to the color plates listed for each of them and read their descriptions to decide which appeal to you most.

Using the Color Plates to Plan Your Garden

Browse through the color plates looking for plants that appeal to you. No doubt you will recognize many that you have seen before. Perhaps you have problem spots in the garden that only a ground cover with dense, lush foliage can solve. Do you want small, round, shiny leaves, or needlelike ones? Look for possibilities among the foliage ground covers in the color plates; examine the range of shapes, textures, and colors available and consider how you might mix and match different plants. Check the captions to see how hardy the plants are, how high they grow, what seasons they work best in, and what special conditions they can tolerate. Finally, turn to the plant descriptions for cultivation details, color or size variations, and related forms that may not be pictured.

Basic Botany

Garden plants can be divided into groups based on the length of time it takes a plant to complete its life cycle, that is, to germinate, mature, produce seeds, and die.

Annuals

An annual completes its life cycle in one growing season. The seed, usually planted in the spring, germinates quickly. The plant blooms the same year. Just before it dies in the fall, it sets seeds, which are either sown naturally (self-seeded), or collected by the gardener to be sown the following year. A few of the grasses and vines considered in this book are annuals.

Biennials

A biennial requires 2 years to complete its life cycle. During the first growing season, the seed is sown and germinates. The plant grows, but produces only foliage. During the second growing season, the plant flowers, and by the fall of that year it sets seeds and dies.

Perennials

Plants that bloom during more than one year are called perennials. They may last for a few years or for decades. Herbaceous perennials include many ground covers, grasses, and vines, most of which die back to the ground in the fall. Although the tops of these plants are dead, their roots remain alive through the winter. It is from these persistent rootstocks that the plants renew themselves in each growing season. Several quick-growing tropical perennials are grown as annuals in North American gardens. These plants flower in their first year, but the roots are winter-killed in cold climates.

Woody perennials include trees and shrubs, many vines, and the subfamily of grasses that comprises the bamboos. These plants do not die back to the ground in winter. Trees and shrubs use the previous years' growth as the starting point to increase their size in height and width. Among the bamboos, each individual stem (culm) completes its growth in one year, living for several more but producing no new growth upon the old.

Shrubs

These woody perennials usually have many stems, rather than a single trunk, and are generally intermediate in height between trees and herbaceous perennials. They mature more quickly than most trees and can begin to flower and set seed by the second or third year. The shrubs considered here as ground covers are low-growing—that is, their growth habit and branching patterns are mainly horizontal. Dwarf shrubs are those that grow very slowly; their landscape form can be either horizontal or vertical. Subshrubs are intermediate between woody and herbaceous perennials; their tops die down for the winter, but a woody base persists aboveground. Die-back shrubs are woody in the warmer parts of their range, but in colder regions are treated as herbaceous perennials because the top growth is winter-killed to the ground and only the roots survive.

Deciduous and Evergreen Plants

Woody plants are classified as deciduous or evergreen, depending on whether or not they lose their leaves in autumn. Deciduous plants are those whose leaves dry up and drop from the branches as the winter season of dormancy approaches. When temperatures rise in spring, the plants produce a new set of leaves. Evergreen plants retain some or all of their green foliage during dormancy. They may shed some of the older leaves or needles the following spring as new growth emerges. Some plants are evergreen in milder regions and deciduous in cold climates. Certain herbaceous (nonwoody) plants, such as *Asarum europaeum,* are evergreen too, making them very valuable as ground covers.

How Vines Climb

Vines reach toward the light by elongating their stems and attaching themselves to whatever support is available. These plants are adapted to adhere to objects by various means, including tendrils, adhesive rootlets, twining stems, and hooks. Tendrils are slender, whiplike appendages that may be derived from modified stems, leaves, or stipules. When the tendril touches a support, it winds around the object, forming an elastic coil that becomes strong enough to support the weight of the plant. In a few kinds of vines, the tendrils terminate in disks that have an adhesive resin to hold the plant in place. Certain climbers like ivy (*Hedera*) attach themselves to almost any surface by producing aerial rootlets that adhere directly to the supporting surface. The largest group of climbers simply have twining stems. As their growing tips elongate, the stems coil around the nearest vertical support. Some vines coil clockwise and others counterclockwise, according to the fixed habit of the species. Some plants, such as roses, have hooks (thorns) that help to attach them to an upright support, but these plants must be tied to the support for proper vertical growth. There is also a small number of weavers— plants that climb by threading their stems in and out of an openwork support such as a trellis or chain link fence.

Grasses

All grasses are members of the grass family, or Gramineae (Poaceae to some botanists). Highly specialized, grasses differ from most other plants in that their stems and leaves grow from the base up, rather than producing new growth at the stem tips. The grasses all have narrow leaves with parallel veins, and each leaf is composed of 2 parts—the blade, which is free from the stem (culm), and the sheath, which wraps around the stem. Stems are usually hollow except at the point where leaves are attached (the node). Nodes are

Basic Botany

Vines adhere to surfaces by various means. Crimson Glory Vine has tendrils that coil readily around objects. English Ivy clings with aerial rootlets.

Boston Ivy's tendrils end in adhesive disks that hold the plant in place. Hall's Honeysuckle twines its stems around vertical supports.

Crimson Glory Vine

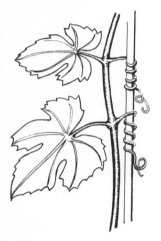

Boston Ivy

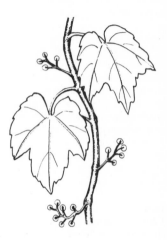

English Ivy

Hall's Honeysuckle

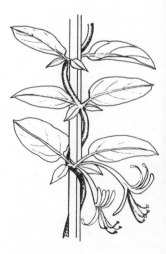

prominent in many grasses, especially in the bamboos. Individual flowers in grasses are generally small, but the inflorescence—the entire arrangement of flowers (or seeds) on the stem—can be very showy. The flowers of some grasses include a long bristle (awn) that adds to the decorative aspect of the plant.

Bamboos

Bamboos are woody-stemmed grasses that constitute a subfamily within the grass family. These plants spread by rhizomes, underground stems that bear buds from which the culms grow. An individual culm attains its full size in one season, hardens, lives for several years, then dies standing.

Bamboos are classed as "running" or "clump," depending on how the rhizomes spread. Running bamboos have long, thin rhizomes that grow quickly to varying distances from the mother plant before sending up new culms. This results in invasive growth habits and open stands. In general, they are hardier than clump-forming bamboos.

Clump bamboos have short, thick rhizomes that travel only short distances before sending up new culms. They form dense, slowly spreading stands. Most are of tropical origin and can be grown only in frost-free climates.

How Ground Covers Spread

A plant's value as a ground cover in a landscape setting is based primarily on its horizontal growth habit. Plants accomplish this in different ways. Many of the low-growing shrubs simply have long branches that extend out to the sides, close to or on the ground, and the shade cast by the branches prevents weeds from germinating. These wide-spreading branches may (cotoneasters) or may not (junipers) root where they touch the ground. Other plants increase in size by producing offshoots, or suckers, that root from the base, gradually increasing the diameter of the plant; *Iberis* is a plant with this type of growth habit. *Vinca minor* is typical of ground covers that send out long runners from the main plant, each runner rooting at several nodes along its length and sending up leaves. A similar method of expansion is by rhizomes, which are stems that grow underground or just at ground level. Rhizomes root at the nodes as they travel, with the tip progressively sending up stems or leaves. Grasses usually spread by runners or rhizomes, vines by runners or offshoots.

The Parts of a Flower

A typical flower is composed of 4 groups of parts. The outermost, the calyx, is usually green; its individual parts are called sepals. Within the calyx is the corolla, which is composed of petals and is usually colorful. Together, the calyx and corolla are termed the perianth. In some plants, the sepals and petals look alike; in others,

Basic Botany

This drawing shows the most common anatomical parts of grasses.

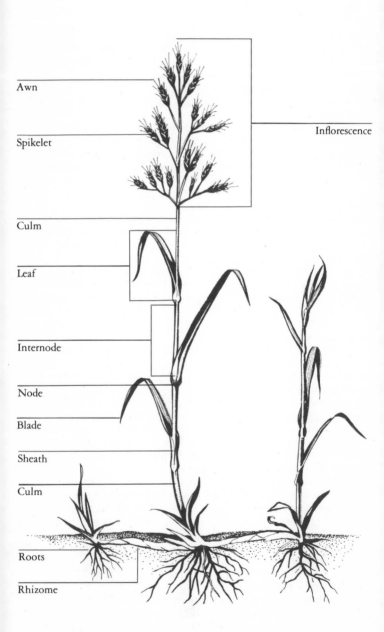

Awn

Spikelet

Inflorescence

Culm

Leaf

Internode

Node

Blade

Sheath

Culm

Roots

Rhizome

the petals may be absent and only the sepals visible. Sometimes the sepals are colorful and resemble petals. The petals may be separate, or united to form a tube. The sepals may also be separate or joined in a tube.

Within the corolla are the stamens, the male reproductive organs. Each stamen consists of a thin filament bearing a saclike anther that contains pollen. Inside the pollen grains are the male germ cells. At the center of the flower are one or more pistils, the female reproductive organs. Each pistil consists of an ovary, a style, and a stigma. The ovary contains ovules; after pollen reaches the stigma, the ovules develop into seeds as the ovary swells and ripens into a fruit.

Flower Clusters

While many flowers are borne singly, clusters of various forms are common in some families. The most common clusters are umbels, corymbs, cymes, panicles, racemes, and spikes.

Leaves

The arrangement and form of leaves can be important in plant identification. If each leaf is attached at a different level along the stem, the leaves are called alternate. If they occur in pairs along the stem, they are considered opposite. If more than 2 are attached at the same level on the stem, they are termed whorled.

Leaves may be simple, consisting of a single blade, or compound, composed of many small leaflets, each with its own blade. If the leaflets radiate from a single point, so that they resemble fingers, the leaf is said to be palmately compound; if the leaflets are arranged along a central axis, the leaf is termed pinnately compound.

The edges, or margins, of leaves and leaflets may be lobed, toothed, or entire (that is, without lobes or teeth). The upper and lower surfaces of leaves may be smooth to hairy.

Common and Scientific Names

Most familiar garden plants have common names, frequently derived from folklore or from some physical attribute of the plant. But common names vary from region to region; the same plant may be known by several different names or the same name may be applied to different plants.

Scientific names avoid this confusion by providing a universal system of nomenclature, accepted and understood throughout the world. According to this system, devised in the 18th century by the Swedish botanist Carolus Linnaeus, every plant is assigned to a species, and every species to a genus. The name of the plant consists of 2 words, the first one (the generic name) being that of the genus, the second (the specific epithet) that of the species. A generic name can be used for only one group of species in the Plant Kingdom, and a specific epithet only once in a particular genus. Both the

Basic Botany

*These drawings show
the most common
anatomical parts of
flowers.*

Stamen
Pistil
Corolla lobe
Throat

Corolla tube
Calyx

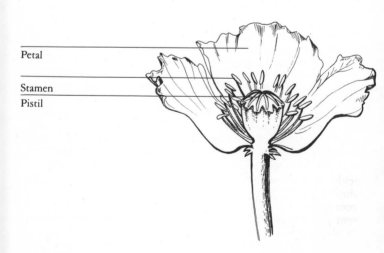

Petal

Stamen
Pistil

generic name and the specific epithet are italicized, and the generic name always begins with a capital letter. The specific epithet begins with a small letter. Scientific names may seem formidable at first, but they are not difficult to learn and are worth knowing, because only by using scientific names can one be absolutely sure what plant one is talking about or buying.

Variety, Cultivar, or Hybrid?

Many gardeners are not clear about the differences between a variety, a cultivar, and a hybrid. Learning a few basics will help you to know what to expect from your garden plants.

Varieties

A variety is a naturally occurring variant of a species. These variants are often called subspecies by some botanists. The scientific name of a variety may contain the abbreviation "var." An example is *Leiophyllum buxifolium* var. *prostratum,* which was found to be a shorter-growing kind than the species. Some botanists omit the abbreviation "var.," and the plant then has a 3-part name: *Leiophyllum buxifolium prostratum*.

Cultivars

Plants in cultivation are often bred with the intention on the part of the breeder of enhancing or minimizing certain inherited traits such as color, fragrance, hardiness, size, or growth habit. These selected plants or groups of plants are known as cultivars, because they are developed under cultivation. They are also commonly, but incorrectly, called varieties.

Cultivars are preserved through vegetative propagation; in some instances, especially in the case of many garden annuals and vegetables, they may be an inbred line of plants that now invariably reproduce from seed.

The name of a cultivar is added to the end of the scientific name of a plant and set off by single quotation marks; the cultivar name is not italicized. An example is *Ilex crenata* 'Helleri', a cultivar of *Ilex crenata*.

Hybrids

A hybrid is the result of a cross between 2 plants belonging to different species, cultivars, varieties, or even—occasionally—different genera. Hybrids are often more disease-resistant than the parent plants, or may have larger or more colorful blooms. The symbol × in a scientific name indicates that the plant is a hybrid. An example is *Hypericum × moseranum,* a cross between *Hypericum calycinum* and *H. patulum*. Many hybrid plants are sterile; others are fertile but produce offspring that differ from their parents. In most cases it is thus necessary to reproduce hybrids by vegetative means.

Getting Started

Every garden has room for experimentation, but planting ground covers may represent a sizable investment in time and money. The key to success is choosing appropriate plants for your environment and giving them proper care.

Where Does Your Garden Grow?

The ground covers that you plant must be able to survive in your garden, be it hot or cold, dry or wet. Some are so hardy that they can survive almost anywhere; others can live only within certain temperatures or humidity ranges.

Plant hardiness is based on 3 factors: temperature, availability of water, and soil conditions. Of these, temperature is by far the most important.

The United States Department of Agriculture has devised a map that divides the country into 10 zones based on average minimum temperatures. (Refer to the map on page 22.) These zones run from north to south and indicate the general limits of plant hardiness. Zone 1 begins in northern Canada, where the average minimum temperature is $-50°$ F. Zone 10, the southernmost zone, ends at the tip of Florida, where the average minimum temperature is $30°$ to $40°$ F. Knowing the zone in which you live is particularly useful when you buy a plant you have never grown before. If the description in this book or in a nursery catalogue contains the notation "zone 4," it means that the plant is hardy as far north as the northernmost areas of zone 4. If the note says "zones 4 to 7," it means that the plant probably will not grow north of zone 4 or south of zone 7.

Microclimates

Within each zone, conditions can fluctuate because of variations in temperature, rainfall, or soil type. These microclimates can occur within states, cities, or even on a small plot of land. Successful gardening is based, in part, on understanding how these variations affect your garden.

On the north side of your house, the temperature may be colder than it is elsewhere. Similarly, colder-than-normal temperatures often occur at the bottom of hills or on ground that is exposed to wind. Areas that receive plenty of sun are usually warmer than those that do not; so are areas that are protected from the wind and those that get reflected heat in the winter.

By learning to recognize the microclimates on your land, you will be able to grow a wider variety of plants than if you based all your plant choices on zone alone. At first, stick to plants that are known to be hardy in your zone; then begin to experiment. If you live in zone 4, you may find that some plants hardy only to zone 5 survive in a warm, protected area near your house. But use common sense: Do not be tempted to cover large areas with plants of uncertain hardiness.

Sun and Shade

Unlike vegetables or annuals, which almost always need full sun, many shrubs and herbaceous ground covers thrive in shade or partial shade. Even when plants are said to require full sun, they usually don't need sun for the entire day. In the heat of summer, most plants do better when protected from intense sunlight. In the South, this protection is especially important. If a plant gets morning sun, and then receives some shade from the shadow of a building, fence, hedge, or tree in the afternoon, it will flourish. Sun-loving plants will thrive if they get shade during the most intense part of the day, and then late afternoon sun. They will also survive if they get filtered sun throughout the day.

When you are determining how much sun a plant requires, keep latitude in mind. In the Deep South, midsummer days are relatively short and the nights are long. In the far North, midsummer days are very long. This extra light can make plants grow rapidly in the North, while those in the South may grow more slowly.

Although some plants actually prefer shade and grow beautifully in it, none can flower in deep shade beneath dense tree canopies or in areas shadowed by buildings all day long. Either grow your flowering plants somewhere else, or be content with plants that have handsome foliage. If shade is caused by a tree, you can "limb up the tree"—cut off the lower branches and remove some of the inner branches to allow light to reach the plant. If that doesn't let enough light in, you may have to remove the tree altogether, or grow other plants.

Soil

Most plants prefer soils that are loamy, well drained, and high in organic matter. Many of those that do well in poor soil will grow even better in richer soil.

Soil is made up of 3 main components: sand, silt, and clay. These components all consist of particles; sand particles are the largest, clay the smallest. If the soil is too sandy, water will pass between the large sand particles and the soil will become dry rapidly. If the soil has too much clay, the small clay particles will trap the water, and the soil will remain wet and sticky. The ideal soil contains some sand, some clay, and some silt.

Organic Matter

Good soil also contains organic matter—humus, rotted leaves or plants, or composted material. This organic matter acts like a sponge to help the soil retain water and nutrients, yet allows adequate air to pass to the roots of the plants. Organic matter also activates organisms in the soil that break down soil particles and fertilizers to release plant nutrients. It is easy to add organic matter to soil. Peat moss, which is actually the decomposed remains of various mosses, is most commonly used. Avoid using very fine peat moss, however,

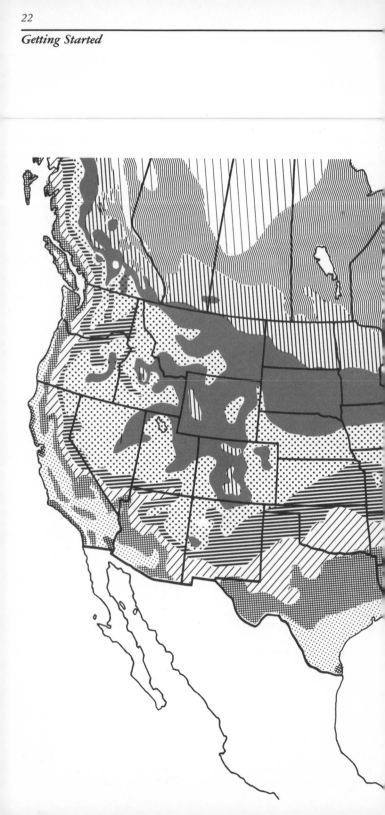

This map was compiled by the United States Department of Agriculture as a broad guideline to temperature extremes in your area.

The key below gives you the average minimum temperatures of the ten zones. Determine if your area corresponds to its zone allocation by comparing your

coldest temperatures with those given in the key.

Minimum Temperatures

Zone 1	Below −50°F
Zone 2	−50 to −40°F
Zone 3	−40 to −30°F
Zone 4	−30 to −20°F
Zone 5	−20 to −10°F
Zone 6	−10 to 0°F
Zone 7	0 to 10°F
Zone 8	10 to 20°F
Zone 9	20 to 30°F
Zone 10	30 to 40°F

Getting Started

because it decomposes rapidly. Rotted leaves and composted garden wastes are also good sources of organic matter.

pH Levels

A soil's pH level measures its degree of acidity or alkalinity, factors that influence the uptake of secondary and micro-nutrients such as iron, calcium, manganese, zinc, and copper. pH is rated on a scale from 1 to 14, with 7 representing a neutral level, the level of pure water. The lower numbers indicate acidity, the higher ones alkalinity.

Although most plants are not overly fussy, most prefer a slightly acidic to neutral soil (pH 5.5 to 7.0). If you live in the East and have oak trees, azaleas, and rhododendrons on your property, you have acidic soil and probably should add lime to it. If you live in an area that has a good deal of limestone, like much of the Midwest, your soil is alkaline. Use the agricultural grade of sulfur or add a generous amount of sphagnum moss to make your soil more acid.

To discover the pH level of your soil, either buy a simple soil test kit or send a soil sample to a local soil test lab. Most of these labs are associated with land-grant universities or with the Cooperative Extension Service. The test lab will analyze your soil and tell you what additives are necessary for the plants you want to grow.

Fertilizer

A complete fertilizer contains nitrogen, phosphorus, and potassium. The amounts of each of these elements are described by the 3 numbers on the package; they may be 5-10-5, 10-10-10, 10-6-4, or some other formula. The first number refers to the percentage of nitrogen the fertilizer contains, the second to its phosphate, and the third to its potash.

Ground covers are grown primarily for their foliage and should have a balanced fertilizer—nitrogen for green growth, phosphorus for root growth, and potash for cell-wall integrity. With ornamental grasses or plants grown mainly for their flowers, avoid high-nitrogen fertilizers, which cause excess green growth. Fertilizer can be applied in granular form during initial soil preparation, as a liquid for quick-acting, short-term results, or in time-release pellets. In subsequent years, a light scattering in spring of 10-10-10 on established plantings should make up for any deficiencies and replace nitrogen lost during decomposition of mulch. Spring rains will carry the fertilizer down into the soil.

Preparing the Soil

Because ground covers live for many years in the same spot, it is worth the effort to prepare the soil well before you plant them. This allows plants to establish good root systems. Adequate soil preparation is important for vines too, especially those planted near house foundations, where construction debris is often present.

To prepare a new bed, first remove the sod, if necessary; then turn the soil over to a depth of one spade (about 18 to 20 inches). Next, spread a layer of compost, peat moss, or other organic material over the soil surface. The amount of granular fertilizer you add depends upon the amount of organic matter already in the soil. If your soil is very acid you may want to add lime, following the recommendations on the package. Since most soils in the eastern United States are low in phosphorus, gardeners customarily add 5 pounds of superphosphate (0-46-0) per 100 square feet of bed. Mix the phosphorus in thoroughly, since it tends to stay where it is placed.

Incorporate the organic material, fertilizer, lime, and phosphorus into the soil by turning them in with a spade or by rototilling. Rake the soil to level it. Allow the ground to settle for a few days before planting, or set a sprinkler on the bed for a few hours to hasten settling.

Planting Ground Covers

If you are planting a new bed, lay the plants out on the ground in their pots according to your design and move them around until you are satisfied with the arrangement. A staggered row pattern gives a better visual impression and helps control erosion on slopes. If the bed is too wide to reach across without stepping into the freshly prepared soil, place a board across the bed and use it as a bridge. Dig a hole for each plant using a hand trowel or shovel. Remove the plant from its pot by turning it over and hitting the bottom sharply to loosen it—never pull it out by the stem. It may be necessary to cut down the sides of shrub containers if the pots are crowded with roots. Loosen and spread out any roots that are tightly wound around the plant, and set the plant in the hole. Refill the hole with soil, firming it in place with your fingers. For larger shrubs refill the hole halfway, water well to settle the soil and eliminate air pockets, then finish filling the hole.

Once the plants are in the ground, water them well with either a watering can or a hose with a water breaker. Carefully soak each plant at the base, and avoid wetting the foliage to prevent the spread of diseases such as mildew and fungal leafspots. Be sure to soak the plants thoroughly and deeply. If the weather is hot or especially dry, water the plants regularly until they are established and new growth begins.

The water requirements of plant species vary widely. As a rule of thumb, you can equate water requirements to the size and color of leaves. Narrow or needlelike leaves, especially those that are gray, silvery, or furry, indicate that the plant may be of dryland origin and needs relatively little water. On the other hand, plants with big, dark green leaves usually require generous amounts of water. During dry spells, a thorough watering every 7 to 10 days should be sufficient, but drooping leaves are an obvious sign that more water is needed.

Getting Started

When planting ground covers, first lay plants out on the ground in their pots according to your design. Then dig planting holes.

To remove a plant from its pot, turn the pot over and hit the bottom sharply; never pull a plant by its stem. Next, loosen and spread out the roots.

Set the plant in its hole with the crown at or just above soil level.

Refill the hole and firm soil gently in place, forming a watering basin around the plant. Then carefully water the plant.

Mulches

Buckwheat hulls	Clean, lightweight, and easy to apply, but can blow about in areas with high winds.
Shredded hardwood bark	Easy to apply, lightweight, and resistant to wind. However, some bark may be acidic, and the size of the pieces varies.
Corncobs	Ground into small pieces, corncobs are a serviceable mulch, but not very attractive. Easy to apply but requires extra nitrogen as it decomposes.
Leaves	Leaves are an excellent natural mulch if they are ground up and come from several different types of trees. Oak leaves tend to be acidic, maple leaves alkaline. Unshredded, the leaves will mat.
Redwood bark	An extremely rot-resistant mulch. Good looking, but expensive and often overly coarse.
Pine needles	Pine needles are attractive, but too acidic for general use, unless a little lime is added now and then. In periods of heat or drought, they are a fire hazard.
Peat moss	An attractive mulch, but not recommended because it becomes a waterproof cover when it dries.
Sawdust	Easy to apply, but a potential fire hazard. It ties up nitrogen as it decomposes, and can form a waterproof cover when dry.
Grass clippings	Readily available, but clippings break down rapidly. They tie up nitrogen and may burn plant crowns if applied too thickly.
Hay	Easy to apply, but susceptible to fire and wind. Hay can be mixed with leaves or similar materials to provide a better mulch.
Wood chips	Chips can vary in coarseness and require extra nitrogen as they decompose.
Rotted manure or half-rotted compost	Both are excellent mulches that also provide food for the plants but may contain weed seeds.

When to Plant

The best time to plant ground covers depends on where you live. In cold climates, spring planting is preferred because plants then have a long growing season to become established before winter comes. New plants whose roots are not well secured may heave out of the ground during late winter due to alternate freezing and thawing of the soil. Dry roots will result, killing the plants. Late summer and early autumn are second choices for planting time. Be sure plants begin winter well watered and mulched. After the ground freezes, apply a light covering of evergreen boughs or salt hay for winter protection. Do not remove this covering in spring until the weather is settled and new growth has begun.

Where winters are mild, early autumn planting gives ground covers a long, cool growing season with usually abundant rainfall during which they can become established before summer heat arrives.

Mulching

Mulching covers the soil surface with a porous layer of material that acts as insulation and slows down changes in soil temperature. It also retards water loss from evaporation, while permitting water to percolate through the soil. Finally, it helps retard the growth of weeds by keeping the soil too dark and cool for weed seeds to germinate; and the light, airy structure of the mulch and uncompacted nature of the protected soil combine to make any weeds that do develop easy to pull out.

This is particularly important with ground covers, where the object is to establish a weed-free carpet of greenery. Apply the mulch thickly—it will mat down—but keep it away from plant crowns, where it may encourage diseases and slugs.

When choosing a mulch, consider availability, cost, appearance, and durability. Make sure it is free of weeds and diseases. Most organic mulches use nitrogen from the soil as they decompose. This can be counteracted by an annual light application of fertilizer.

Spacing Ground Covers

The number of plants it takes to cover a given area depends on several factors—the plants' growth rate, how quickly you want complete coverage, and funds available for the project.

The closer you space plants, the faster they will cover an area, but some conifers and low-growing azaleas tend to mound up instead of spreading if planted too close together. Keep the plants' growth rate and mature size in mind. As a guide, ground covers like ivy (*Hedera*) and periwinkle (*Vinca*) are usually planted on 1-foot centers—that is, planted 1 foot apart. Spreading shrubs such as cotoneasters and junipers are planted on 3-foot centers (3 feet apart). Most vines and fast spreaders are planted no closer than 5 feet apart. Mulch well to keep weed growth under control until plantings completely cover the area. If the planting seems sparse during the first year or two, annuals can be interplanted to add interest and color and help suppress weeds until the permanent planting fills in. Some ground covers will fill in faster if you cut back old leggy top growth in late winter to encourage dense new growth.

Planting on Slopes

In addition to providing an attractive cover on bare soil slopes, plants can help solve erosion problems. Until plants are well established, however, they may contribute to the problem if they are not properly situated. The degree of slope will determine the planting method. On all slopes, staggered-row planting will help prevent gullies that form when water runs straight downhill. On gentle slopes of 20° or less, creating a small basin or berm to catch water on the downhill side of each plant should provide adequate erosion control. On somewhat steeper grades, terraces across the width of the slope, reinforced with boards and stakes, will control runoff. To control erosion on steep slopes, it is necessary to build a series of low retaining walls of stone backed with sand. Another way to minimize runoff is to plant ground covers in pockets of improved soil rather than tilling and disturbing an entire area; any roots already present will lend stability. If all else fails, you can cover the slope with a water-permeable polyethylene film or jute mesh and cut planting holes in it. The best plants to use on difficult sites are those with long, tenacious roots and those that quickly send out stolons or rhizomes that bind the soil.

Weed Control

Weeds are inevitable in every garden and there is no quick remedy. You can make the job of weeding less time-consuming, however, if you catch weeds when they are young. Left alone to grow, flower, and set seed, weeds will become worse with each passing year. Adding a layer of mulch to the bed will help keep weeds in check, but until the planting develops into a cover thick enough to choke them out, you must spend some time weeding by hand. Weeds are easier to pull out after a rain, when the softened soil allows you to get all the pieces of root. It is possible to use certain pre-emergent or post-emergent herbicides on planted areas, but there is always the danger of misuse or runoff to other parts of the garden.

To clear weeds from an area prior to planting, you can cultivate the soil repeatedly, removing all weeds that grow after each cultivation, until fewer and fewer appear. Or you can remove all vegetation by using a nonselective herbicide; however, some products have a long-lasting residual effect in the soil, making it unsafe to plant for extended periods. Glyphosate-type herbicides have a residual effect that lasts only a few weeks, but drift or runoff is still possible. The simplest way to rid an area of unwanted vegetation is to cover it for a few weeks with black polyethylene film, which creates heat and darkness that will eventually eradicate even the toughest weeds.

To help control erosion on gentle slopes of 20° or less, create a small basin or berm on the downhill side of each plant to catch water.

On somewhat steeper grades, you can build terraces reinforced with boards and stakes to control runoff.

Keeping Ground Covers Tidy

Early spring is usually the best time to prune ground covers because new growth will quickly cover the bare stubs. The amount of pruning required depends on how tidy the area must appear. Cut out dead branches with hand pruners or loppers and remove winter-damaged branch tips to encourage dense new growth. Shrubs that have become too tall or lanky should be cut back to acceptable height. To rejuvenate *Pachysandra* and other herbaceous evergreen ground covers that have suffered winter burn, use a rotary mower on its highest setting. Avoid severe pruning in late summer or autumn, since it can force tender growth that will not have time to harden off properly before winter.

Training and Pruning Vines

Training vines consists of pruning out all unwanted new growth during the growing season, pruning out old woody or diseased growth during the dormant season, and guiding and securing the plants so they will grow only where you want them.

You can avoid the need to constantly hack back and tie up overzealous vines by choosing plants to suit their location. Select those that grow rapidly to cover large areas, and slower-growing ones to cover small trellises or areas where pruning would be difficult. The next step is to match the plant to its support, according to the vine's climbing habit.

Trellises

Vines that cling by aerial rootlets or adhesive disks climb well on rough masonry or brick surfaces, but they should not be allowed to climb on wooden houses because they will damage the surface and must be removed when the house needs painting. A good support for a twining or tendril-climbing vine is a hinged trellis, secured about 6 inches from a wooden wall and designed to swing away during painting or pruning. This type of trellis is also useful for climbing roses or other vines that must be tied to their supports. Attach such plants by fastening soft cloth or polyethylene ties first to the support, then loosely to the vine.

To make a portable trellis, thread a dowel through the ends of a length of chicken wire or chain link and suspend it from hooks attached to the eaves of a house or from the top of a stockade fence, securing the bottom with J-hooks driven into the ground. You can also mold wire mesh over a stone wall that you want a tendril climber or weaver to cover.

Other Supports

Twiners also climb well on wires, drainpipes, lampposts, and other vertical supports of small to medium diameter. They will not, however, twine around thick columns or large trees. It is important to know whether the vine you have chosen twines right-to-left or left-to-right so that it gets started in the proper direction. Do not plant vigorous twiners near small trees, which some vines can kill by grasping tightly enough to cut off the flow of nutrients and water. Tendril-climbing vines will readily clamber over shrubs; plant them on the shrub's windward side so that their climbing stems are blown in the right direction. These vines are also appropriate for climbing multi-stem trees. Rootlet climbers can grow up tree trunks without causing damage, as long as they do not cover the tree's foliage crown. Vines are most successful in trees that do not cast dense shade.

Training Growth

No matter what type of support you use, your vine will probably need a little help getting started on its climb. A short length of string, polyfilament, or netting will guide the plant to the first foot or two of its support.

As they grow upward toward the light, some vines produce a mass of foliage at the top, leaving their bottom stems bare. This can be prevented by training the stems horizontally at first and forcing vertical growth from lateral shoots. Moderate pruning in the first year or so will also encourage low branching.

Pruning

Once their basic framework is established, most vines are best pruned only to the extent necessary to keep them healthy and within bounds. But prune annually so that plants do not get out of hand, requiring drastic measures later. Your reward will be improved appearance, easier maintenance, and increased flowering.

Large-flowered clematis, climbing roses, and other vines that flower on new wood should be pruned, if necessary, in late winter. Remove old woody or diseased stems to the base and other shoots to 2 or 3 buds from the base to eliminate messy tangles. New, young canes are the best climbers and bear the most flowers. After climbing roses have finished blooming, cut off the spent flowers and the laterals on which they were borne to within 2 or 3 buds of the main canes. This increases the chances of repeat flowering.

Vines that flower on old wood (usually spring bloomers), like *Clematis montana* and *Wisteria* species, are pruned after they blossom. If necessary, you can cut back the previous year's growth by as much as one-half. On wisteria vines, pinch back long, new shoots to 6 to 12 inches several times during the remainder of the growing season. Save only those shoots needed to extend the length of the vine, and tie them to the support. This will improve flowering the following year and keep the vigorous plants under control.

Propagating Plants

The anticipated expense of installing ground covers may seem overwhelming, but you can easily economize if you buy just enough plants to cover a small area and then gradually increase their number by propagating additional ones.

Division

Division is the easiest way to increase herbaceous plants, even though other methods will produce them in larger numbers. Herbaceous perennials vary in their root formation and habit, but the majority spread by the development of growth buds, or eyes. Each bud, although attached to the parent plant, grows independently the following season. Propagation by division involves the separation of these growth buds to increase the number of plants. Early spring and late summer are the best times to divide established clumps of herbaceous ground covers.

Plants like *Hemerocallis* have fleshy rootstocks. When you dig them out, you'll notice that the roots intertwine and that there are several growth buds on each root. Pull these roots apart gently or cut them with a knife to get several independent pieces, each with one or more growth buds. Plant the pieces in a prepared bed.

In rhizomatous plants, the stem branches out at or below the surface of the ground. At each underground node on the stem you will find a bud and one or more roots. If the clump is large, pull the stems apart, making sure that each stem has one or more growth buds. If the clump has only one stem, cut the individual growth buds apart, making sure that each bud has one or more roots.

Perennials like *Heuchera* and *Ajuga* develop many crowns. Dig up the plant and carefully pull the crowns apart.

Cuttings

Both herbaceous and woody ground covers as well as some vines can be increased by cuttings. These will yield a larger number of plants than division, but require more care. For most herbaceous plants the optimum time to take cuttings is mid- to late summer, when new growth is not too soft and not too firm—about like a fresh green bean. For broadleaf evergreens, take cuttings from hardened new growth in autumn. Choose a shoot that is 3 to 6 inches long and has no flower buds, preferably a side-shoot. Shrub cuttings should include a small section of the parent stem, or heel.

Your cuttings will be more successful if they have a minimum of 3 leaf joints. With a razor blade or sharp knife, cut the shoot one-quarter to one-half inch below a leaf or pair of leaves. The new roots will come out below the node where the stem buds are located in the axils of the leaves.

Caring for Cuttings

To keep the cuttings moist and prevent them from wilting, immediately place them in a damp towel or in a plastic bag. Fill a pot or flat with an equal-parts mixture of peat moss and coarse sand. Smooth the surface of the mix, taking care not to firm it, and

To divide a clump of tangled roots, first dig the roots up, then pry them apart with two cultivating forks. Continue dividing the smaller clusters until you have the number of divisions that you want.

Getting Started

To propagate new plants from stem cuttings, choose a shoot that is 3 to 6 in. long, with at least 3 leaf joints and no flower buds.

Cut just below a leaf joint, then remove the leaves at the base. Plant the stem cuttings upright in flats or individual pots filled with peat moss and coarse sand.

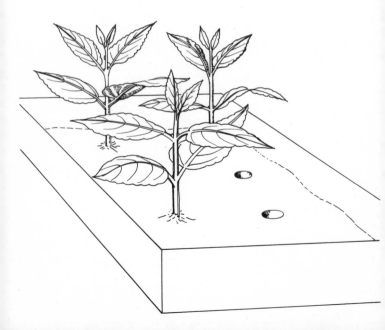

moisten it with a fine mist of water. Insert the cuttings in rows, spacing them so their leaves barely touch. Remove the lowest leaves of the cutting and push the stem gently down; this prevents the development of air spaces around the cutting. After you have inserted all the cuttings, water them to make the planting medium firm.

After the pot or flat is filled, cover it with plastic film, using a wire frame or wooden stakes to keep the bag from touching the cuttings. Place the container in indirect light, never in sunlight. Watch for signs of discoloration or disease, and remove any plants with these symptoms. After the plants are rooted, remove the bag. You will know that roots have formed (4 to 6 weeks for herbaceous plants) when you see new growth and when the cuttings resist a gentle tug. In mild climates plant cuttings outdoors once they are well rooted; in cold climates, protect them in a cold frame during the first winter.

Layering

Woody and herbaceous ground covers and some vines can be increased by layering. In fact, many of them root and produce new plants naturally wherever their trailing stems touch the ground. Well-rooted stems can be separated from the parent plant and transplanted.

The best time to begin layering is in spring. To encourage a runner to root where it touches the ground, secure the trailing stem to the soil with a forked stick or U-shaped wire and cover it with several inches of soil. Apply a top mulch to help keep the soil damp until rooting occurs. You can make a series of layers by weaving long stems in and out of the soil. To layer a woody plant, notch the stem partway through on the underside and dust it with rooting hormone powder, then cover it with soil. Shrub layers may require as long as a year to become rooted well enough to sever from the parent plant.

Seeds

Ground covers are sometimes propagated by seeds, but this method is limited to true species and the occasional cultivars that breed "true" from seed. Although this may be the least expensive way to propagate plants, other methods are usually easier and faster. Outdoors you can sow seeds directly into a bed or a cold frame; inside you can start them in pots or flats under fluorescent lights or on a windowsill.

Sowing Seeds Outdoors

If you plan to sow seeds directly into a bed or cold frame, the soil should be thoroughly prepared with organic matter. Add sand if drainage is not adequate, and try to choose a location with partial shade. Sow the seeds thinly and uniformly in blocks or rows and cover them with a layer of fine soil to a depth of about 3 times the

Getting Started

Many ground covers and some vines can be increased by layering, which works best in spring. To encourage a runner to root where it touches the ground, secure the trailing stem to the soil with a U-shaped wire. Cover it with soil and add top mulch. To make a series of layers, weave long stems in and out of the soil.

Serial layering

Simple layering

thickness of the seed. Firm the soil lightly over the seeds and water them with a fine mist. Keep the seeds moist and remove competing weeds after the seeds have germinated. Transplant the seedlings to their permanent place in the garden after they are well established. For summer-sown seeds, transplant them the following spring. If your climate is mild, they can be transplanted in early autumn.

Starting Seeds Indoors
Indoors, sow seeds in a flat or a pot. Fill the container with a light mix of one-half peat moss and one-half horticultural-grade perlite or vermiculite. You can substitute coarse, sharp sand for the perlite, or you can buy a seed-starting mixture. Whatever you use, be sure it has been pasteurized to prevent damping-off, the fungus that kills seedlings before or shortly after they emerge.

Starting Seeds Under Fluorescent Lights
To control the light that seeds and seedlings receive, consider starting them under fluorescent lights. Use a 2-tube fluorescent light fixture, consisting of 40 watts per tube. You should rotate the pots occasionally because the end position receives less intense light than the center. When the tiny seedlings have sprouted, transplant them. Hang the lights in a cool spot, 50° to 65°F, protected from cold and drafts. Rooms that are warmer, 65° to 75°F or more, may result in tall, spindly plants. Hang the lights so they can be lowered to within 2 inches of the top of seeded pots. When the seedlings are the size of a dime, raise the lights so that they hang about 6 inches above the seedlings. If the seedlings start to stretch and appear spindly, lower the lights and, if possible, the room temperature as well.

Transplanting Seedlings
Once the seeds have germinated, watch for the development of the first set of true leaves. This is the time for the young seedlings to be transplanted from the seed flat or pot to a new pot or an outdoor bed. Carefully loosen the soil around the roots of the seedlings with a small, pointed stick, then lift the young seedling out of the flat or pot using the stick, holding the plant by a leaf, not the stem. Transplant the seedling to its new location and firm the soil around the roots to close up any air pockets. Water it very carefully after transplanting. Be sure to allow plenty of space between the plants.

Hardening Off Seedlings
Tender seedlings must be acclimatized before they are set outside. The process of hardening off is simple. A week before you wish to transplant the seedlings, find an area that is protected from wind, yet open to sunlight and fluctuations in temperature. Move the transplants there. Water them twice a day if they seem to dry out rapidly. After they have been outside for 3 or 4 days, place them in a

fully exposed outdoor location. Beware of cold night temperatures; if the thermometer is supposed to plunge, move them indoors. Cold frames are ideal locations for hardening off seedlings, since their covers can be opened gradually.

Cold Frames

If you are going to grow plants from seed or do any form of plant propagation, a cold frame is a useful and versatile device. Basically a cold frame is a bottomless box with a top made of a transparent material like glass, polyethylene plastic, or fiberglass that can be opened or removed. Some prefabricated units come with temperature-sensitive devices that open the cover automatically. Cold frames are unheated and vary in size; most are 3 feet by 6 feet. They can be portable or permanent. For maximum use a frame should slope to the south to allow it to trap as much sun as possible early in the year. It should be on ground that is high enough to prevent surface water from seeping in under normal conditions. Since wind will lower the temperature inside the frame, try to place it in a protected area.

If you plan to grow seeds directly in the cold frame, the soil must be well drained and should have a quantity of leaf-mold or similar organic matter incorporated into it. If the plants are to be grown in pots, then line the bottom of the frame with builder's sand, fine gravel, or coal ash.

Ventilating the Cold Frame

As the weather begins to warm in the spring, control excess heat and humidity by opening the cover gradually. As you ventilate the frame, water the plants. Before the frame is totally opened, water the plants in the morning, just enough to keep the soil evenly moist. Once the frame is uncovered, this is not as critical.

Gardening Tools

Gardening is more enjoyable and less tiring when you have the proper tools. There is no need to start with an expensive collection, but do invest in the best quality tools you can afford. Clean your tools regularly and sharpen those that require it. Store them in a safe place protected from the weather.

The lid of a cold frame should prop open securely to three positions: slightly open, half-open, and fully open. Sink the frame into the ground or build a bank of soil part way up the sides.

Starter Tools

Shovel	This implement has a slightly curved blade and a round-pointed end, and is available with a long, straight handle or one that is D-shaped. Good all-purpose tool for moving soil or digging planting holes.
Spade	Unlike a shovel, a spade has a flat blade with a square-pointed end, and usually a D-shaped handle. Useful for deep digging or for straightening the edge of a border.
Steel rake	Use this tool for leveling the soil and for breaking up small clods.
Cultivator	A 3-pronged, forklike hand tool useful for loosening soil to remove weeds and their roots.
Pruning shears	Hand clippers are essential for deadheading and light pruning. Shears with bypass action are preferable to anvil shears because they make a cleaner cut and the blades can be sharpened. Choose a pair that feels comfortable in your hand and is not too large to grasp when open.
Hand trowel	An essential tool for planting. It should have a durable, solid shaft. For large projects, a trowel with a curved, pistol-grip handle will prevent some blisters in the palm of your hand.
Watering can	Use this to water individual plants and those in the cold frame. Galvanized metal is more durable than plastic, but also more expensive.
Hose	Make sure the hose you buy is long enough to reach all parts of the garden. Rubber-base hoses remain more flexible and manageable in cool weather than vinyl-base ones, but are more expensive. Whichever you choose, attach a water breaker, not a jet nozzle, when you are watering plants.

Garden Design

Creating a garden that will suit your needs is a continuing process that may be divided into 3 main stages: selecting the plants; making use of them as elements of design; and maintenance. Ultimately, the element that makes or breaks a garden is maintenance—the ongoing attention that you give your plants.

Right Plant, Right Site

Many gardeners fall into the trap of buying a plant in full flower because it is beautiful or cute. Then the plant is taken home and put in the first available spot with no awareness of its habit, growth rate, or environmental needs. This "plunkitis" always results in chaos. As you build your garden, remember that plants not only occupy space but also create it. It is the manipulation and organization of this space that turns a collection of plants into a garden.

Gardening is much simpler if you choose plants that will readily adapt to the conditions on your property. Consider sunlight, soil conditions (wet or dry, acid or alkaline), exposure to wind and salt spray, and other important factors. Some plants will thrive in a wide range of site conditions; most, however, are more specific in their requirements, and a major part of good gardening is developing the talent to match the right plant to the right site.

Analyzing Your Site

Site analysis is the first task of the professional garden designer. To analyze your own site, take an inventory of the conditions in the front, back, and side yards. Are the conditions the same? If not, how do they differ? Are these conditions constant throughout the year? How do they change? How does the sun's intensity and angle change from hour to hour or season to season? What are the soil conditions? Is the soil clay or sandy? Are there low, poorly drained spots? Is there seasonal wind or salt spray that might be overlooked during clear, calm days?

Consider the 5 greatest strengths and worst problems of your grounds. Positive features may include scenic views, distinctive architectural features that should not be obscured, or significant existing plants, such as mature trees, handsome shrubs, or majestic vines. Negative features include existing plants that lack unity or continuity, steep slopes, rocky outcroppings, or seasonal springs that keep a section of the lawn wet. Look out of every window in the house to determine the characteristics of your view.

Next, organize your property around traffic patterns within the garden. Assess how much space you need for living—for lawns, a vegetable garden, terraces, pools, parties, or games, as well as utility areas for garbage cans, firewood storage, and laundry lines.

Remember that space is 3-dimensional. In envisioning the vertical dimension, project the height, width, and volume required to fulfill a spatial function. Then choose specific plants to function as ground covers, walls, and ceilings that fit the existing habitat conditions.

There is an easy way to get a feel for this process. On a table, place a large magazine to represent your house. Then use plastic cups of varying sizes to represent plantings. Group the cups together in both large and small clusters to create and enclose space around the house. Always keep in mind how you will get from the house to areas such as the street, the swimming pool, or the vegetable garden. Rearrange the cups several ways to discover the many spaces one might capture within the large space of the table. Once you arrive at groupings you think will work, you can begin to add ground covers to unify the plantings. This can be done by taking a piece of colored string and using it to surround and connect all the plants (cups) in one area or cluster.

Designing with Ground Covers
Ground covers can be thought of as carpets of the outdoors. They can be used, like lawn grasses, to cover a large area, or for smaller patches of color, much as one would use an area rug. Ground covers can be grown alone to define or enclose space, or combined with shrubs, trees, and structural elements. Where you want to maintain a feeling of openness, select a low-growing or prostrate plant. In another area you might want a taller plant to screen the base of a leggy shrub or fill in a barren space beneath a tall tree. Ground covers knee-high or taller will help define the edges of pathways where people are invited to walk.

Vigor, Density, and Year-round Appearance
Many people select ground covers only on the basis of flowering potential, failing to consider year-round appearance. It is important to think about vigor, density, texture, or leaf color, whether the plant is evergreen or deciduous, and how the plant looks during the winter or dormant season.

Vigor is important for 2 reasons. Some plants are slow to become established or have specialized environmental needs for optimum growth. If your site doesn't meet these needs, the plant will languish or be slow to fill in, allowing weeds to invade. Once weeds arrive, your maintenance must escalate markedly.

Many ground covers are invasive, and the best are in truth little more than weeds that have been well chosen, placed, and restrained. Some plants need a controlling agent—such as barriers, hand weeding, or regular treatment with herbicides—to restrict and control their outward spread. Examples of these are *Lamiastrum galeobdolon* 'Variegatum' and *Aegopodium podograria*. Be especially cautious of ground covers that can seed or spread themselves into adjacent garden areas or the lawn. *Ajuga reptans* or *Arundinaria viridistriata* invade quickly and become impossible to eradicate without taking up the lawn.

Density is another important factor. Some ground covers may be dense and aggressive in one place but thin and sparse in another. A plant's density can change from year to year depending on soil fertility, rainfall, winter stress, or garden pests. Grow less vigorous, sparser plants sparingly, for they will probably require special maintenance to be at their best.

It is also important to consider the look of a plant—its leaf color or texture—apart from its tendency to flower. Even plants with exceptionally long bloom periods rarely flower for more than 4 to 6 weeks, and you are left with foliage for the rest of the summer—or, if the plant is evergreen, the whole year. Good gardeners first attempt to create patterns of height, texture, and form, regarding the flowers only as an added benefit. Leaf texture can vary from short, fine, and grasslike, as in *Ophiopogon,* to bold or coarse in plants such as *Hosta sieboldiana*. In constantly shaded gardens, consider selecting plants with variegated or colorful leaves or distinctive textures to create tapestry effects.

Whether you choose deciduous or evergreen plants depends on how you want the garden to look year-round. Where only deciduous ground covers are used, the whole effect may disappear with the first frost; if only evergreen ground covers are employed, the changing seasons produce little variation, and your garden may look static or monotonous. Usually a combination works best; the deciduous plants will lose their leaves, providing a change of scene, but the evergreen materials will give backbone and structure for winter.

Choosing Plants

Flowers are the reward of a well-designed garden and should be considered only after other criteria are satisfied. Evaluate the existing environment and determine what height, form, and texture you require for your design; then you can determine what plants will work, and what ornamental opportunities they present. Blossoms can be selected for color, form, bloom time, length of flowering, repeat flowering, or the plant's ability to shed spent flowers cleanly and gracefully. Some ground covers bear pleasantly scented flowers, and others are useful in attracting birds or butterflies.

Imagine that you want to plant a ground cover 3 to 4 feet tall with bold texture. You have determined that you need a plant that will tolerate winter temperatures of −10° F for a seasonally wet, shaded site. You would like flowers if possible, but will be satisfied with a plant with interesting-looking foliage. Of the plants discussed in this book, only the following fit your criteria: *Hosta sieboldiana, Sasa palmata, Sasa veitchii,* and *Xanthorhiza simplicissima*. Of these, 2 have distinctive leaves; one is the deciduous *Hosta sieboldiana* 'Frances Williams', with gold markings in the leaf. *Sasa veitchii* is evergreen to semievergreen, and its leaves bear a tan marginal band during the short, cool days of autumn.

Now that we have considered factors of plant selection, how do we bring the individual players together as a cast of characters? Ground covers are rarely grown independently of other landscape elements.

In designing an area, first envision shapes on the ground. You can use formal geometric shapes—a square, rectangle, circle, or oval—or less formal, soft, flowing curves. Beds can be created where there are no existing plants, or they can unify a miscellaneous array of trees and shrubs.

There are several ways to visualize these beds without spending any money. If you live where winters are snowy, you can wait for snowfall to blanket your yard, and then sculpt potential planting beds into the snow. In other seasons, use a garden hose or colorful extension cord to create design patterns in the grass or mulch. One good method is to take bamboo stakes 2 to 4 feet high, tie colorful plastic ribbons to the top of each, and use them to mark off beds that fit the site and the contours of the land.

Once you arrive at a design you like, allow the grass within the space to grow for several weeks while keeping edges and area around the space closely mowed. The height of the grass clearly depicts how ground cover plantings might look in the space. Particularly on large sites, practice mowing along the edges to determine if you have created nooks and crannies that will make mowing the lawn cumbersome. Slight alterations can generally be made without any noticeable negative impact on the design itself.

When you make the final decision about the perimeter, mark the edge permanently with a herbicide that will kill the grass and retain the design in place until it is time to begin work. As soon as the edges are clearly defined, use stakes with plastic ribbons or other objects—such as flower pots, boxes, and chairs—to help you visualize the vertical arrangement of the plantings.

Having decided upon a master plan for the whole property, you can divide it into portions or stages, taking into consideration your budget and the time available.

Tapestry Ground Covers

Every gardener's goal, for large areas, is reliable and dependable coverage; to achieve this effect, it is possible to mix ground covers together right from the beginning, much as you might blend different grass seeds to produce a beautiful, full lawn. Mixtures such as these are known as tapestry ground covers. In a shaded site, you might try mixing *Pachysandra terminalis, Vinca minor,* and *Hedera helix* together. In some areas there may be solid patches of *Pachysandra,* while in others there will be mixes and the mix may change from season to season depending on light, soil fertility, and soil moisture. In a sunny site, it is delightful to combine *Cerastium tomentosum,* which has grayish foliage and produces single white flowers in early summer, with *Ceratostigma plumbaginoides,* which produces a colorful carpet of cobalt-blue flowers in midsummer. These plants can be massed around a grouping of the low shrub *Potentilla fruticosa* 'Gold Finger', and the combination will flower for a minimum of 10 to 12 weeks. For a year-round evergreen effect, consider creating a large mass planting of *Juniperus horizontalis* 'Wiltonii', which grows 4 to 6 inches high, and interplanting it with clusters or colonies of *Yucca filamentosa* 'Golden Sword' or 'Bright Edge', whose dramatic variegated leaves are especially striking during drab winter days. Many ground cover plantings are enhanced by interplanting with flowering bulbs.

Recording New Ideas
Garden designers are constantly on the lookout for appealing combinations; it is helpful to record them photographically or in a card file, where the information is retrievable. Ideas about using and combining plants are everywhere—not only in the gardens of specialists, but also in the grounds of office buildings, churches, and local public gardens. Look around your neighborhood.

Landscaping with Vines
Vines are among the most underrated landscape plants. Because they can twist, climb, and cling, vines can add color to places where there isn't room for other types of plants and in areas where people rarely envision a plant being used. Vines soften or screen harsh, blank walls; overhead, they function as garlands, canopies, or ceilings on trellises, arbors, and pergolas. Does your house need to be dressed up a bit? Is your terrace exposed to the sun and the view of neighbors? Does your dining-room table look out at a blank wall? Is part of your yard uninviting? Imagine how a climbing garland of green would improve the space and visual image.

Vines are unpopular chiefly because of the widespread belief that they harm buildings. Yet rarely is damage to stone, brick, concrete, or cinderblock attributable to the growth of a vine. It is true, however, that the aerial rootlets of vines cluster around frost cracks and settling cracks, where the plant obtains additional anchorage and better support. It is perhaps unwise to grow vines directly along a wooden or frame structure, because the higher moisture level between the leaves and the wall may accelerate deterioration of the wall. Instead, you can grow vines against a trellis held away from the wall by 4- to 8-inch spacers. Don't allow vines that form aerial rootlets—such as *Hedera helix, Parthenocissus tricuspidata,* and *Campsis radicans*—to grow under the eaves or onto the roof of a building, because they can invade and raise the edges of the shingles.

Growth Habit
Knowing how a vine climbs is often a clue to its use. Some vines, such as *Hedera helix, Hydrangea anomala petiolaris,* and *Campsis radicans,* climb by clinging or aerial holdfasts; these plants need no special support and can attach themselves directly to masonry, tree trunks, wooden fences, or any stationary support. Vines such as these produce vertical lawns of green that ameliorate the harshness of large blank walls.

Other vines twine or twist; these require support to climb upward, and are perfect with trellises and arbors. Some, such as *Aristolochia durior* and *Clematis paniculata,* produce relatively thin, light stems, so the structural support can be made of light material. Others, including *Actinidia* and *Wisteria,* form heavy, massive trunks and require strong supports.

Twining vines are well suited to masking barrier structures like chain link or cyclone fences with wire mesh, which allows the plants to weave in and about, gradually filling in with a leafy screen. In sunny, well-drained locations, try *Clematis montana* cultivars, *Clematis paniculata, Ipomoea* species, *Kadsura japonica, Lonicera* species, *Menispermum canadense, Polygonum aubertii,* and *Thunbergia alata.* Fences in shady sites can be covered with *Akebia quinata, Decumaria barbara, Euonymus fortunei, Hedera* species, *Lonicera japonica* 'Halliana', and *Parthenocissus* species. To keep vines on chain link fences tidy, shear them occasionally; certain vines, like *Euonymus fortunei* cultivars, can be fashioned into a narrow evergreen hedge. Some vines used in this way, such as *Aristolochia durior,* shape themselves tightly to the fence and need little pruning to stay attractive. Others, such as *Wisteria* and *Celastrus,* misbehave—their long growth grabs people who walk nearby. Keeping these plants in bounds requires frequent pruning.

Members of the third group of vines have either tendrils, as in *Vitis* species, or holdfasts, as in *Parthenocissus tricuspidata.* Plants with tendrils will latch onto any thin object or support—wire, shrubs, or the branches of trees. Grapes (*Vitis*) will climb to great heights and then traverse a horizontal support such as a thick wire or cable.

New houses are often plunked down on sites from which all vegetation has been stripped, and new owners often plant for privacy and shade. A simple trellis paired with a fast-growing vine makes a good solution, providing quick shade on a porch, over a patio or walkway, or on one side of the house.

Trees in many established gardens produce tall, massive trunks before beginning any branch or leaf growth. These stems are often ideal as supports for clinging vines, such as *Campsis radicans, Decumaria barbara, Euonymus fortunei, Hedera* species, *Parthenocissus* species, and *Schizophragma* species. Unless they grow along the branches and keep sunlight from reaching the foliage, these vines will not harm the tree. It is wise not to use twisting vines such as *Actinidia, Celastrus,* and *Wisteria,* for they may strangle the tree.

Designing with Ornamental Grasses

Ornamental grasses provide the landscape designer with unusual opportunities. Grasses can contribute exciting color and texture to the garden, and wind blowing through the leaves produces animation and pleasing sound.

Some grasses form clumps; others spread. Clump-forming grasses are much easier to manage in the landscape because, with proper use, they tend not to invade or overgrow their neighboring plants. Yet spaced incorrectly, these species will produce bald spots where plants fail to overlap—and bald sites are perfect for the growth of weeds, so pay careful attention to spacing. One distinct advantage of designing with clump-type grasses is that their height is fairly predictable, and they reach their full growth in one or two growing seasons.

Grasses that spread by stolons or run underground can be strongly invasive and may take over sections of a garden never intended for them to occupy. When using spreading grasses, always consider how the plants will be contained or restrained once they reach the limit allowed for their growth. Strong grasses such as *Sasa, Arundinaria,* and *Glyceria* require a solid, in-ground mechanical barrier; sheets of fiberglass or aluminum set on end and dug in to a depth of 2 feet will work. Other stoloniferous grasses that lack the potential for strong underground growth—such as *Phalaris, Hakonechloa,* and *Calamagrostis*—are easily contained by occasionally grubbing them out and pushing back the advancing edge.

You can use grasses in the landscape for a variety of purposes. You may wish to grow a specimen plant in the middle of a lawn; *Cortaderia selloana, Miscanthus sinensis* cultivars, and *Phyllostachys aurea* adapt to this type of use. Smaller grasses such as *Calamagrostis, Festuca, Helictotrichon, Molinia,* and *Pennisetum* can be used as accents in perennial and rock gardens or mixed into a shrub border. Several types of the larger clump-type grasses, set in straight lines or sweeping curves, make unusual summertime screens for enclosure and privacy. Hedging choices include *Calamagrostis, Cortaderia, Erianthus, Helictotrichon, Miscanthus,* and *Pennisetum.*

Grasses are ideal along drives and walkways; they can be cut to the soil level each fall, creating space to shovel snow without any harm to the grass planting itself, and they regrow quickly in spring.

Certain grasses can be planted in a large mass to serve as a ground cover. These include *Arundinaria, Hakonechloa, Phalaris,* and *Sasa.* Generally, grasses used as ground covers are best managed and most dense if mowed to the ground once or twice, depending on how the plant grows.

Two grasses serve as delightful edges along walks and planting beds. *Hakonechloa macra* 'Aureola' is ideal as a border along a shaded walkway. The variegated leaves brighten the space by daylight; at night, the yellow stripes pick up ambient light from nearby street lamps, defining the edge of the paving. *Molinia caerulea* 'Variegata' makes a wonderful border along a perennial garden, or a miniature hedge for lightly shaded sites; it can be substituted for less hardy plants like *Liriope muscari.*

Many grasses are most dramatic when dormant in the late fall and winter; they change from their normal green summer color to tan, bronze, copper, or golden-brown. In colder areas, planting these grasses where they can be seen from indoors provides inviting winter views for housebound occupants.

Design for a Mixed Planting

The garden design on the following pages combines ground covers and ornamental grasses in a foundation planting and a mixed border that will remain effective throughout the seasons. It shows you how to use a variety of spatial relationships within the home landscape, while allowing for normal traffic patterns. The taller plants used in the border, such as the grass *Miscanthus sacchariflorus,* create enclosure and privacy from the street and help delineate property lines. The low-growing shrub *Cotoneaster horizontalis* carpets the ground in place of lawn and supplies bright autumn color.

To provide further seasonal, textural, and color variety in the landscape, several of the plants included here may be combined with other species. For example, beneath the grass *Miscanthus sinensis* 'Gracillimus' are planted small, early-spring-blooming bulbs of crocus (*Crocus chrysanthus*) and snowdrop (*Galanthus nivalis*). This grass should be cut to soil level before the bulbs emerge. Elsewhere in the border, *Vinca minor* planted beneath the grass *Molinia caerulea* 'Variegata' offers contrasting color, height, and texture. Underneath the Allegheny Serviceberry (*Amelanchier laevis*) trees flanking the entrance to the house are sweeps of *Liriope spicata* interspersed with spring-flowering *Narcissus* and fall crocus (*Colchicum autumnale*). Directly adjacent to the house, a planting of *Hosta sieboldiana* 'Elegans' is preceded in early spring by *Narcissus* bulbs, and the grasslike, evergreen *Liriope spicata* is planted beneath the deciduous hostas for textural contrast and year-round cover.

Garden Design

Key to a mixed
planting:

1. *Miscanthus
   sacchariflorus*
2. *Miscanthus
   sinensis* 'Gracillimus'
3. *Juniperus chinensis
   sargentii*
4. *Paxistima canbyi*
5. *Alchemilla mollis*
6. **Sedum**
   'Weihenstephaner
   Gold'

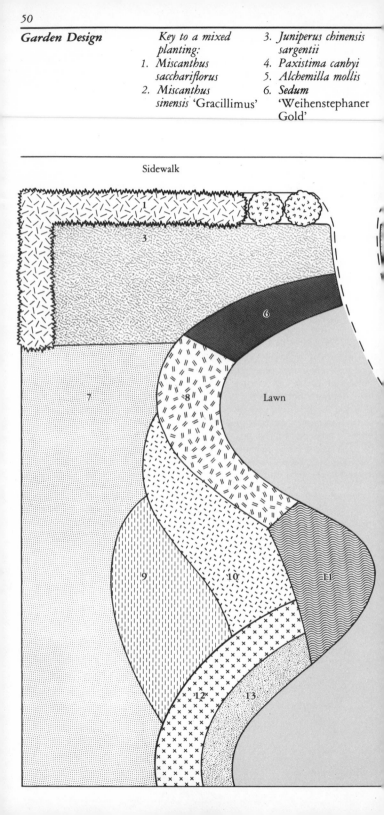

Sidewalk

Lawn

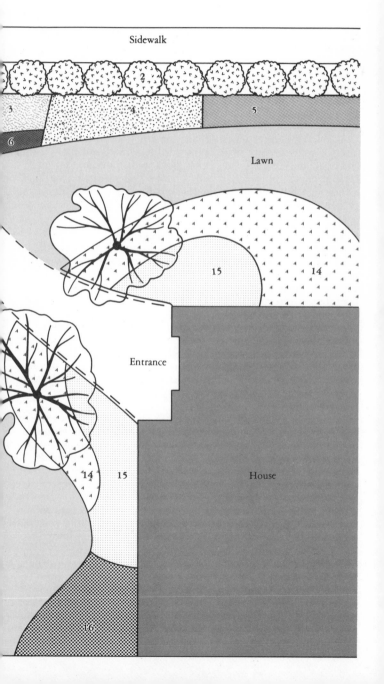

Lawn Care

Many gardeners consider a lush, green turfgrass lawn the ultimate ground cover and will accept no substitutes.

General Guidelines

There are a few rules for successfully establishing and maintaining a lawn in any location. First, seek the advice of a local nurseryman or the Cooperative Extension Service, and choose a type of grass known to grow well in the area. Buy top-quality, weed-free seeds or sod from reliable sources—inferior components yield an inferior lawn. Use the right amount of recommended fertilizers, and apply them at the best time for your area. Lawn grass needs the equivalent of 1 inch of rainfall per week; if rain is in short supply, give your lawn a thorough soaking. Be on the lookout for insect and disease problems, and treat them immediately.

Cool-Season and Warm-Season Grasses

There are 2 basic kinds of grasses, cool-season and warm-season. Cool-season grasses, grown from zone 7 northward, are also adapted to the Pacific Northwest and in western mountains where rainfall is adequate. These grasses include Kentucky Bluegrass, fescues, bentgrasses, and ryegrasses; they tolerate cold but dislike summer heat, and grow best in spring and fall.

Cool-season grasses are usually started from seed available either individually or in blends. For cool temperate regions with adequate summer rainfall, the basis of all mixtures is Kentucky Bluegrass (*Poa pratensis*). Because this grass is not thoroughly established the first season, it is mixed with other, fast-growing species that make a good early showing but are ultimately crowded out by Kentucky Bluegrass.

Warm-season grasses are at their best in zones 9 and 10 in the South and Southwest. They grow well during hot weather and become dormant when temperatures drop below freezing, turning brown. Even when dormant, the thick carpet acts as a barrier to weeds. The most widely grown warm-season grasses are Bermuda, St. Augustine, zoysia, and centipede. Improved selections and hybrids are available, and are sold as sod, plugs, sprigs, or stolons, depending on the type. The dormant brown grass can be overseeded for the winter with green annual ryegrass. If annual rye persists the following year, mow it very short in late spring to encourage the permanent lawn.

Soil Preparation

Any good garden loam will grow a good lawn. However, lawn grasses will not tolerate soil that is markedly acid or predominantly sand. If soil acidity is below pH 5.5, you must raise the pH before trying to establish a lawn. Usually all that is necessary is to broadcast just enough agricultural lime to cover the soil—50 to 75 pounds per 1000 square feet; then rake it in thoroughly. If your soil is too sandy, add organic matter.

Good permanent lawns that will survive summer heat and dryness should be grown on at least 8 inches of topsoil, and 12 inches is better. In deep soil the grasses get a firm, deep hold with their roots in the coolest and moistest layer of the topsoil. If you do not have at least 8 inches of topsoil, add some from another place.

Prepare lawn soil as you would garden soil. Incorporate organic matter and lawn fertilizer, following directions on the bag. Thoroughly mix the soil amendments—including lime, if needed—by turning over the soil.

Rototilling saves time but only a final hand-raking will leave the soil smooth and fine enough for a good lawn. See that all lumps are broken up. Seeds, sod, and plugs "take" better on freshly raked land. If the yard is large, work in small areas at one time.

Planting Grass Seed

Cool-season grasses grow best from seed; fall is the best time to begin, with spring planting the second choice. Seed on a still day, because grass seed is fine and can be carried to other areas by the wind. You may seed by hand or by mechanical spreader. The amount of seed required depends on soil type and the kind of grass mixture; follow package instructions.

For thorough distribution, divide the grass seed in half. While sowing the first half, walk back and forth in parallel lines; then sow the second half on the same area by walking in lines at right angles to the first lines. Rake the seeds in lightly and tamp the area down with a board, the back of a spade, or a roller. Keep the area well watered, but not soggy, until new growth is well established.

Sod, Plugs, and Sprigs

Warm-season grasses are best grown from sod, plugs, or sprigs. They grow rapidly in hot weather, so spring is the best time to start or repair this type of lawn. To establish a sod lawn, prepare the soil as previously described, with topsoil 7 to 7½ inches deep, to allow for sod thickness. Unroll the sod and lay the strips parallel, with the ends staggered in a bricklike pattern. Water thoroughly and frequently until the roots knit with the underlying soil.

Plugs are small squares of sod used to establish zoysia grass or to patch some established lawns. Plant plugs 6 to 12 inches apart in a pattern of alternating rows.

Sprigs and stolons can be planted in 2 ways. In a small area, plant them 6 to 12 inches apart in shallow parallel trenches; cover them with soil and tamp it down. On larger areas, scatter sprigs or stolons over the ground and cover with soil. Keep the soil moist until the grass takes root and begins to grow.

Watering

One of the keys to success with your lawn is to provide adequate moisture, but not to the point where waterborne diseases develop.

Various kinds of soaker hoses and sprinklers make watering easy. Soaker hoses can be laid out to fit oddly shaped areas, and oscillating and turret sprinklers cover areas of different sizes and shapes without waste. Avoid running sprinklers during the hottest part of the day, when much water will be lost to evaporation. Early-morning watering, especially where humidity is high, allows grass to dry quickly, decreasing the incidence of fungus diseases.

Underground water systems—drip irrigation or sprinklers—save labor but are expensive and require advance planning. Drip irrigation systems provide water by capillary action; they consist of plastic tubes with periodic emitters buried under the turf. Sprinklers have underground pipes with heads that pop up when the water is turned on and drop down when not in use. The best time to install an underground system is after your soil has been prepared, but before planting. Consult an irrigation systems designer.

No matter which system you use, soak your lawn so thoroughly that the soil will be wet to a depth of 7 to 8 inches—where the roots ought to be. One soaking each week is all you need, and one thorough watering is of the greatest benefit during a long dry spell.

Surface sprinkling causes roots to seek moisture near the surface, making constant sprinkling necessary. If you have adequate summer rainfall, and if your lawn is grown on a proper depth of topsoil, it ought not to need watering except in periods of extreme heat and drought. (Creeping Bentgrass, however, needs constant watering.)

Fertilizer

Supplement nutrients twice a year. Since green foliage is the goal, a high-nitrogen fertilizer is more economical than a balanced formula. Follow package instructions for amounts, and water the fertilizer in well if rain is not expected. Feed cool-season grasses in early spring and fall, warm-season grasses in late spring and early fall.

Mowing

No hard-and-fast rule governs the frequency of mowing. During rainy spring weather in the East, you may need to mow every 5 days; later in the summer, mow only as often as absolutely necessary to keep an even carpet. This may mean mowing twice a month during a dry August. A rotary mower will do an adequate job on most lawns, especially those with cool-season grasses; reel-type mowers may give warm-season lawns a better appearance.

Mow often enough that a properly set mower will clip only about one-half to three-quarters of an inch off the top. Do not set the blades too low; cutting too close exposes the crown of the plant to too much direct sunlight, dries out the soil, and encourages weeds. (In the case of Creeping Bentgrass, however, the machine cannot be set too low.) After an ordinary cutting, do not rake the lawn; short clippings will filter down and help create a mulch over the roots, conserving moisture. Decaying clippings also contribute nitrogen. If the grass is very long, the clippings will have to be raked or caught in a bag; too heavy a mat of clippings blocks air and water from the roots and can harbor diseases.

Mow new lawns for the first time when the grass is 3 inches high; follow general mowing directions thereafter. Grass seed is certain to settle unevenly, so after the first mowing, fill all depressions with fine topsoil and reseed immediately.

Weeds

Regular mowing prevents annual weeds from ever flowering or seeding. Mowing also keeps most upright perennials from seeding, but a few deep-rooted perennials—dock, dandelion, and any other weed with a deep taproot—will not be discouraged. Use a knife to cut out these weeds as deeply as possible below ground level.

If weeds are numerous, use a commercial weed killer. Selective herbicides kill only the target weeds without injuring the lawn; nonselective types kill both weeds and grass without distinction. For small areas, try spot treatment with aerosols, which place the chemical exactly where you want it, with little danger of drift.

Control broadleaf weeds—such as dandelions, plantain, and veronica—in cool-season lawns by spraying with selective herbicides containing 2, 4-D and dicamba. (Most warm-season grasses are somewhat sensitive to these remedies.) Pre-emergent herbicides can prevent seed germination of certain weeds, notably crabgrass.

Before planting your lawn, treat weedy areas with nonselective weed killers. Be sure to use a herbicide with a short-term residual effect in the soil, such as glyphosate. Applied to bare ground, mixtures containing diphenamid and trifluralin can control future weed seed germination.

Always use herbicides with caution; be sure to use the right one, and carefully follow label directions concerning amounts, timing, and disposal. Spray only on windless days and protect nearby ornamentals from drift.

Insects and Diseases

The best defense against insects and diseases is preventive care. Diagnosis and treatment varies considerably; consult your local nurseryman or Cooperative Extension Service for specific information.

Restoration

Sometimes lawns deteriorate as a result of poor maintenance, excess wear, or overtreatment with herbicides. You should renovate in the same season that is best for planting lawns in your area—fall for cool-season grasses, late spring for warm-season grasses. Top-dress minor damage with 2 to 3 inches of topsoil; then seed, sprig, or plug, and keep the area moist until the new grass is established. For major repairs, remove existing sod, and proceed as for a new lawn.

Garden Diary

Keeping track of plant and seed orders, weather conditions, and plant performance doesn't have to involve mountains of paperwork. A notebook can serve as a diary or journal. Good notes include not only the tasks you undertook and the weather, but also your personal impressions of the garden. Is that evergreen vine getting sun-scorched on the south wall of the house? Did you like the color of the new epimedium? Entries need not be elaborate, but they should include the date and be neat so you can read them later.

Weather
Note such unusual features as late or early frosts, heavy rain or wind, high and low temperatures, and the date of each rainfall.

Plant Records
Note new plants you grow and describe how they perform. Are they spreading too vigorously? Would you plant them again?

Seed and Plant Orders
Keep a record of mail orders as a reminder of where you obtained a specific plant and when you ordered it. The copy will serve as a checklist against the actual plants or seeds received.

Propagation Records
Record when seeds were stratified and planted, what cuttings were taken, what percentage rooted, how long it took, the method you used to root them, and when you divided any plants.

Pests and Diseases
Which pests and diseases plagued your garden and when did they appear? What did you use to treat them, how much, and when?

Soil Improvement
Log all soil improvements you make and record results of any tests.

Fertilizers
Which did you use, how much, and when?

Books and Articles
Keep a record of gardening articles you may want to refer to again. Also note any new (or old) gardening books you want to read.

New Ideas
What did you hear from another gardener, read, or see that might be interesting or helpful to try in your own garden?

Personal Events
Record personal experiences. What did you grow that was new or "impossible?" What aspect of the garden pleases you the most?

& Calendar

Ground covers, once established, are among the least demanding of plants, but they do need special attention from time to time to remain in peak condition. Think of the tasks outlined here as guidelines rather than as hard-and-fast rules.

Whatever the timing and length of the seasons are in your location, use common sense and don't be too rigid in planning your seasonal gardening tasks. If the winter has been particularly mild, you may be able to begin spring gardening activities several weeks sooner than usual. Likewise, in a long, mild autumn, cleanup may be delayed for a while, but don't be caught unprepared by that first cold snap. Remember, the dates of the first and last frosts in your region are the best indicators of when winter actually begins and spring ends.

Early Spring

Most gardeners think of this time as the beginning of the year. As the weather settles and new growth begins, remove pine boughs and other winter protection. Check shrubs as they begin to leaf out and remove any winter-damaged twigs. Heaths and heathers should be pruned hard to encourage compact growth. Prune summer-flowering vines and climbing roses to remove old growth and maintain shape. Cut ornamental grasses to the ground before new growth begins. Scatter a small amount of balanced fertilizer around established plantings of ground covers, preferably before a rain. Treat lawns with pre-emergent herbicide and give cool-season lawns 25 percent of their annual fertilizer. Sow grass seed in bare spots, but delay major lawn renovations until fall. Sow seeds of annual vines and grasses indoors 6 to 8 weeks before last average frost date. Or, start them directly in the garden after the danger of frost is past. As the sun grows more intense, watch for rising temperatures and dryness in cold frames.

Spring

As temperatures rise and spring rains arrive, the garden tempo increases. Remove remaining winter protection and clear away debris and accumulated leaves. When the top growth of ground covers and ornamental grasses, including bamboos, is 3 to 4 inches tall, clumps can be divided and reset.

Prepare garden beds for planting, if possible allowing a few days for the soil to settle before putting in the plants. Begin weed patrol in ground cover plantings, because many weeds (especially chickweed) flower and set seeds early. Supplement mulch as needed. Cool-season lawns are growing rapidly now and require frequent mowing. Cut often enough so that no more than one-third of the height is removed at any given time.

Late Spring–Early Summer

Continue spring planting and division of ground covers, grasses, and vines. Seeds started earlier may be ready for thinning or transplanting, either to cold frames or to the garden. Plants wintered over in cold frames can be planted out now. Begin propagating ground covers and vines by layering, mulching the layer to ensure continued soil moisture. As soon as new growth firms up, begin propagation by cuttings, using side-shoots without flower buds whenever possible. Prune spring-flowering vines as needed after they finish blooming to maintain size and shape.

Now is the time to renovate warm-season lawns, control weeds, and routinely apply fertilizer. Mow and water lawns as needed, providing 1 inch of water per week if rainfall is insufficient. Watch for early signs of disease or insect problems in lawn and garden plantings and treat promptly to prevent severe infestations.

Summer

In the coolest climates planting can continue except during hot spells and drought, but do give extra attention to watering and mulching. In all areas watering and weeding the garden are major concerns; mulch will facilitate both. Remove spent flowers to keep plants tidy and prevent excess seedling formation. Prune back excess green growth on vigorous vines such as wisteria.

Continue propagating herbaceous perennials by cuttings, placing flats of cuttings away from direct sunlight.

Growth of cool-season lawns has slowed down now; raise mower height and reduce mowing frequency so that grass will better tolerate dryness and heat. Check lawns for grub and larvae infestations and treat if needed.

Note which plants are doing well and which are not; record ideas for future improvements. Above all, take time to enjoy your garden.

Late Summer

Continue with ongoing maintenance tasks: weeding, watering, and mowing. New growth of woody plants is ripe enough now for propagation by cuttings. Cut any flowers or ornamental grasses you want to dry; simply hang them upside down in a cool, dry area away from sunlight for several weeks. Prepare beds for fall planting, working organic matter into the soil. If seedlings and rooted cuttings are sturdy enough, transplant them to their permanent location. Order plants from catalogues for fall delivery.

Fall

In early fall when plants begin to look shabby, begin garden cleanup. Add leaves and clippings to the compost pile, but discard any material that is disease- or insect-infested. To hasten decomposition, sprinkle some complete fertilizer over materials as they are stacked on the compost pile. Plant ground covers, grasses, and vines in all areas. Where winters are cold, new plants need a minimum of 6 weeks to become established before the ground freezes. As temperatures drop, begin renovating and seeding cool-season lawns and apply 75 percent of their annual fertilizer allotment. For warm-season grasses, apply fall fertilizer 1 month before the lawn goes dormant. Continue mowing and watering as long as grass shows growth.

Late Fall–Early Winter
Complete cleanup of garden debris, since dead materials lying on the ground can harbor insects and diseases over the winter. Leave attractive foliage of ornamental grasses standing for winter effect. Before the ground freezes, thoroughly water woody evergreens to minimize winter desiccation. Newly planted evergreens can be sprayed with antidesiccants. Before closing cold frames down for the winter, water them well and add a container of rodent bait. Keep weeding until the ground freezes—you will be ahead of weeds in spring. Collect evergreen boughs for winter mulching, but do not place them on the beds until the ground has frozen. Secure vines to their supports so they will not be damaged by winter winds.
Clean, repair, oil, and sharpen garden tools and mowers, noting in your garden diary those that need to be replaced. Label and date all chemicals, discarding any that are more than 2 years old.
As warm-season grasses go dormant, you can overseed with annual ryegrass for a green lawn through the winter.

Winter
Winter is the time to review your garden diary for the successes and failures of the past year. With these observations in mind, send in plant and seed orders to mail-order suppliers. Look around the garden to see if you need more evergreens or ornamental grasses for winter interest. Watch sun patterns to see if evergreens are becoming sun-scorched; if so, note in your diary to move them in the spring. Take time to catch up on reading gardening articles and books, looking for new ideas to put to work. During thaws, check to see if plants are heaving and need more winter protection.

Late Winter
This is a time when many gardeners are overzealous and try to do too much too soon in the garden. The soil is still too wet to dig. On mild days, prune vines and shrubs, but be careful not to step on dormant perennials while you work. If any plants have heaved from the ground as a result of alternate freezing and thawing, carefully press them back into the soil.
Sharpen and repair garden tools not attended to earlier. Make sure you have adequate supplies for starting seeds and for garden bed improvement. This is the last call for the best selection of mail-order seeds and plants for spring delivery.
You have now arrived back at the beginning of a new gardening year. Using the calendar and diary as guidelines, you should find that your garden becomes more satisfying with each passing year.

Buying Plants

Gardeners are generous people, and plants, which grow and multiply, foster these generous instincts. The plants you receive as gifts from neighboring gardeners are likely to grow well for you because they were successful in your area. However, be wary of accepting gift plants that may be too invasive for your garden. Determine how fast they spread before using them in your garden. In the beginning you will probably buy most of the plants you need. They are available from local garden centers and specialty nurseries or by mail order.

Ordering Through the Mail

Many mail-order nurseries advertise their catalogues in the classified section of gardening magazines. If you don't know the company, judge it by the descriptions and other information the catalogue gives on plants, not by the color photographs. These descriptions should include the botanical name of the plant as well as its hardiness zone and cultural requirements. Ground cover descriptions should also give some indication of whether the plant is too vigorous for small areas.

Plants may be available for either spring or autumn shipping. Nurseries frequently dig up plants for early spring delivery the previous autumn, then store them in refrigerators over winter. Plants for fall delivery are freshly dug and packed just as they begin to go dormant. Consequently they can make the transfer into your garden with less shock than plants that have been out of the ground for a long time.

Study catalogues in advance to become familiar with the suppliers' policy on terms of sale, shipping dates, and plant guarantees. It is helpful to specify a shipping date that coordinates with the best planting time in your area, especially if the supplier is located in another section of the country. At present, delivery by United Parcel Service seems to be more reliable than the U.S. Postal Service.

Do not expect too much initially from mail-order plants, woody or herbaceous. You are basically buying rootstocks, and the plants you receive will not look like the glowing catalogue pictures. Give them some time and proper care, however, and they will soon become established and grow well. Do not be influenced too much by low prices, as plants offered at inexpensive rates may be small and take additional time to become established. This is especially important for fall planting, because small plants with inadequate root systems will probably succumb the first winter. If you need large numbers of ground covers to fill in a big area, purchase a few good-size stock plants and propagate your own rather than buying a quantity of undersize plants.

Unpack mail-order plants immediately upon their arrival. If they appear desiccated, soak them in a one-quarter-strength solution of soluble fertilizer before planting or potting up. Clip off any broken stems or roots.

It is important for fellow gardeners that you report to the supplier any plants that are unsatisfactory. Most nurserymen are honest and anxious to protect their reputations. Write a letter specifically describing the problem (plant dead, dried out, or unusually small) and indicate whether you want a refund or replacement. The catalogue should state the firm's policy on refunds.

Shopping at Local Nurseries

Local garden centers and nurseries sell most of their plants in containers; sometimes larger specimens are sold balled and burlapped. You will find the best selections in spring, but visit your garden center in summer or early fall as well to see herbaceous plants at their mature height, woody plants showing autumn color, and ornamental grasses at their peak.

The most widely used ground covers are available in flats containing 6, 12, or even 50 or 100 plants. These are more economical to buy than individual pots, and the plants are usually well rooted. They can be cut into cubes for easy removal and planting. Know the size of the area you need to cover; the garden center staff should be able to help you calculate how many plants you need, which will vary according to the ground cover you choose. If the salesperson does not answer your questions, or at least offer to find an answer, look elsewhere for your plants.

Choose plants that appear healthy and well cared for. Look for deep green foliage and dense, compact growth. Avoid tall, wiry plants that have been growing in a container so long they are shedding their lower leaves. If roots appear through the drainage holes or seem to spiral around inside the container, the plant is potbound and will adjust slowly when transplanted, no matter how carefully you untangle and spread out the roots.

Mail-Order Nurseries versus Garden Centers

When you buy plants locally, you can see what you are getting and choose the plants individually. Locally available specimens are likely to be larger than those bought through the mail. Multi-plant flats of ground covers are difficult to ship and so are available only from local sources, although small plants may be available in cell-packs from mail sources. Since plants in garden centers are usually sold potted, they can be kept in a shady spot until it suits your schedule to plant them.

Mail-order sources frequently offer a wider selection of plants. These plants, however, are usually shipped bare root, have been out of the ground for long periods of time, and demand immediate attention upon their arrival.

Whether you buy plants from a local garden center or a mail-order nursery, beware of extravagant claims for plant performance. Reading about various plants and talking with other gardeners will help you form realistic expectations.

Nurseries

Bluebird Nursery Inc.
515 Linden Street, Clarkson, NE 68629
Kurt Bluemel Inc.
2740 Greene Lane, Baldwin, MD 21013
The Bovees Nursery
1737 S.W. Coronado, Portland, OR 97210
Busse Gardens
Route 2, Box 13, Cokato, MN 55321
Caprice Farm Nursery
15425 S.W. Pleasant Hill Road, Sherwood, OR 97140
Carlson's Gardens
Box 305, South Salem, NY 10509
Carroll Gardens
Box 310, Westminster, MD 21157
Clifford's Perennial and Vine
Box 320, Route 2, East Troy, WI 53120
Crownsville Nursery
1241 Generals Highway, Crownsville, MD 21032
The Cummins Garden
22 Robertsville Road, Marlboro, NJ 07446
Daystar (formerly The Rock Garden)
R.F.D. #2, Litchfield, ME 04350
DeGiorgi Co., Inc.
P.O. Box 413, Council Bluffs, IA 51502
Endangered Species
12571 Red Hill Avenue, Tustin, CA 92680
Englerth Gardens
2461 22nd Street, Hopkins, MI 49328
Far North Gardens
16785 Harrison, Livonia, MI 48154
Ferbert Garden Center
806 South Belt Highway, St. Joseph, MO 64507
Forestfarm
990 Tetherow Road, Williams, OR 97544
Foxborough Nursery
3611 Miller Road, Street, MD 21154
D. S. George Nurseries
2515 Penfield Road, Fairport, NY 14450
Gilson Gardens
P.O. Box 277, Perry, OH 44081
Russell Graham
4030 Eagle Crest Road, N.W., Salem, OR 97304
Greer Gardens
1280 Goodpasture Island Road, Eugene, OR 97401
Heaths and Heathers
Box 850, Elma, WA 98541
Holbrook Farm
Route 2, Box 223B, Fletcher, NC 28732

The following nurseries are among the retail sources for plants included in this book.

All firms listed will ship and all issue a retail catalogue; some charge for the catalogue.

Homestead Division of Sunnybrook Farms
9448 Mayfield Road, Chesterland, OH 44026
Charles Klehm & Son Nursery
2E Algonquin Road, Arlington Heights, IL 60005
Lamb Nurseries
E. 101 Sharp Avenue, Spokane, WA 99202
Louisiana Nursery
Route 7, Box 43, Opelousas, LA 70570
Maver's Rare Plant Nursery
R.R. #2, Box 265B, Price Road, Asheville, NC 28805
Mellingers
2310 W. South Range Road, North Lima, OH 44452
Milaeger's Gardens
4848 Douglas Avenue, Racine, WI 53402
Morningside Farm Nursery
Route 1, Box 151E, Morrilton, AR 72110
Park Seed Co., Inc.
Greenwood, SC 29647
Powell's Gardens
Route 3, Box 21, Princeton, NC 27569
Rakestraw's Gardens
3094 S. Term Street, Burton, MI 48529
Steve Ray's Bamboo Gardens
909 79th Place South, Birmingham, AL 35206
Rice Creek Gardens
1315 66th Avenue N.E., Minneapolis, MN 55432
Rocknoll Nursery
9210 Highway 50, Hillsboro, OH 45133
Roses of Yesterday & Today
802 Brown's Valley Road, Watsonville, CA 95076
Jim & Irene Russ
H.C.R. #1, Box 6450, Igo, CA 96047
Shady Oaks Nursery
700 19th Avenue N.E., Waseca, MN 56093
Siskiyou Rare Plant Nursery
2825 Cummings Road, Medford, OR 97501
Spring Hill Nurseries
110 West Elm Street, Tipp City, OH 45371
Thompson & Morgan
P.O. Box 1308, Jackson, NJ 08527
Upper Bank Nurseries
P.O. Box 486, Media, PA 19063
Andre Viette Farm & Nursery
Route 1, Box 16, Fisherville, VA 22939
Wayside Gardens
Hodges, SC 29695
White Flower Farm
Route 63, Litchfield, CT 06759

The plates on the following pages are
divided into four groups: foliage ground
covers; flowering ground covers; vines; and
grasses. The flowering ground covers are
arranged by color.

Visual Key
The visual key adds another dimension to
the color plates by providing an overview
of the various plant, leaf, and flower
shapes.
The first group represents ground covers that
are grown primarily for their foliage. They
include a wide range of leaf types and plant
shapes, from creeping evergreen junipers
with tiny, needlelike leaves to clump-forming
perennial hostas with broad, heart-shaped
leaves. The second group represents ground
covers that are grown for their flowers.
Among them are such favorites as primroses,
azaleas, and phlox. Next are the vines,
divided into two sections: those grown
mainly for foliage, such as the familiar
English ivy; and many others, such as
bougainvillea and clematis, known best for
their handsome flowers. Ornamental grasses
make up the last group. They range from
low, narrow-leaf tufts of silvery-blue sheep's
fescue to tall, majestic bamboos with
patterned stems.

Visual Key

Ground Covers

The plants in this group are grown chiefly for their foliage and include both deciduous and evergreen species. Some of these foliage plants also bear striking flowers or fruit.

Ground Covers: Flowers

This section features ground covers that are grown mainly for their attractive flowers. The photographs are arranged by flower color and shape.

This chart shows the
range of plants in each
group of color plates.

Pages 70–143

Pages 144–209

Vines

Versatile plants, vines can be trained to climb arbors, trellises, or porches, trailed over rocks or walls, or trimmed to ground cover size. Included here are herbaceous perennials and annuals as well as woody plants. The flowering vines are arranged by color.

Grasses

Ornamental grasses exist in a wide array of shapes, sizes, and colors. This group includes both herbaceous and woody-stemmed grasses, as well as a few plants that are not grasses at all but resemble them in form and use in the landscape.

Ground Covers

Opuntia humifusa *Prickly Pear* *Effective spring to*
Plant height: to 6 in. *summer*
p. 347 *Tolerates dry soil*
Zone 5

Lysimachia *Moneywort* *Effective spring to fall*
nummularia *Plant height: to 2 in.* *Tolerates shade and*
'Aurea' *p. 340* *wet soil*
Zone 4

Herniaria glabra   Rupturewort   Effective summer to
                         Plant height: to 3 in.   winter
                         p. 329   Zone 6

Baccharis pilularis   Dwarf Coyote Brush   Effective spring to fall
                            Plant height: 1–2 ft.   Tolerates dry soil
                            p. 303   Zone 7

Sedum cauticola   *Shortleaf Stonecrop*   *Effective spring to fall*
                         Plant height: to 3 in. *Tolerates dry soil*
                         p. 362   *Zone 5*

Sedum anglicum   *English Stonecrop*   *Effective spring to fall*
                        Plant height: to 2 in. *Tolerates dry soil*
                        p. 362   *Zone 4*

| *Saxifraga* × *urbium* | London Pride
Plant height: to 6 in.
p. 361 | Effective spring to fall
Tolerates shade
Zone 5 |

| *Sedum brevifolium* | Shortleaf Stonecrop
Plant height: to 3 in.
p. 362 | Effective spring to summer
Tolerates dry soil
Zone 4 |

Sedum
'Weihenstephaner
Gold'

Stonecrop
Plant height: to 6 in.
p. 363

Effective spring to fall
Tolerates dry soil
Zone 4

Sedum spurium
'Dragon's Blood'

Two-row Stonecrop
Plant height: to 6 in.
p. 363

Effective year-round
Tolerates dry soil
Zone 3

Sedum kamtschaticum

Stonecrop
Plant height: 6–9 in.
p. 362

Effective year-round
Tolerates dry soil
Zone 4

Sedum × rubrotinctum

Pork and Beans
Plant height: to 8 in.
p. 363

Effective spring to fall
Tolerates dry soil
Zone 8

Sagina subulata 'Aurea'

Scotch Moss
Plant height: to 4 in.
p. 359

Effective spring to fall
Tolerates shade
Zone 5

Thymus pseudolanuginosus

Woolly Thyme
Plant height: to 1 in.
p. 368

Effective spring to summer
Tolerates dry soil
Zone 4

Arenaria verna   Irish Moss
Plant height: to 2 in.
p. 299

Effective spring to summer
Tolerates shade
Zone 3

Sedum reflexum   Yellow Stonecrop
Plant height: to 3 in.
p. 363

Effective spring to summer
Tolerates dry soil
Zone 5

Arctostaphylos
'Emerald Carpet'

Emerald Carpet
Manzanita
Plant height: to 15 in.
p. 297

Effective year-round
Tolerates dry soil
Zone 8

Sedum lineare
'Variegatum'

Stringy Stonecrop
Plant height: to 6 in.
p. 362

Effective spring to
summer
Tolerates dry soil
Zone 5

| ***Teucrium chamaedrys* 'Prostratum'** | *Wall Germander*
Plant height: to 6 in.
p. 367 | *Effective spring to summer*
Tolerates dry soil
Zones 5–6 |

| ***Cerastium tomentosum*** | *Snow-in-Summer*
Plant height: to 6 in.
p. 309 | *Effective spring to summer*
Tolerates dry soil
Zone 4 |

Rosmarinus officinalis 'Prostratus'

Trailing Rosemary
Plant height: to 2 ft.
p. 357

Effective year-round
Tolerates dry soil
Zone 7

Galium odoratum

Sweet Woodruff
Plant height: to 12 in.
p. 321

Effective spring to fall
Tolerates shade
Zone 5

Paxistima canbyi   Rat-Stripper   Effective year-round
                       Plant height: to 12 in.   Tolerates shade
                       p. 349   Zone 5

Thymus serpyllum   Creeping Thyme   Effective spring to
                       Plant height: to 4 in.   summer
                       p. 368   Tolerates dry soil
                                                    Zone 4

Santolina chamaecyparissus

Lavender Cotton
Plant height: 1–2 ft.
p. 359

Effective spring to summer
Tolerates dry soil
Zone 6

Dianthus gratianopolitanus

Cheddar Pink
Plant height: 6–8 in.
p. 315

Effective spring to summer
Tolerates dry soil
Zone 5

Chamaemelum nobile	*Chamomile* *Plant height: to 12 in.* *p. 310*	*Effective spring to summer* *Zone 6*

Santolina virens	*Green Lavender Cotton* *Plant height: 10–18 in.* *p. 360*	*Effective spring to summer* *Tolerates dry soil* *Zone 6*

Taxus baccata 'Repandens'	*Spreading English Yew* *Plant height: to 2 ft.* *p. 366*	*Effective year-round* *Tolerates shade and dry soil* *Zone 5*

Microbiota decussata	*Siberian Carpet Cypress* *Plant height: to 2 ft.* *p. 342*	*Effective year-round* *Tolerates shade and dry soil* *Zone 3*

| ***Taxus cuspidata*** **'Densa'** | *Cushion Japanese Yew* *Plant height: to 18 in.* *p. 366* | *Effective year-round* *Tolerates shade and dry soil* *Zone 5* |

| ***Juniperus chinensis*** ***sargentii*** | *Sargent Juniper* *Plant height: to 18 in.* *p. 334* | *Effective year-round* *Zone 5* |

Juniperus conferta Shore Juniper *Effective year-round*
  Plant height: to 18 in. *Tolerates dry soil*
  p. 334 *Zone 6*

Juniperus sabina Savin *Effective year-round*
'Tamariscifolia' *Plant height: to 2 ft.* *Zone 4*
  p. 335

Juniperus conferta
Shore Juniper
Plant height: to 18 in.
p. 334

Effective year-round
Tolerates dry soil
Zone 6

Juniperus procumbens 'Nana'
Dwarf Japanese Juniper
Plant height: to 18 in.
p. 334

Effective year-round
Zone 5

Juniperus
horizontalis
'Plumosa'

Andorra Juniper
Plant height: to 18 in.
p. 334

Effective year-round
Tolerates dry soil
Zone 3

Juniperus
horizontalis
'Wiltonii'

Blue Rug Juniper
Plant height: to 6 in.
p. 334

Effective year-round
Tolerates dry soil
Zone 3

Juniperus
horizontalis
'Bar Harbor'

Bar Harbor Juniper
Plant height: to 12 in.
p. 334

Effective year-round
Tolerates dry soil
Zone 3

Juniperus
horizontalis
'Wiltonii'

Blue Rug Juniper
Plant height: to 6 in.
p. 334

Effective year-round
Tolerates dry soil
Zone 3

Leucothoe axillaris   Coast Leucothoe
Plant height: to 5 ft.
p. 339

Effective year-round
Tolerates shade
Zone 6

Mahonia repens   Creeping Mahonia
Plant height: to 12 in.
p. 341

Effective spring to fall
Tolerates shade
Zone 6

| *Xanthorhiza simplicissima* | Yellowroot
Plant height: to 2 ft.
p. 375 | Effective spring to fall
Tolerates shade and
wet soil
Zone 5 |

| *Rhus aromatica* 'Gro-Low' | Fragrant Sumac
Plant height: to 2 ft.
p. 356 | Effective summer to
fall
Tolerates dry soil
Zone 3 |

Arctostaphylos edmundsii

Little Sur Manzanita
Plant height: to 2 ft.
p. 297

Effective year-round
Tolerates shade
Zone 8

Gaultheria shallon

Salal
Plant height: to 3 ft.
p. 321

Effective year-round
Tolerates shade
Zone 6

Vaccinium	Low-Bush Blueberry	Effective spring to fall
angustifolium	Plant height: 1–2 ft.	Tolerates dry soil
	p. 370	Zone 3

Gaultheria shallon	Salal	Effective year-round
	Plant height: to 3 ft.	Tolerates shade
	p. 321	Zone 6

***Arctostaphylos
hookeri***
Monterey Manzanita
Plant height: to 4 ft.
p. 297
Effective year-round
Tolerates shade
Zone 8

***Gaylussacia
brachycera***
Box-Huckleberry
Plant height: 8–16 in.
p. 322
Effective year-round
Tolerates shade
Zone 5

Berberis verruculosa   *Warty Barberry*   *Effective year-round*
                           Plant height: to 3 ft.   *Zone 6*
                           p. 304

Paxistima myrsinites   *Oregon Boxwood*   *Effective year-round*
                           Plant height: to 2 ft.   *Tolerates shade*
                           p. 349   *Zone 5*

Arctostaphylos uva-ursi

Bearberry
Plant height: to 12 in.
p. 297

Effective year-round
Zone 3

Gaultheria procumbens

Wintergreen
Plant height: to 4 in.
p. 321

Effective year-round
Tolerates shade
Zone 5

Arctostaphylos uva-ursi

Bearberry
Plant height: to 12 in.
p. 297

Effective year-round
Zone 3

Gaultheria procumbens

Wintergreen
Plant height: to 4 in.
p. 321

Effective year-round
Tolerates shade
Zone 5

**Cotoneaster
horizontalis**

*Rock Cotoneaster
Plant height: to 3 ft.
p. 313*

*Effective spring to fall
Zone 5*

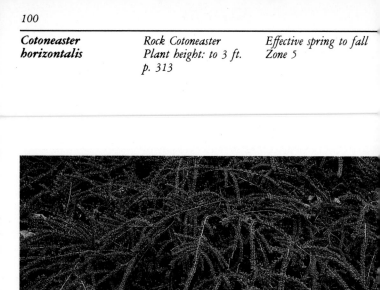

**Cotoneaster
apiculatus**

*Cranberry Cotoneaster
Plant height: to 3 ft.
p. 313*

*Effective spring to fall
Zone 5*

Cotoneaster horizontalis   *Rock Cotoneaster*   *Effective spring to fall*
                               Plant height: to 3 ft.   *Zone 5*
                               p. 313

Cotoneaster adpressus praecox   *Creeping Cotoneaster*   *Effective spring to fall*
                                    Plant height: to 12 in.   *Zone 5*
                                    p. 313

Ilex crenata
'Helleri'

Japanese Holly
Plant height: to 3 ft.
p. 332

Effective year-round
Zone 6

Skimmia reevesiana

Reeves Skimmia
Plant height: to 2 ft.
p. 364

Effective year-round
Tolerates shade
Zone 7

Cotoneaster
dammeri
'Skogsholm'

Bearberry Cotoneaster
Plant height: to 12 in.
p. 313

Effective spring to fall
Zone 5

Vaccinium
vitis-idaea minus

Mountain Cranberry
Plant height: to 6 in.
p. 370

Effective year-round
Zone 3

Euonymus fortunei
'Colorata'

Purple Winter Creeper
Plant height: to 18 in.
p. 319

Effective year-round
Tolerates shade
Zone 4

Mazus reptans

Plant height: to 2 in.
p. 341

Effective spring to
summer
Tolerates shade and
wet soil
Zone 6

Euonymus fortunei **'Kewensis'**　*Kew Winter Creeper*　*Effective year-round*
　　　　　　　　　　Plant height: to 2 in.　*Tolerates shade*
　　　　　　　　　　p. 319　　　　　　　　*Zone 4*

Mitchella repens　　*Partridge-Berry*　　　*Effective year-round*
　　　　　　　　　　Plant height: to 2 in.　*Tolerates shade*
　　　　　　　　　　p. 342　　　　　　　　*Zone 4*

Nandina domestica
'Harbor Dwarf'

Heavenly Bamboo
Plant height: 1½–2 ft.
p. 343

Effective spring to fall
Tolerates shade
Zone 7

Vinca minor

Periwinkle
Plant height: to 10 in.
p. 373

Effective year-round
Tolerates shade
Zone 5

Sarcococca
hookerana humilis

Sweet Box
Plant height: 6–24 in.
p. 360

Effective year-round
Tolerates shade
Zone 6

Vinca major

Big Periwinkle
Plant height: to 18 in.
p. 373

Effective year-round
Tolerates shade
Zone 7

***Lysimachia
nummularia***

*Moneywort
Plant height: to 2 in.
p. 340*

*Effective spring to fall
Tolerates shade and
wet soil
Zone 4*

***Geranium
macrorrhizum***

*Bigroot Cranesbill
Plant height: 12–18 in.
p. 325*

*Effective spring to fall
Tolerates shade
Zone 5*

Baccharis pilularis 'Twin Peaks'

Dwarf Coyote Brush
Plant height: to 20 in.
p. 303

Effective spring to fall
Tolerates dry soil
Zone 7

Potentilla tridentata

Three-toothed
Cinquefoil
Plant height: to 9 in.
p. 352

Effective spring to fall
Tolerates dry soil
Zone 3

Waldsteinia ternata Barren Strawberry   Effective year-round
Plant height: to 6 in.   Tolerates shade
p. 375   Zone 4

Duchesnea indica Mock Strawberry   Effective spring to fall
Plant height: 2–3 in.   Zone 4
p. 316

Potentilla tabernaemontani

Spring Cinquefoil
Plant height: to 4 in.
p. 351

Effective spring to summer
Tolerates dry soil
Zone 4

Waldsteinia fragarioides

Barren Strawberry
Plant height: 4–6 in.
p. 375

Effective year-round
Tolerates shade
Zone 5

Cornus canadensis   *Bunchberry*   *Effective spring to fall*
  Plant height: to 6 in.   *Tolerates shade*
  p. 312   *Zone 2*

Pachysandra   *Alleghany Spurge*   *Effective spring to*
procumbens   *Plant height: 8–10 in.*   *summer*
  p. 348   *Tolerates shade*
  Zone 5

| ***Cornus canadensis*** | *Bunchberry*
Plant height: to 6 in.
p. 312 | *Effective spring to fall*
Tolerates shade
Zone 2 |

| ***Fragaria chiloensis*** | *Beach Strawberry*
Plant height: 6–8 in.
p. 320 | *Effective spring to*
summer
Zone 5 |

Antennaria dioica   *Pussytoes*   *Effective spring to fall*
   Plant height: 4–12 in.   *Tolerates dry soil*
   p. 296   *Zones 4–5*

Pachysandra   *Japanese Spurge*   *Effective year-round*
terminalis   *Plant height: to 9 in.*   *Tolerates shade*
'Silver Edge'   *p. 348*   *Zone 5*

Pachysandra terminalis

Japanese Spurge
Plant height: to 9 in.
p. 348

Effective year-round
Tolerates shade
Zone 5

Ajuga reptans 'Bronze Beauty'

Bugleweed
Plant height: to 6 in.
p. 293

Effective spring to fall
Tolerates shade
Zone 3

Ajuga reptans   *Bugleweed*   *Effective spring to fall*
Purple-leaf form   *Tolerates shade*
Plant height: to 6 in.   *Zone 3*
p. 293

Ajuga pyramidalis   *Bugleweed*   *Effective spring to fall*
Plant height: to 10 in.   *Tolerates shade*
p. 293   *Zone 4*

| *Ajuga reptans* 'Multicolor Rainbow' | *Bugleweed* Plant height: to 6 in. p. 293 | *Effective spring to fall* Tolerates shade Zone 3 |

| *Ajuga reptans* 'Burgundy Glow' | *Bugleweed* Plant height: to 6 in. p. 293 | *Effective spring to fall* Tolerates shade Zone 3 |

Euonymus fortunei
'Silver Queen'

*Variegated Winter
Creeper
Plant height: to 2 ft.
p. 319*

*Effective year-round
Tolerates shade
Zone 4*

**Pulmonaria
saccharata**
'Mrs. Moon'

*Bethlehem Sage
Plant height: 8–14 in.
p. 354*

*Effective spring to fall
Tolerates shade
Zone 4*

| *Aegopodium podagraria* 'Variegatum' | *Goutweed*
Plant height: to 12 in.
p. 293 | *Effective spring to fall*
Tolerates shade
Zone 4 |

| **Lamium maculatum** | *Spotted Dead Nettle*
Plant height: to 12 in.
p. 336 | *Effective spring to fall*
Tolerates shade
Zone 4 |

Lamiastrum
galeobdolon
'Variegatum'

Variegated Yellow
Archangel
Plant height: to 12 in.
p. 335

Effective spring to fall
Tolerates shade
Zone 4

Lamium maculatum
'Beacon Silver'

Spotted Dead Nettle
Plant height: to 9 in.
p. 336

Effective spring to fall
Tolerates shade
Zone 4

Lamiastrum   *Yellow Archangel*   *Effective spring to fall*
galeobdolon *Plant height: to 12 in.* *Tolerates shade*
'Herman's Pride' *p. 335*   *Zone 4*

Lamium maculatum   *Spotted Dead Nettle*   *Effective spring to fall*
'White Nancy'   *Plant height: to 9 in.* *Tolerates shade*
                         p. 336   *Zone 4*

***Asarum
shuttleworthii*
'Callaway'**

*Southern Wild Ginger
Plant height: to 5 in.
p. 301*

*Effective spring to fall
Tolerates shade
Zone 6*

Asarum caudatum

*British Columbia
Wild Ginger
Plant height: to 6 in.
p. 301*

*Effective year-round
Tolerates shade
Zone 6*

Asarum europaeum   European Wild Ginger   Effective year-round
Plant height: to 7 in.   Tolerates shade
p. 301   Zone 5

Asarum canadense   Wild Ginger   Effective spring to
Plant height: 6–8 in.   summer
p. 301   Tolerates shade
Zone 4

Rubus calycinoides
Bramble
Plant height: to 2 in.
p. 358

Effective year-round
Tolerates dry soil
Zone 7

***Saxifraga
stolonifera***
Strawberry Geranium
Plant height: to 5 in.
p. 361

Effective spring to
summer
Tolerates shade
Zone 7

| *Vancouveria hexandra* | American Barrenwort Plant height: to 18 in. p. 370 | Effective spring to summer Tolerates shade Zone 5 |

| *Epimedium* × *versicolor* 'Sulphureum' | Epimedium Plant height: to 12 in. p. 317 | Effective spring to fall Tolerates shade and dry soil Zone 5 |

Epimedium
grandiflorum
'Rose Queen'

Longspur Epimedium
Plant height: to 12 in.
p. 317

Effective spring to fall
Tolerates shade and
dry soil
Zone 5

Epimedium ×
rubrum

Red Epimedium
Plant height: to 12 in.
p. 317

Effective spring to fall
Tolerates shade and
dry soil
Zone 5

Epimedium ×
warleyense

Warley Epimedium
Plant height: 9–12 in.
p. 317

Effective spring to fall
Tolerates shade and
dry soil
Zone 5

Epimedium alpinum

Alpine Epimedium
Plant height: to 10 in.
p. 317

Effective spring to fall
Tolerates shade and
dry soil
Zone 4

128

Viburnum davidii	David Viburnum Plant height: 1–2½ ft. p. 373	Effective year-round Tolerates shade Zone 8

Stachys byzantina 'Silver Carpet'	Lamb's-Ears Plant height: to 8 in. p. 364	Effective year-round Tolerates dry soil Zone 5

Omphalodes verna

Blue-Eyed Mary
Plant height: to 8 in.
p. 345

Effective spring to
summer
Tolerates shade
Zone 5

Stachys byzantina

Lamb's-Ears
Plant height: to 8 in.
p. 364

Effective year-round
Tolerates dry soil
Zone 5

Artemisia stellerana   Beach Wormwood   *Effective spring to fall*
                          Plant height: to 2 ft.   *Tolerates dry soil*
                          p. 300   *Zones 3–4*

Heuchera sanguinea   Coralbells   *Effective spring to fall*
'Coral Cloud'   *Plant height: to 12 in.*   *Tolerates shade*
                          p. 329   *Zone 5*

Alchemilla mollis	*Lady's-Mantle* *Plant height: to 15 in.* *p. 294*	*Effective spring to fall* *Tolerates shade and* *wet soil* *Zone 4*

Tolmiea menziesii	*Piggyback Plant* *Plant height: to 9 in.* *p. 369*	*Effective spring to* *summer* *Tolerates shade and* *wet soil* *Zone 8*

Tellima grandiflora
Fringe-Cups
Plant height: to 12 in.
p. 366

Effective spring to
summer
Tolerates shade
Zone 5

**Brunnera
macrophylla**
Siberian Bugloss
Plant height: 12–18 in.
p. 306

Effective spring to
summer
Tolerates shade
Zone 4

Galax urceolata   *Galax*   *Effective spring to fall*
                             Plant height: to 6 in.   *Tolerates shade*
                             p. 320   *Zone 5*

Hedera canariensis   *Algerian Ivy*   *Effective year-round*
                             Plant height: to 12 in.   *Tolerates shade*
                             p. 327   *Zone 8*

Hosta sieboldiana   *Siebold Plantain-lily*   *Effective summer to*
'Elegans'   *Plant height: to 2½ ft.*   *fall*
    p. 330   *Tolerates shade*
    Zone 4

Bergenia cordifolia   *Heartleaf Bergenia*   *Effective year-round*
    Plant height: 12–18 in.   *Tolerates shade*
    p. 304   *Zone 3*

Hosta sieboldiana | *Siebold Plantain-lily* | *Effective summer to*
| *Plant height: to 2½ ft.* | *fall*
| *p. 330* | *Tolerates shade*
| | *Zone 4*

Bergenia ciliata | *Bergenia* | *Effective year-round*
| *Plant height: to 12 in.* | *Tolerates shade*
| *p. 304* | *Zone 6*

Bergenia ciliata
Bergenia
Plant height: to 12 in.
p. 304

Effective year-round
Tolerates shade
Zone 6

Bergenia cordifolia
'Profusion'
Heartleaf Bergenia
Plant height: 12–18 in.
p. 304

Effective year-round
Tolerates shade
Zone 3

Bergenia crassifolia **hybrid**	*Siberian Tea* *Plant height: to 18 in.* *p. 305·*	*Effective year-round* *Tolerates shade* *Zone 3*

Bergenia crassifolia	*Siberian Tea* *Plant height: to 18 in.* *p. 305*	*Effective year-round* *Tolerates shade* *Zone 3*

Aspidistra elatior   Cast-Iron Plant
Plant height: to 2 ft.
p. 302

Effective year-round
Tolerates shade and
dry soil
Zone 8

Convallaria majalis   Lily-of-the-Valley
Plant height: 6–12 in.
p. 311

Effective spring to
summer
Tolerates shade
Zone 4

Hosta lancifolia

Narrow Plantain-lily
Plant height: to 12 in.
p. 330

Effective summer to
fall
Tolerates shade
Zone 4

Hosta
'Golden Tiara'

Plantain-lily
Plant height: to 10 in.
p. 330

Effective spring to
summer
Tolerates shade
Zone 4

Hosta
'Gold Standard'

Plantain-lily
Plant height: to 18 in.
p. 330

Effective spring to
summer
Tolerates shade
Zone 4

Hosta
'Ginko Craig'

Plantain-lily
Plant height: to 10 in.
p. 330

Effective spring to
summer
Tolerates shade
Zone 4

| *Hosta* 'Francee' | Plantain-lily
Plant height: to 15 in.
p. 330 | *Effective spring to summer*
Tolerates shade
Zone 4 |

| *Disporum sessile* 'Variegatum' | *Variegated Japanese Fairy-Bells*
Plant height: 1–2 ft.
p. 316 | *Effective spring to summer*
Tolerates shade
Zone 5 |

Liriope muscari
'Variegata'

Blue Lily-Turf
Plant height: to 18 in.
p. 339

Effective year-round
Tolerates shade and
dry soil
Zone 6

Ophiopogon
japonicus

Mondo Grass
Plant height: to 12 in.
p. 346

Effective year-round
Tolerates shade
Zone 7

Liriope spicata

Creeping Lily-Turf
Plant height: to 10 in.
p. 339

Effective year-round
Tolerates shade and
dry soil
Zone 5

Ophiopogon
planiscapus
'**Arabicus**'

Black Mondo Grass
Plant height: to 10 in.
p. 346

Effective year-round
Tolerates shade
Zone 7

Ground Covers.

Flowers

Primula ×
polyantha

Primrose
Plant height: to 12 in.
p. 352

Effective in spring
Tolerates shade
Zone 5

Primula ×
polyantha

Primrose
Plant height: to 12 in.
p. 352

Effective in spring
Tolerates shade
Zone 5

| Primula ×
polyantha | Primrose
Plant height: to 12 in.
p. 352 | Effective in spring
Tolerates shade
Zone 5 |

| Primula veris | Cowslip
Plant height: to 8 in.
p. 352 | Effective in spring
Tolerates shade
Zone 5 |

| **Hemerocallis** 'Hyperion' | Daylily Plant height: 1–5 ft. p. 328 | Effective spring to summer Tolerates shade and wet or dry soil Zone 3 |

| **Hemerocallis** hybrids | Daylily Plant height: 1–5 ft. p. 328 | Effective spring to summer Tolerates shade and wet or dry soil Zone 3 |

| *Hemerocallis* **hybrids** | *Daylily* *Plant height: 1–5 ft.* *p. 328* | *Effective spring to summer* *Tolerates shade and wet or dry soil* *Zone 3* |

| *Hemerocallis* **hybrid** | *Daylily* *Plant height: 1–5 ft.* *p. 328* | *Effective spring to summer* *Tolerates shade and wet or dry soil* *Zone 3* |

Arctotis
hybrids

African Daisy
Plant height: to 15 in.
p. 299

Effective spring to
summer
Tolerates dry soil
Zone 9

Gazania rigens
leucolaena

Treasure Flower
Plant height: to 16 in.
p. 323

Effective spring to fall
Zone 9

**Arctotheca
calendula**

Cape Weed
Plant height: to 12 in.
p. 298

*Effective spring to
summer
Tolerates dry soil
Zone 9*

**Eriophyllum
lanatum**

Woolly Eriophyllum
Plant height: to 2 ft.
p. 318

*Effective spring to
summer
Tolerates dry soil
Zone 5*

Lampranthus | Ice Plant | Effective in spring
aureus | Plant height: to 18 in. | Tolerates dry soil
| p. 337 | Zone 9

Helianthemum | Rock Rose | Effective spring to
nummularium | Plant height: to 12 in. | summer
'Firedragon' | p. 327 | Tolerates dry soil
| | Zone 6

Lampranthus
'Gold Bush'

Ice Plant
Plant height: to 18 in.
p. 337

Effective in spring
Tolerates dry soil
Zone 9

Helianthemum
nummularium

Rock Rose
Plant height: to 12 in.
p. 327

Effective spring to
summer
Tolerates dry soil
Zone 6

Potentilla
tabernaemontani

Spring Cinquefoil
Plant height: to 4 in.
p. 351

Effective spring to
summer
Tolerates dry soil
Zone 4

Chrysogonum
virginianum

Green-and-Gold
Plant height: 4–10 in.
p. 310

Effective spring to
summer
Tolerates shade
Zone 5

Genista pilosa
Broom
Plant height: to 20 in.
p. 323

Effective year-round
Tolerates dry soil
Zone 6

Oenothera tetragona
Sundrops
Plant height: 1–2 ft.
p. 345

Effective in summer
Tolerates dry soil
Zone 5

Santolina chamaecyparissus   *Lavender Cotton*
Plant height: 1–2 ft.
p. 359

Effective spring to summer
Tolerates dry soil
Zone 6

Achillea tomentosa   *Woolly Yarrow*
Plant height: to 8 in.
p. 292

Effective spring to summer
Zone 3

Santolina virens   Green Lavender Cotton   *Effective spring to*
                          Plant height: 10–18 in.   *summer*
                          p. 360   *Tolerates dry soil*
                                                     Zone 6

Genista sagittalis   Broom   *Effective year-round*
                            Plant height: to 20 in. *Zone 6*
                            p. 324

Sedum kamtschaticum

Stonecrop
Plant height: 6–9 in.
p. 362

Effective year-round
Tolerates dry soil
Zone 4

Lysimachia nummularia

Moneywort
Plant height: to 2 in.
p. 340

Effective spring to fall
Tolerates shade and
wet soil
Zone 4

| **Sedum** 'Weihenstephaner Gold' | *Stonecrop* *Plant height: to 6 in.* *p. 363* | *Effective spring to fall* *Tolerates dry soil* *Zone 4* |

| **Lysimachia nummularia** 'Aurea' | *Moneywort* *Plant height: to 2 in.* *p. 340* | *Effective spring to fall* *Tolerates shade and wet soil* *Zone 4* |

Opuntia humifusa
Prickly Pear
Plant height: to 6 in.
p. 347

Effective spring to summer
Tolerates dry soil
Zone 5

Waldsteinia fragarioides
Barren Strawberry
Plant height: 4–6 in.
p. 375

Effective year-round
Tolerates shade
Zone 5

Hypericum calycinum

Aaron's-Beard
Plant height: to 12 in.
p. 331

Effective in summer
Tolerates shade and
dry soil
Zone 5

Duchesnea indica

Mock Strawberry
Plant height: 2–3 in.
p. 316

Effective spring to fall
Zone 4

Phlox subulata
Moss Pink
Plant height: to 6 in.
p. 350

Effective spring to fall
Tolerates dry soil
Zone 4

Arenaria montana
Mountain Sandwort
Plant height: to 4 in.
p. 299

Effective spring to
summer
Zone 4

Phlox nivalis

Trailing Phlox
Plant height: to 6 in.
p. 350

Effective in spring
Tolerates dry soil
Zone 6

Leiophyllum
buxifolium
prostratum

Allegheny Sand
Myrtle
Plant height: to 4 in.
p. 338

Effective in spring
Tolerates wet soil
Zone 6

Potentilla tridentata   *Three-toothed*   *Effective spring to fall*
                             Cinquefoil   *Tolerates dry soil*
                             Plant height: to 9 in. *Zone 3*
                             p. 352

Arenaria verna   *Irish Moss*   *Effective spring to*
                      Plant height: to 2 in. *summer*
                      p. 299   *Tolerates shade*
                                                Zone 3

Arabis procurrens	*Rock Cress* *Plant height: to 12 in.* *p. 296*	*Effective spring to* *summer* *Tolerates dry soil* *Zone 5*

Arabis caucasica **'Flore Pleno'**	*Wall Cress* *Plant height: to 12 in.* *p. 296*	*Effective spring to* *summer* *Tolerates dry soil* *Zone 4*

Cornus canadensis   *Bunchberry*   *Effective spring to fall*
                            Plant height: to 6 in.   *Tolerates shade*
                            p. 312   *Zone 2*

Anemone canadensis   *Canada Anemone*   *Effective spring to*
                           Plant height: to 2 ft.   *summer*
                           p. 295   *Tolerates shade*
                                                      Zone 4

| *Campanula carpatica* 'Alba' | Carpathian Harebell
Plant height: 6–12 in.
p. 307 | *Effective spring to summer*
Zone 4 |

| *Galium odoratum* | Sweet Woodruff
Plant height: to 12 in.
p. 321 | *Effective spring to fall*
Tolerates shade
Zone 5 |

Hebe menziesii   *Plant height: to 3 ft.*   *Effective year-round*
                      p. 326   *Zone 8*

Calluna vulgaris   Heather   *Effective year-round*
'Silver Knight'   *Plant height: to 18 in.*   *Zone 5*
                      p. 306

Iberis sempervirens | *Perennial Candytuft* | *Effective spring to*
Plant height: to 12 in. | *summer*
p. 332 | *Zone 5*

Calluna vulgaris | *Heather* | *Effective year-round*
'Kinlochruel' | *Plant height: to 18 in.* | *Zone 5*
p. 306

Erica carnea

Spring Heath
Plant height: to 12 in.
p. 318

Effective year-round
Zone 5

Symphytum grandiflorum

Plant height: 8–12 in.
p. 365

Effective spring to
summer
Tolerates shade and
dry soil
Zone 5

Daboecia cantabrica
'Alba'

Irish Heath
Plant height: to 2 ft.
p. 314

Effective year-round
Zone 5

Viola odorata
'White Czar'

Sweet Violet
Plant height: to 6 in.
p. 374

Effective spring to
summer
Tolerates shade
Zone 6

| **Convallaria majalis** | Lily-of-the-Valley
Plant height: 6–12 in.
p. 311 | Effective spring to
summer
Tolerates shade
Zone 4 |

| **Tiarella cordifolia** | Foamflower
Plant height: to 6 in.
p. 368 | Effective spring to
summer
Tolerates shade
Zone 5 |

Saxifraga stolonifera

Strawberry Geranium
Plant height: to 5 in.
p. 361

Effective spring to summer
Tolerates shade
Zone 7

Ajuga reptans 'Alba'

Bugleweed
Plant height: to 6 in.
p. 293

Effective spring to fall
Tolerates shade
Zone 3

Rhododendron
'Snow'

Kurume Azalea
Plant height: to 3 ft.
p. 355

Effective year-round
Tolerates shade
Zone 7

Leucothoe axillaris

Coast Leucothoe
Plant height: to 5 ft.
p. 339

Effective year-round
Tolerates shade
Zone 6

Rhododendron
kiusianum
'Album'

Kurume Azalea
Plant height: to 3 ft.
p. 355

Effective year-round
Tolerates shade
Zone 7

Epimedium ×
youngianum
'Niveum'

Snowy Epimedium
Plant height: to 10 in.
p. 317

Effective spring to fall
Zone 5

Robinia hispida

Rose Acacia
Plant height: 3–4 ft.
p. 357

Effective spring to summer
Tolerates dry soil
Zone 5

Rhododendron
'Hilda Niblett'

Robin Hill Azalea
Plant height: to 12 in.
p. 355

Effective year-round
Zone 6

Rhododendron
'Balsaminiflorum'

Indicum Dwarf
Azalea
Plant height: to 18 in.
p. 355

Effective year-round
Tolerates shade
Zone 6

Rhododendron
'Coral Bells'

Kurume Azalea
Plant height: to 3 ft.
p. 355

Effective year-round
Tolerates shade
Zone 7

Rhododendron kiusianum

Kurume Azalea
Plant height: to 3 ft.
p. 355

Effective year-round
Tolerates shade
Zone 7

Rhododendron 'Flame Creeper'

Indicum Dwarf
Azalea
Plant height: to 10 in.
p. 355

Effective year-round
Tolerates shade
Zone 6

Rhododendron | *North Tisbury Azalea* | *Effective year-round*
'Pink Pancake' | *Plant height: to 10 in.* | *Tolerates shade*
  | *p. 355* | *Zone 6*

Rhododendron | *Kurume Azalea* | *Effective year-round*
'Hino-crimson' | *Plant height: to 3 ft.* | *Tolerates shade*
  | *p. 355* | *Zone 7*

Verbena peruviana   *Verbena*
Plant height: 3–4 in.
p. 371

Effective spring to
summer
Tolerates dry soil
Zone 8

Sedum spurium   *Two-row Stonecrop*
'Dragon's Blood'   *Plant height: to 6 in.*
p. 363

Effective year-round
Tolerates dry soil
Zone 3

Verbena peruviana
Verbena
Plant height: 3–4 in.
p. 371

Effective spring to summer
Tolerates dry soil
Zone 8

Lantana montevidensis
Weeping Lantana
Plant height: to 18 in.
p. 337

Effective year-round
Tolerates dry soil
Zone 9

Daphne cneorum   *Rose Daphne*   *Effective spring to*
Plant height: to 12 in.   *summer*
p. 314   *Zone 5*

Andromeda   *Bog Rosemary*   *Effective year-round*
polifolia   *Plant height: to 12 in.*   *Tolerates wet soil*
p. 294   *Zone 3*

Coronilla varia
Crown Vetch
Plant height: to 18 in.
p. 312

Effective spring to summer
Tolerates dry soil
Zone 4

Antennaria dioica rosea
Pussytoes
Plant height: 4–12 in.
p. 296

Effective spring to fall
Tolerates dry soil
Zones 4–5

***Saxifraga* ×
*urbium***

London Pride
Plant height: to 6 in.
p. 361

Effective spring to fall
Tolerates shade
Zone 5

***Thymus
pseudolanuginosus***

Woolly Thyme
Plant height: to 1 in.
p. 368

Effective spring to
summer
Tolerates dry soil
Zone 4

| *Gypsophila repens* 'Rosea' | Creeping Baby's-Breath Plant height: to 6 in. p. 326 | Effective spring to fall Zone 4 |

| *Thymus serpyllum* | Creeping Thyme Plant height: to 4 in. p. 368 | Effective spring to summer Tolerates dry soil Zone 4 |

Veronica prostrata
'Rosea'

Rock Speedwell
Plant height: to 10 in.
p. 372

Effective spring to
summer
Zone 4

Teucrium
chamaedrys
'Prostratum'

Wall Germander
Plant height: to 6 in.
p. 367

Effective spring to
summer
Tolerates dry soil
Zones 5–6

***Astilbe chinensis* 'Pumila'**	*Chinese Astilbe* *Plant height: 8–12 in.* *p. 302*	*Effective spring to summer* *Tolerates shade* *Zone 5*

Bruckenthalia spiculifolia	*Spike-Heath* *Plant height: to 10 in.* *p. 305*	*Effective year-round* *Zone 5*

Erica carnea
'Springwood Pink'

Spring Heath
Plant height: to 12 in.
p. 318

Effective year-round
Zone 5

Calluna vulgaris
'Tib'

Heather
Plant height: to 18 in.
p. 306

Effective year-round
Zone 5

Calluna vulgaris
'County Wicklow'

Heather
Plant height: to 18 in.
p. 306

Effective year-round
Zone 5

Calluna vulgaris
'J. H. Hamilton'

Heather
Plant height: to 18 in.
p. 306

Effective year-round
Zone 5

***Polygonum
cuspidatum
compactum***

Dwarf Japanese
Fleece-Flower
Plant height: to 3 ft.
p. 351

*Effective spring to fall
Tolerates dry soil
Zone 4*

Daboecia cantabrica

Irish Heath
Plant height: to 2 ft.
p. 314

*Effective year-round
Zone 5*

Polygonum cuspidatum compactum

Dwarf Japanese
Fleece-Flower
Plant height: to 3 ft.
p. 351

Effective spring to fall
Tolerates dry soil
Zone 4

Pulmonaria montana 'Salmon Glow'

Mountain Lungwort
Plant height: to 15 in.
p. 353

Effective spring to
summer
Tolerates shade
Zone 4

Primula vulgaris

English Primrose
Plant height: to 6 in.
p. 353

Effective in spring
Tolerates shade
Zone 5

Osteospermum fruticosum

Trailing African
Daisy
Plant height: to 12 in.
p. 347

Effective year-round
Tolerates dry soil
Zone 9

| *Dianthus* *gratianopolitanus* | Cheddar Pink
Plant height: 6–8 in.
p. 315 | Effective spring to summer
Tolerates dry soil
Zone 5 |

| *Lampranthus* *spectabilis* | Ice Plant
Plant height: to 18 in.
p. 337 | Effective in spring
Tolerates dry soil
Zone 9 |

| ***Phlox subulata*** | Moss Pink
Plant height: to 6 in.
p. 350 | *Effective spring to fall*
Tolerates dry soil
Zone 4 |

| **Helianthemum**
nummularium
'Raspberry Ripple' | Rock Rose
Plant height: to 12 in.
p. 327 | *Effective spring to*
summer
Tolerates dry soil
Zone 6 |

Phlox subulata
'Millstream
Coral-eye'

Moss Pink
Plant height: to 6 in.
p. 350

Effective spring to fall
Tolerates dry soil
Zone 4

Helianthemum
nummularium
'Wisley Pink'

Rock Rose
Plant height: to 12 in.
p. 327

Effective spring to
summer
Tolerates dry soil
Zone 6

Geranium
'Claridge Druce'

*Claridge Druce
Cranesbill
Plant height: to 20 in.
p. 324*

*Effective spring to
summer
Tolerates shade
Zone 4*

Geranium endressii
'A. T. Johnson'

*Pyrenean Cranesbill
Plant height: to 12 in.
p. 324*

*Effective spring to
summer
Tolerates shade
Zone 4*

| ***Geranium sanguineum striatum*** | Plant height: to 10 in. p. 325 | Effective spring to summer Tolerates dry soil Zone 4 |

| ***Geranium sanguineum*** | Blood-red Cranesbill Plant height: 12–18 in. p. 325 | Effective spring to fall Tolerates shade Zone 4 |

Campanula carpatica Carpathian Harebell *Effective spring to*
Plant height: 6–12 in. *summer*
p. 307 Zone 4

Geranium 'Johnson's Blue' *Johnson's Blue* *Effective spring to*
Cranesbill *summer*
Plant height: to 2 ft. *Tolerates shade*
p. 325 Zone 4

Pulmonaria
angustifolia
'Johnson's Blue'

Blue Lungwort
Plant height: 6–9 in.
p. 353

Effective spring to
summer
Tolerates shade
Zone 4

Ceratostigma
plumbaginoides

Leadwort
Plant height: to 12 in.
p. 309

Effective spring to fall
Tolerates shade
Zone 5

Veronica repens Creeping Speedwell
Plant height: to 4 in.
p. 372
Effective spring to
summer
Zone 5

***Campanula elatines
garganica*** Bellflower
Plant height: 6–10 in.
p. 307
Effective spring to
summer
Zone 5

Mazus reptans	Plant height: to 2 in. p. 341	Effective spring to summer Tolerates shade and wet soil Zone 6

Campanula poscharskyana	Serbian Bellflower Plant height: 4–6 in. p. 307	Effective spring to summer Zone 4

Phlox divaricata   *Wild Sweet William*   *Effective in spring*
Plant height: to 12 in.   *Tolerates shade*
p. 350   *Zone 4*

Vinca minor   *Periwinkle*   *Effective year-round*
Plant height: to 10 in.   *Tolerates shade*
p. 373   *Zone 5*

| ***Phlox stolonifera*** **'Blue Ridge'** | *Creeping Phlox* *Plant height: to 10 in.* *p. 350* | *Effective spring to summer* *Tolerates shade* *Zone 4* |

| ***Myosotis scorpioides*** ***semperflorens*** | *True Forget-Me-Not* *Plant height: to 18 in.* *p. 343* | *Effective spring to summer* *Tolerates wet soil* *Zone 5* |

Viola labradorica	Labrador Violet Plant height: to 4 in. p. 374	Effective spring to summer Tolerates shade Zone 5

Campanula *portenschlagiana*	Dalmatian Bellflower Plant height: 6–8 in. p. 307	Effective spring to summer Zone 5

Viola sororia	*Woolly Blue Violet* *Plant height: to 6 in.* *p. 374*	*Effective spring to* *summer* *Tolerates shade* *Zone 5*

Iris cristata	*Crested Iris* *Plant height: 4–6 in.* *p. 333*	*Effective spring to* *summer* *Tolerates shade* *Zone 4*

| **Hosta lancifolia** | Narrow Plantain-lily
Plant height: to 12 in.
p. 330 | Effective summer to fall
Tolerates shade
Zone 4 |

| **Ceanothus gloriosus** | Point Reyes Ceanothus
Plant height: to 18 in.
p. 308 | Effective spring to fall
Zone 7 |

Brunnera macrophylla

Siberian Bugloss
Plant height: 12–18 in.
p. 306

Effective spring to summer
Tolerates shade
Zone 4

Ceanothus griseus horizontalis

Carmel Creeper
Plant height: to 2½ ft.
p. 308

Effective spring to fall
Zone 7

Ajuga reptans

Bugleweed
Plant height: to 6 in.
p. 293

Effective spring to fall
Tolerates shade
Zone 3

Nepeta
'Blue Wonder'

Catmint
Plant height: to 2 ft.
p. 344

Effective spring to
summer
Zone 5

Veronica incana   *Woolly Speedwell*   *Effective year-round*
Plant height: to 15 in.   *Zone 4*
p. 372

Veronica prostrata   *Rock Speedwell*   *Effective spring to*
Plant height: to 10 in.   *summer*
p. 372   *Zone 4*

Vines

| *Adlumia fungosa* | Climbing Fumitory
Plant height: to 25 ft.
p. 379 | Effective spring to
summer
Tolerates shade
Zone 5 |

| *Muehlenbeckia
complexa* | Wire-Vine
Plant height: to 20 ft.
p. 400 | Effective in summer
Tolerates dry soil
Zone 6 |

Actinidia kolomikta   Kolomikta Vine   Effective spring to fall
                           Plant height: to 20 ft.   Zone 5
                           p. 378

Ficus pumila   Creeping Fig   Effective year-round
                          Plant height: to 40 ft.   Tolerates shade
                          p. 391   Zone 9

Kadsura japonica   *Scarlet Kadsura*   *Effective year-round*
                          Plant height: to 15 ft.   *Zone 7*
                          p. 396

Euonymus fortunei   *Winter Creeper*   *Effective year-round*
radicans   *Plant height: to 12 ft.*   *Tolerates shade*
'Variegata'   *p. 390*   *Zone 5*

Hedera helix
'Ivalace'

English Ivy
Plant height: to 50 ft.
p. 392

Effective year-round
Tolerates shade
Zone 6

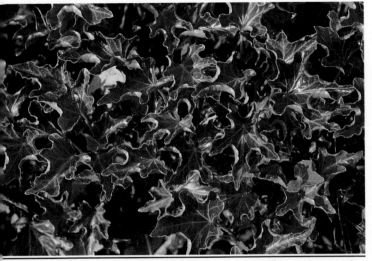

Hedera helix
'Baltica'

English Ivy
Plant height: to 50 ft.
p. 392

Effective year-round
Tolerates shade
Zone 6

Hedera helix
'Gold Heart'

English Ivy
Plant height: to 50 ft.
p. 392

Effective year-round
Tolerates shade
Zone 6

Hedera colchica

Persian Ivy
Plant height: to 50 ft.
p. 392

Effective year-round
Tolerates shade
Zone 8

Hedera colchica
'**Dentato-variegata**'

Persian Ivy
Plant height: to 50 ft.
p. 392

Effective year-round
Tolerates shade
Zone 8

Hedera helix

English Ivy
Plant height: to 50 ft.
p. 392

Effective year-round
Tolerates shade
Zone 6

| *Aristolochia durior* | Dutchman's-Pipe
Plant height: to 30 ft.
p. 381 | Effective spring to
summer
Tolerates shade
Zone 5 |

| *Vitis coignetiae* | Crimson Glory Vine
Plant height: to 50 ft.
p. 410 | Effective summer to
fall
Zone 5 |

Menispermum
canadense

Moonseed
Plant height: to 12 ft.
p. 400

Effective in summer
Tolerates shade and
wet soil
Zone 5

Parthenocissus
tricuspidata

Boston Ivy
Plant height: to 60 ft.
p. 401

Effective spring to fall
Tolerates shade
Zone 5

Humulus lupulus
'Aureus'

Common Hop
Plant height: to 25 ft.
p. 393

Effective in summer
Zone 6

Parthenocissus
henryana

Silver-vein Creeper
Plant height: to 20 ft.
p. 401

Effective summer to
fall
Tolerates shade
Zone 8

Akebia quinata *Fiveleaf Akebia* *Effective spring to*
Plant height: to 30 ft. *summer*
p. 379 *Zone 5*

Parthenocissus *Virginia Creeper* *Effective summer to*
quinquefolia *Plant height: to 50 ft.* *fall*
p. 401 *Tolerates shade*
Zone 4

Ampelopsis
brevipedunculata

Porcelain Vine
Plant height: to 25 ft.
p. 380

Effective spring to fall
Zone 5

Celastrus scandens

American Bittersweet
Plant height: to 20 ft.
p. 384

Effective year-round
Zone 3

Actinidia arguta   *Bower Actinidia*   *Effective spring to fall*
                      Plant height: to 50 ft.   *Zone 5*
                      p. 378

Celastrus orbiculatus   *Oriental Bittersweet*   *Effective year-round*
                      Plant height: to 30 ft.   *Zone 5*
                      p. 384

| *Lonicera japonica* 'Halliana' | Hall's Honeysuckle
Plant height: to 30 ft.
p. 398 | Effective spring to fall
Tolerates shade and
dry soil
Zone 5 |

| *Clematis tangutica* | Golden Clematis
Plant height: to 10 ft.
p. 386 | Effective spring to fall
Zone 4 |

| *Tropaeolum peregrinum* | Canary-Bird Vine Plant height: *to 8 ft.* p. 410 | *Effective in summer Annual* |

| *Lonicera sempervirens* 'Sulphurea' | Trumpet Honeysuckle Plant height: *to 50 ft.* p. 398 | *Effective spring to fall Zone 4* |

**Gelsemium
sempervirens**

Carolina Jessamine
Plant height: 10–20 ft.
p. 391

Effective year-round
Zone 7

Tropaeolum majus

Nasturtium
Plant height: 8–12 ft.
p. 409

Effective in summer
Annual

Bignonia capreolata   Cross Vine   *Effective year-round*
                      Plant height: to 50 ft.   *Tolerates shade and*
                      p. 382   *wet soil*
                                                 Zone 7

Thunbergia alata   Black-eyed Susan Vine   *Effective in summer*
                    Plant height: to 6 ft.   *Annual*
                    p. 408

Campsis radicans
'Mme. Galen'

*Trumpet Creeper
Plant height: to 30 ft.
p. 383*

*Effective spring to
summer
Zone 4*

Campsis radicans

*Trumpet Creeper
Plant height: to 30 ft.
p. 383*

*Effective spring to
summer
Zone 4*

Tecomaria capensis | *Cape Honeysuckle*
Plant height: to 20 ft.
p. 407 | *Effective year-round*
Tolerates dry soil
Zone 9

Distictis | *Blood-red Trumpet*
buccinatoria | *Vine*
Plant height: to 18 ft.
p. 389 | *Effective year-round*
Zone 9

**Ipomoea ×
multifida**

Cardinal Climber
Plant height: to 10 ft.
p. 395

Effective in summer
Annual

Clematis texensis

Scarlet Clematis
Plant height: 5–8 ft.
p. 386

*Effective summer to
fall*
Zone 5

Ipomoea quamoclit   Cypress Vine   *Effective in summer*
                        Plant height: to 20 ft. Zone 8
                        p. 395

Clerodendrum ×   Pagoda Flower   *Effective summer to*
speciosum   *Plant height: to 8 ft.* *fall*
                        p. 387   Zone 10

Antigonon leptopus
Coral Vine
Plant height: to 30 ft.
p. 380

Effective spring to fall
Zone 8

**Lonicera ×
heckrottii**
Goldflame Honeysuckle
Plant height: to 12 ft.
p. 397

*Effective spring to
summer*
Zone 4

Lonicera
sempervirens

Trumpet Honeysuckle
Plant height: to 50 ft.
p. 398

Effective spring to fall
Zone 4

Lonicera
periclymenum
belgica

Woodbine
Plant height: to 15 ft.
p. 398

Effective summer to
fall
Zone 5

Jasminum polyanthum Pink Jasmine Effective spring to
Plant height: to 20 ft. summer
p. 395 Zone 9

***Clematis montana* 'Tetrarose'** Anemone Clematis Effective spring to fall
Plant height: to 25 ft. Zone 5
p. 386

| Clytostoma callistegioides | Violet Trumpet Vine Plant height: to 8 ft. p. 388 | Effective spring to summer Zone 8 |

| Clematis montana rubens | Anemone Clematis Plant height: to 25 ft. p. 386 | Effective spring to fall Zone 5 |

Mandevilla
'Alice du Pont'

Plant height: to 20 ft.
p. 399

Effective spring to fall
Zone 10

Lathyrus odoratus

Sweet Pea
Plant height: 4–6 ft.
p. 397

Effective spring,
summer
Annual

| *Clematis texensis* 'Duchess of Albany' | *Scarlet Clematis* *Plant height: 5–8 ft.* *p. 386* | *Effective summer to fall* *Zone 5* |

| *Lathyrus latifolius* | *Perennial Sweet Pea* *Plant height: to 10 ft.* *p. 397* | *Effective spring to summer* *Tolerates dry soil* *Zone 5* |

***Bougainvillea
spectabilis***

*Plant height: to 30 ft.
p. 382*

*Effective spring to fall
Zone 9*

Passiflora caerulea

*Blue Passion-Flower
Plant height: to 20 ft.
p. 402*

*Effective in summer
Zone 8*

Rosa
'Don Juan'
Climbing Cultivar
Plant height: 8–10 ft.
p. 405
Effective summer to fall
Zone 6

Passiflora incarnata
Maypop
Plant height: to 20 ft.
p. 402
Effective year-round
Zone 7

***Clematis
macropetala***

*Downy Clematis
Plant height: to 10 ft.
p. 385*

*Effective spring to fall
Zone 5*

***Clematis
'Jackmanii'***

*Hybrid Clematis
Plant height: to 15 ft.
p. 385*

*Effective spring to fall
Zone 5*

Clematis **'The President'**	*Hybrid Clematis* *Plant height: to 15 ft.* *p. 385*	*Effective spring to fall* *Zone 5*

Clematis **'Mrs. Cholmondeley'**	*Hybrid Clematis* *Plant height: to 15 ft.* *p. 385*	*Effective spring to fall* *Zone 5*

Ipomoea tricolor Morning Glory
Plant height: *to 10 ft.*
p. 395

Effective in summer
Tolerates dry soil
Zone 8

Wisteria floribunda Japanese Wisteria
Plant height: *to 30 ft.*
p. 411

Effective summer to
fall
Zone 5

Cobaea scandens   Cup-and-Saucer Vine   Effective summer to
                       Plant height: to 25 ft. fall
                       p. 388   Zone 9

Wisteria sinensis   Chinese Wisteria   Effective spring to
                        Plant height: to 40 ft. summer
                        p. 411   Zone 5

Wisteria sinensis
'Alba'

Chinese Wisteria
Plant height: to 40 ft.
p. 411

Effective spring to
summer
Zone 5

Polygonum aubertii

Silver-Lace Vine
Plant height: to 25 ft.
p. 404

Effective summer to
fall
Tolerates dry soil
Zone 5

Wisteria venusta   *Silky Wisteria*   *Effective spring to*
    Plant height: to 30 ft.   *summer*
    p. 411   *Zone 5*

Decumaria barbara   *Climbing Hydrangea*   *Effective spring to fall*
    Plant height: to 30 ft.   *Zone 7*
    p. 389

Hydrangea anomala petiolaris Climbing Hydrangea
Plant height: 50–60 ft.
p. 394
Effective summer to
fall
Zone 4

Clerodendrum thomsoniae Glory Bower
Plant height: to 8 ft.
p. 387
Effective summer to
fall
Zone 10

Schizophragma hydrangeoides

Japanese Hydrangea Vine
Plant height: to 30 ft.
p. 406

Effective summer to fall
Zone 5

Mandevilla laxa

Chilean Jasmine
Plant height: to 15 ft.
p. 399

Effective in summer
Zone 8

Stephanotis floribunda

Madagascar Jasmine
Plant height: to 15 ft.
p. 407

Effective in summer
Zone 9

Trachelospermum jasminoides

Star Jasmine
Plant height: to 30 ft.
p. 409

Effective year-round
Zone 9

**Plumbago
auriculata**

Cape Plumbago
Plant height: to 10 ft.
p. 403

Effective spring to fall
Zone 9

Clematis virginiana

Virgin's Bower
Plant height: to 18 ft.
p. 386

Effective summer to
fall
Zone 4

Clematis armandii *Armand Clematis* *Effective spring to*
Plant height: to 20 ft. *summer*
p. 385 *Zone 7*

Clematis *Hybrid Clematis* *Effective spring to fall*
'Henryi' *Plant height: to 15 ft.* *Zone 5*
p. 385

Clematis paniculata   Sweet Autumn   Effective summer to
                           Clematis   fall
                           Plant height: to 30 ft. Zone 5
                           p. 386

Ipomoea alba   Moon-Flower   Effective in summer
                           Plant height: to 8 ft. Zone 9
                           p. 394

Rosa wichuraiana Memorial Rose
Plant height: to 20 ft.
p. 405

*Effective summer to
fall*
Zone 6

Rosa banksiae Lady Banks' Rose
Plant height: 15–30 ft.
p. 404

*Effective summer to
fall*
Zone 7

Rosa laevigata   Cherokee Rose   Effective summer to
                      Plant height: to 15 ft. fall
                      p. 405   Zone 6

Rosa banksiae   Lady Banks' Rose   Effective summer to
                     Plant height: 15–30 ft. fall
                     p. 404   Zone 7

Grasses

| *Arundo donax* | Giant Reed
Plant height: to 12 ft.
p. 416 | Effective spring to
summer
Zone 7 |

| *Miscanthus
floridulus* | Giant Miscanthus
Plant height: to 10 ft.
p. 432 | Effective spring to
summer
Zone 5 |

| **Miscanthus** **sacchariflorus** | *Eulalia Grass* *Plant height: to 6 ft.* *p. 433* | *Effective year-round* *Tolerates wet soil* *Zone 5* |

| **Spartina pectinata** **'Aureo-marginata'** | *Prairie Cord Grass* *Plant height: to 6 ft.* *p. 439* | *Effective spring to fall* *Tolerates wet or dry* *soil* *Zone 5* |

Miscanthus sinensis
'Silver Feather'

Silver Feather Grass
Plant height: 4–8 ft.
p. 433

Effective year-round
Tolerates wet soil
Zone 5

Stipa gigantea

Feather Grass
Plant height: to 6 ft.
p. 440

Effective spring to fall
Zone 5

Erianthus ravennae   Ravenna Grass   *Effective fall to winter*
                         Plant height: to 14 ft.   *Zone 6*
                         p. 426

Cyperus papyrus   Paper Plant   *Effective year-round*
                         Plant height: 6–8 ft.   *Tolerates wet soil*
                         p. 423   *Zone 10*

***Helictotrichon
sempervirens***

*Blue Oat Grass
Plant height: to 2 ft.
p. 428*

*Effective year-round
Zone 4*

Panicum virgatum

*Switch Grass
Plant height: 5–6 ft.
p. 434*

*Effective spring to fall
Zone 5*

Carex buchananii   *Leatherleaf Sedge*   *Effective year-round*
                            Plant height: to 2 ft.   *Zone 6*
                            p. 420

Calamagrostis   *Feather Reed Grass*   *Effective year-round*
acutiflora stricta   *Plant height: to 5 ft.* *Tolerates wet soil*
                            p. 419   *Zone 5*

| **Pennisetum setaceum** | *Fountain Grass*
 Plant height: to 3 ft.
 p. 435 | *Effective spring to*
 summer
 Zone 8 |

| **Pennisetum**
 alopecuroides | *Fountain Grass*
 Plant height: 2–3 ft.
 p. 435 | *Effective spring to*
 summer
 Zone 5 |

Cortaderia selloana Pampas Grass Effective year-round
Plant height: 8–12 ft. Tolerates dry soil
p. 422 Zone 8

Pennisetum villosum Feathertop Effective spring to
Plant height: to 2 ft. summer
p. 435 Zone 9

Miscanthus sinensis
'Gracillimus'

Maiden Grass
Plant height: to 5 ft.
p. 433

Effective year-round
Tolerates wet soil
Zone 5

Calamagrostis
arundinacea
brachytricha

Feather Reed Grass
Plant height: to 3 ft.
p. 419

Effective spring to fall
Zone 5

Miscanthus sinensis **'Zebrinus'**

Zebra Grass
Plant height: to 7 ft.
p. 433

Effective year-round
Tolerates wet soil
Zone 5

Koeleria glauca

Blue Hair Grass
Plant height: to 18 in.
p. 430

Effective spring to fall
Tolerates dry soil
Zone 5

Festuca amethystina | Large Blue Fescue | Effective year-round
 | Plant height: to 18 in. | Tolerates dry soil
 | p. 426 | Zone 4

Elymus glaucus | Blue Lyme Grass | Effective spring to
 | Plant height: to 3 ft. | summer
 | p. 425 | Tolerates dry soil
 | | Zone 4

Festuca ovina glauca   Blue Fescue
Plant height: to 12 in.
p. 427

Effective year-round
Tolerates dry soil
Zone 4

Luzula nivea   Snowy Wood Rush
Plant height: to 2 ft.
p. 431

Effective year-round
Tolerates shade
Zone 4

Carex pendula

Drooping Sedge
Plant height: to 2 ft.
p. 420

Effective year-round
Tolerates shade and
wet soil
Zone 5

Deschampsia
caespitosa

Tufted Hair Grass
Plant height: to 2 ft.
p. 424

Effective spring to fall
Tolerates shade
Zone 5

Carex grayi
Gray's Sedge
Plant height: to 2 ft.
p. 420

Effective summer to fall
Tolerates wet soil
Zone 3

Luzula sylvatica
Greater Wood Rush
Plant height: to 12 in.
p. 431

Effective year-round
Tolerates shade
Zone 5

Juncus effusus spiralis
Corkscrew Rush
Plant height: 2–3 ft.
p. 430
Effective spring to summer
Tolerates wet soil
Zone 5

***Carex conica* 'Variegata'**
Miniature Variegated Sedge
Plant height: to 6 in.
p. 420
Effective year-round
Tolerates shade and wet soil
Zone 5

Dactylis glomerata **'Variegata'**	Orchard Grass Plant height: to 18 in. p. 423	Effective spring to summer Zone 5

Arrhenatherum **elatius bulbosum** **'Variegatum'**	Bulbous Oat Grass Plant height: to 12 in. p. 415	Effective spring to fall Tolerates dry soil Zone 5

| ***Miscanthus sinensis*** **'Variegatus'** | *Variegated Silver Grass* *Plant height: to 5 ft.* *p. 433* | *Effective year-round* *Tolerates wet soil* *Zone 5* |

| ***Holcus mollis*** **'Albo-variegatus'** | *Variegated Velvet Grass* *Plant height: to 12 in.* *p. 429* | *Effective spring to summer* *Zone 5* |

Phalaris arundinacea picta

Ribbon Grass
Plant height: to 3 ft.
p. 436

Effective spring to summer
Tolerates shade and wet or dry soil
Zone 4

Phormium tenax 'Variegatum'

New Zealand Flax
Plant height: to 15 ft.
p. 436

Effective year-round
Tolerates dry soil
Zone 8

Acorus gramineus
'Variegatus'

Japanese Sweet Flag
Plant height: to 12 in.
p. 414

Effective year-round
Tolerates wet soil
Zone 6

Molinia caerulea
'Variegata'

Variegated Purple
Moor Grass
Plant height: to 3 ft.
p. 434

Effective spring to
summer
Zone 5

Carex morrowii 'Aureo-variegata'

Variegated Japanese
Sedge
Plant height: to 12 in.
p. 420

Effective year-round
Tolerates wet soil
Zone 6

Alopecurus pratensis 'Aureo-variegatus'

Yellow Meadow
Foxtail
Plant height: to 2 ft.
p. 414

Effective spring to fall
Zone 5

Glyceria maxima
'Variegata'

Manna Grass
Plant height: to 2½ ft.
p. 427

Effective spring to
summer
Tolerates wet soil
Zone 5

Imperata cylindrica
rubra

Japanese Blood Grass
Plant height: to 12 in.
p. 429

Effective spring to fall
Zone 5

Hakonechloa macra 'Aureola'

Golden Variegated Hakonechloa
Plant height: to 18 in.
p. 428

Effective spring to fall
Tolerates shade
Zone 5

Phormium tenax 'Rubrum'

New Zealand Flax
Plant height: to 15 ft.
p. 436

Effective year-round
Tolerates dry soil
Zone 8

**Spodiopogon
sibericus**

Silver Spike Grass
Plant height: to 3 ft.
p. 440

Effective spring to fall
Tolerates wet soil
Zone 5

**Milium effusum
'Aureum'**

Bowles' Golden Grass
Plant height: to 18 in.
p. 432

Effective spring to fall
Tolerates shade
Zone 5

Molinia caerulea altissima	Tall Purple Moor Grass Plant height: to 6 ft. p. 434	Effective spring to summer Zone 5

Eragrostis trichodes	Sand Love Grass Plant height: to 4 ft. p. 425	Effective spring to fall Tolerates dry soil Zone 5

Bouteloua gracilis   *Mosquito Grass*   *Effective spring to fall*
Plant height: to 2 ft.   *Tolerates dry soil*
p. 418   *Zone 5*

Briza media   *Quaking Grass*   *Effective spring to fall*
Plant height: 10–18 in.   *Tolerates dry soil*
p. 418   *Zone 5*

Briza maxima

Large Quaking Grass
Plant height: 1–2 ft.
p. 418

Effective spring to fall
Tolerates dry soil
Annual

**Chasmanthium
latifolium**

Northern Sea Oats
Plant height: to 5 ft.
p. 421

Effective summer to
winter
Tolerates shade
Zone 5

Sasa veitchii

Kuma Bamboo
Plant height: to 3 ft.
p. 438

Effective spring to fall
Tolerates shade
Zone 6

Arundinaria pygmaea

Pygmy Bamboo
Plant height: to 12 in.
p. 416

Effective spring to summer
Zone 7

Arundinaria viridistriata   Plant height: to 6 ft.   Effective spring to
                                 p. 416   summer
                                                            Zone 7

Pseudosasa japonica   Arrow Bamboo   Effective year-round
                           Plant height: to 15 ft.   Zone 7
                           p. 438

Sasa palmata Plant height: to 7 ft. Effective spring to fall
p. 438 Tolerates shade
Zone 6

Shibataea kumasaca Ruscus-leaved Bamboo Effective spring to fall
Plant height: to 3 ft. Tolerates shade
p. 439 Zone 6

Bambusa glaucescens

Hedge Bamboo
Plant height: to 20·ft.
p. 417

Effective spring to summer
Zone 8

Coix lacryma-jobi

Job's Tears
Plant height: to 3 ft.
p. 422

Effective in fall
Tolerates wet soil
Annual

Arundo donax
'Variegata'

Striped Giant Reed
Plant height: to 8 ft.
p. 416

Effective spring to
summer
Zone 8

Phyllostachys
aureosulcata

Yellow Groove Bamboo
Plant height: to 30 ft.
p. 437

Effective year-round
Zone 6

Cyperus alternifolius *Umbrella Plant* *Effective year-round*
Plant height: 2–4 ft. *Tolerates wet soil*
p. 423 *Zone 9*

Phyllostachys aurea *Golden Bamboo* *Effective year-round*
Plant height: 10–20 ft. *Zone 7*
p. 437

Encyclopedia of Ground Covers, Vines, and Grasses

Ground Covers

Ground covers are low-growing plants—perennials, shrubs, and even a few vines—used to add interest to the garden, cover bare soil, and prevent the growth of weeds.

Height and Scale
The lower its mature height, the more versatile a plant will be as a ground cover. Taller-growing plants, especially shrubs, are useful but require extra pruning. Generally, "low-growing" means up to 3 feet high, although there really is no definitive height limit for a ground cover. In fact, exact height is usually less important than the relative scale of the plants in an overall garden design. A ground cover that grows only 2 inches high, for example, would be lost if planted in front of a mansion or in broad sweeps down a hillside. Likewise, a stand of spreading junipers 2 feet tall would be out of place in a small rock garden. It is mostly a matter of choosing plants that will be appropriate for the site.

Ground covers are valued for their ability to spread over an area rapidly enough to create a weed-free carpet. This they accomplish by physically smothering the weeds and cutting off their needed light. Most ground covers will tolerate the occasional foot traffic that maintenance requires, but in high-traffic areas, lawn or stone paths are a better choice.

Plant Types
Many low-growing perennials make good ground covers, especially those with a creeping habit that allows them to fill in an area in a short time. Evergreen perennials are a good choice wherever they are hardy, but deciduous ones are best used in climates where snow will blanket the bare ground during most of the plants' dormant period. Woody plants—shrubs and subshrubs—may be deciduous or evergreen; evergreen kinds, with broad or needlelike leaves, provide year-round interest and cover. Some vines are also good as ground covers, but you should use them with caution, preferably in an isolated area, since most immediately climb the first tree or other obstacle they meet.

Choosing Ground Covers
To use ground covers to best advantage, consider the wide variety of colors, textures, and forms available, keeping in mind that the foliage is of primary interest. Foliage colors range from the silvery blue of junipers to the dark green, glossy leaves of Japanese Pachysandra; textures, from the leathery, round leaves of European Wild Ginger to the needle-fine spikes of heathers. Some ground covers, such as the azaleas, have the added attraction of showy flowers; others have colorful fruit or distinctive twigs or bark. By choosing plants with complementary and contrasting ornamental characteristics, you can create interesting ground cover gardens to serve many different purposes.

Ground Covers in the Landscape

Ground covers are problem solvers because they are frequently used in adverse growing conditions or difficult terrain. For example, under the branches of many large trees, where there is little sunlight and the soil is dry and root-filled, ground covers adapted to dry shade compete successfully with the tree for available water and nutrients.

Appropriate ground covers can also decrease the maintenance problems of steep or rocky slopes. These areas may be dangerous or difficult to mow, or rainfall may cause soil erosion. You can stabilize such sites and improve their appearance by planting carpeting. ground covers that have long, fibrous roots.

Although frequently used to solve landscape problems, ground covers have intrinsic beauty you should not overlook. Small-leaved ground-huggers, such as Woolly Thyme, are attractive creeping between paving stones, and low-growing perennials with showy flowers or distinctive foliage make excellent edging plants for flower borders. They can also be used to unify a planting of mixed shrubs and trees, where they help avoid a dot-and-dash effect and protect tree bark from lawn-mower damage.

Care

Traditionally, ground covers other than grass have been associated with carefree gardening, but they do require regular care for the first few years, with particular attention to weed control. Once established, however, they need less maintenance than a lawn.
The culture information and plant descriptions provided in the text accounts that follow will help you to select the right ground covers for your garden.

Achillea
Daisy family
Compositae

A-kil-lee′a. Yarrow. A large genus of
perennial herbs, mostly from the north
temperate zone, a few grown for their
flowers.

Description
Leaves toothed, parted, or divided, and in
some species finely dissected. Flowerheads
small, usually numerous, often in flat-topped
clusters.

How to Grow
Yarrow is easy to grow in a sunny location
in ordinary garden soil with good drainage.
Propagate by dividing roots in spring or
autumn. Many species are rank growers,
crowding out other plants. The taller species
are attractive in borders.

tomentosa p. 156
Woolly Yarrow. To 8 in. (20 cm) high.
Dense carpets of woolly gray-green leaves,
mostly basal, topped by flat corymbs, 1 in.
(2.5 cm) wide, of tiny, bright yellow flowers
borne on 6 in. (15 cm) stems in spring.
Cultivars 'King Edward' and 'Moonlight'
have pale yellow flowers. Europe, Asia.
Prefers sandy soil. Zone 3.

Aegopodium
Carrot family
Umbelliferae

Ee-go-po′di-um. A small group of Eurasian
perennial herbs, one of which, the
Goutweed, is planted (mostly in its
variegated form) as a deciduous edging or
ground cover.

Description
Leaves twice-compound, the ultimate leaflets
toothed. Flowers small, white, in a
compound umbel.

How to Grow
Easy to grow in ordinary soil. Prefers partial
shade, but tolerates sun. Increase by dividing
its slender rootstocks in spring or fall.

podagraria p. 119
Goutweed; Bishop's Weed. Stout, coarse
herb, 12 in. (30 cm) high. Leafstalks,
especially the lower ones, winged and
clasping. Flowers minute, white, in umbels
1½–3 in. (4.0–7.5 cm) wide. 'Variegatum',
which has white-margined leaflets, is most
popular and is a useful foliage plant. Flowers
bloom in early summer, but they should be
removed to prevent self-seeding. Goutweed
can become weedy if not controlled. Zone 4.

Ajuga
Mint family
Labiatae

Aj-oo'ga. Bugleweed. European annual or
perennial herbs, sometimes weedy, but a few
cultivated in borders and rock gardens for
their profusion of blooms.

Description
Leaves opposite, with smooth margins or
blunt teeth, oval, to 2½ in. (6 cm) long.
Flowers irregular and 2-lipped, in close
clusters or spikes, blooming in spring or
early summer.

How to Grow
The bugleweeds are easy to grow in ordinary,
well-drained garden soil. Propagation is by
spring-sown seeds, division, and, in *A.
reptans,* by its free-rooting stems.

pyramidalis p. 116
Rhizomatous, 8–10 in. (20–25 cm) high.
Leaves 4 in. (10 cm) long, hairy, in basal
rosettes. Flowers lavender-blue on spikes,
blooming in early summer. Well behaved.
Zone 4.

reptans pp. 115, 116, 117, 173, 208
The common blue Bugleweed. 3–6 in.
(7.5–15.0 cm) high. Stems usually half-
prostrate and often rooting. Leaves mostly
basal, dark green. In the typical form,
flowers are ¼ in. (6 mm) wide and blue or
purplish. Preferred garden sorts include
'Alba', with white flowers; 'Bronze Beauty',
with bronze foliage and blue flowers;
'Burgundy Glow', which is less robust and
has green, white, and dark pink to purple
foliage; and 'Multicolor Rainbow', which is
less vigorous than the species and has red,
white, yellow, and purple foliage. Zone 3.

Alchemilla
Rose family
Rosaceae

Al-ke-mill´a. Of the 200 species in this genus, only a few are of any garden importance.

Description
Somewhat weedy plants with lobed or compound leaves and small greenish-yellow flowers without petals. Grown primarily for the silvery or grayish leaves. Individual plants form spreading clumps.

How to Grow
Very easy to grow in any ordinary garden soil in sun or light shade. In hot or dry climates, plant them in moist, humus-enriched soil. Increase by division or seeds.

mollis p. 131
Lady's-Mantle. Rootstock stout and horizontal. Plant grows to 15 in. (38 cm) high. Leaves erect, long-stalked, grayish, with shallow rounded lobes that are toothed. Flower clusters 2–3 in. (5.0–7.5 cm) wide. Bears many chartreuse or yellowish flowers in early summer. Europe. Also sold as *A. vulgaris*. Zone 4.

Andromeda
Heath family
Ericaceae

An-drom´i-da. Two species of low-growing evergreen shrubs native to North America, Europe, and Asia. The name is often misapplied to the genus *Pieris*.

Description
Leaves alternate and simple, leathery on top, glaucous beneath. Flowers pink or white, in nodding terminal umbels.

How to Grow
Andromedas are best suited for acid, humus-rich soil with plenty of moisture, in sun or light shade. Can be increased by rooting the creeping runners or top cuttings. Seed may be sown in moist peat moss.

polifolia p. 182
Bog Rosemary. Evergreen shrub to 12 in. (30 cm) high, with creeping rootstock.

Leaves 1–1½ in. (2.5–4.0 cm) long, narrow.
Flowers bell-shaped. Blooms in spring. Good
plant for the damp garden. 'Nana' is a more
compact form. Zone 3.

Anemone
Buttercup family
Ranunculaceae

A-nem′o-nee. These popular garden plants,
which include windflowers and pasque-
flowers, constitute a large genus of perennial
herbs, mostly confined to the north
temperate zone.

Description
Leaves compound or, if simple, divided or
dissected; mostly basal. Flowers usually
showy, with petal-like sepals in a wide range
of colors.

How to Grow
Culture and propagation vary. The species
below prefers a rich, moist soil and light
shade. Easy to increase by division of the
creeping rootstock in spring.

canadensis p. 166
Canada Anemone. To 2 ft. (60 cm) high.
Leaves basal, 5–7-parted. Flowers 2 in.
(5 cm) long, white, on stalks held above the
foliage. Blooms in early summer. An invasive
plant not suitable for small areas. Zone 4.

Antennaria
Daisy family
Compositae

An-ten-ar′i-a. A large genus of white-woolly
perennial herbs, very common as wild plants.

Description
Leaves mostly basal. Flowers small, tubular,
off-white, in loose clusters; flowerheads
sometimes used for dried arrangements.

How to Grow
Very easy to grow in sunny, dry, sandy
places. Most species are somewhat weedy and
spread so rapidly that they may become a
nuisance. Propagate by division or seeds.

dioica *pp. 114, 183*
Pussytoes. 4–12 in. (10–30 cm) high. Leaves
hairy, 1½ in. (4 cm) long. Flowerheads
pink-tipped, ¼ in. (6 mm) wide. Eurasia. A
good mat-former for rock gardens in full sun
and other well-drained sites. Var. *rosea* has
pink flowerheads. Blooms in early summer.
Zones 4–5.

Arabis
Mustard family
Cruciferae

Ar'a-bis. The rock cresses are a large genus of
herbs much grown for ornament, especially
on walls and in rock gardens.

Description
Leaves basal or along stem, usually hairy.
Flowers small, white or purple, often in
ample spikes or racemes, blooming in
spring.

How to Grow
Easy to grow, especially in open sunlight and
warm, sandy soil. Propagate by division in
spring or fall.

caucasica *p. 165*
Wall Cress. A tufted species from the
Caucasus. To 12 in. (30 cm) high. Leaves
gray-green, toothed. Flowers white, fragrant,
½ in. (13 mm) wide, in loose clusters.
'Flore Pleno' is a double-flowered form; there
are also variegated-leaf forms. Prefers good
drainage. In climates with hot, humid
summers, it may rot. Zone 4.

procurrens *p. 165*
Rock Cress. To 12 in. (30 cm) high,
creeping by short runners. Flowers
white, showy, ⁷⁄₁₆ in. (12 mm) wide, in
racemes. Se. Europe. It thrives in relatively
poor soils. There is a variegated-leaf form.
Zone 5.

Arctostaphylos
Heath family
Ericaceae

Ark-to-staff'i-los. About 50 species of
evergreen woody plants, mostly North
American, ranging in size from small trees to

a prostrate ground cover. Includes the
Bearberry and Manzanita.

Description
Low-growing or erect plants with smooth,
crooked stems. Leaves handsome, evergreen,
without marginal teeth. Flowers small and
urn- or bell-shaped, often nodding. Fruit
fleshy, red or dull, often showy.

How to Grow
All species perform best in sandy or rocky
acid soil in full sun or partial shade. Can be
successfully propagated by top cuttings or, in
the creeping species, by transplanting sods.

edmundsii p. 94
Little Sur Manzanita. Creeping shrub
6–24 in. (15–60 cm) high, with rooting
stems and a span to 12 ft. (3.5 m). Leaves
light green, 1–1¼ in. (2.5–3.0 cm) long, on
red stems. Pink flowers in winter. The lower-
growing cultivar 'Carmel Sur', to 12 in.
(30 cm) high, has gray-green leaves.
Zone 8.

'Emerald Carpet' p. 80
Emerald Carpet Manzanita. Dense, uniform,
wide-spreading carpet to 15 in. (38 cm)
high. Leaves oval, with pointed tips, to ½
in. (13 mm) long, shiny emerald-green.
Flowers pale pink, in midwinter. Tolerates
heat and dry conditions. Resists fungus if
watered deeply and infrequently. Prefers
neutral or slightly acid soil. 'Sea Spray' is
dense, compact, and hugs the ground, with
leaves shiny bronze when new, turning dark
green. 'Winter Glow' has round leaves with
reddish margins, the entire leaf turning
copper in winter. All zone 8.

hookeri p. 96
Monterey Manzanita. Mound-forming shrub
2–4 ft. (60–120 cm) high, slowly spreading
to 6 ft. (1.8 m) wide. Leaves 1 in. (2.5 cm)
long, bright green, glossy. Flowers white to
pink, in late winter. Fruit bright red, shiny.
Zone 8.

uva-ursi pp. 98, 99

Bearberry; Kinnikinnick. To 12 in. (30 cm)
high; prostrate, the stems often 5–6 ft.
(1.5–1.8 m) long and rooting at the joints.
Forms large patches of handsome evergreen
foliage that turns bronze in winter. Leaves
leathery, to 1 in. (2.5 cm) long. Flowers
bell-shaped, waxy pink, blooming in spring,

followed by long-lasting red fruit. 'Point Reyes', a popular West Coast cultivar, has dense, dark green foliage. Zone 3.

Arctotheca
Daisy family
Compositae

Arc-to-thee′ca. African Daisy. Native to South Africa, only one species of particular garden interest. Grown almost exclusively in Calif.

Description
Leaves grayish green, deeply divided. Flowers yellow, showy, resembling daisies. Usually acts like a ground cover, but growth habit depends on wind and humidity.

How to Grow
The species below does not tolerate heavy frost, but when established it will tolerate heat and drought. Ideal temperature is 50°F (10°C). Self-seeds readily. Easy to grow in sunny, moderately fertile, well-drained soil. Can be mowed or thinned annually to improve appearance.

calendula p. 151
Cape Weed; Cape-Dandelion. To 12 in. (30 cm) high. Flowers yellow, 1–2 in. (2.5–5.0 cm) wide, blooming best in spring, but sporadically all year. Needs a lot of space; good choice for wild gardens and hillsides. Zone 9.

Arctotis
Daisy family
Compositae

Ark-toe′tis. A South African genus of white-woolly, tender annual or perennial herbs. Grown primarily in Calif. for their early spring flowers.

Description
Leaves alternate, usually toothed or deeply cut. Flowerheads handsome, long-stalked, in bright colors.

How to Grow
Arctotis prefers full sun and well-drained soil. In mild climates where it will winter over,

plant in autumn. In colder areas where it is tender plant in spring and treat as an annual. To maintain flower color, propagate from cuttings, since self-sown plants revert to species flower color.

hybrids *p. 150*

African Daisy. Flowers large, red, orange, yellow, pink, or white, usually with a contrasting color ring, on stems 12–15 in. (30–38 cm) high. Plants bloom in spring and early summer. They tolerate drought but require cool nights for best flowering. Zone 9.

Arenaria
Pink family
Caryophyllaceae

A-re-nay′ri-a. Sandwort. A genus of about 150 species of annual and perennial herbs of the north temperate zone and arctic regions. Some are offered as *Alsine* or *Minuartia*.

Description
Most sandworts form grassy mats or low tufts, either upright or creeping. Leaves narrow, opposite. Flowers abundant, small, white, either in terminal clusters or in the leaf axils.

How to Grow
Sandworts grow best in well-drained, ordinary soil. They are well suited to the sunny rock garden or the cracks between paving stones.

montana p. 162

Mountain Sandwort. To 4 in. (10 cm) high. Leaves trailing, grasslike, to 1 in. (2.5 cm) long. Flowers a profusion of white, 5-petaled stars blooming in spring. Europe. Best propagated by seeds. Zone 4.

verna pp. 79, 164
Irish Moss. To 2 in. (5 cm) high, in dense, mosslike clumps. Leaves linear, smooth. Flowers star-shaped, white, in terminal heads. The cultivar 'Aurea' has yellow-green foliage. Zone 3.

Artemisia
Daisy family
Compositae

Ar-te-miz'i-a. The wormwoods are a very
large genus of bitter or aromatic herbs and
low shrubs, found in most countries.
Cultivated since ancient times for their
aromatic qualities, for ornament, or as
seasoning.

Description
Leaves alternate, mostly divided or dissected.
Flowers in small heads, usually not showy.
Grown primarily for the ornamental silvery
leaves.

How to Grow
Most species do not tolerate much winter
moisture. They need full sun and well-
drained soil; they rot in wet soil or in areas
with high humidity. Otherwise they are
generally easy to grow and do better in poor
and sandy soil than in rich soil. Easy to
increase by root division or cuttings. To
promote dense growth, prune occasionally.

stellerana p. 130
Beach Wormwood. A densely white-woolly
rhizomatous herb, to 2 ft. (60 cm) high.
Flowerheads tiny, yellow, crowded in dense
racemes. A splendid beach plant. One of the
best gray foliage plants and also one of the
least inclined to rot in humid conditions.
Zones 3–4. Two other useful species, both
hardy to zone 6, are *P. caucasica* (Silver
Spreader) and *P. pycnocephala* (Sandhill
Sage).

Asarum
Birthwort family
Aristolochiaceae

Ass'a-rum. Woodland plants with aromatic
rootstocks, useful as a ground cover in shady
places. Most below from North America.
Usually called wild ginger because of their
strong scent and flavor. Some botanists
consider the southern species to be a separate
genus, *Hexastylis.*

Description
Leaves stalked, heart- or kidney-shaped.
Flowers borne at or near the ground and
hidden by the relatively dense foliage.

How to Grow
Given shade, humus soil, and plenty of
moisture, the wild gingers spread readily
and will cover large areas in a few years.
Easy to increase by division of creeping
rootstocks or by seeds. The flowers are
slug-pollinated.

canadense p. 123
Wild Ginger. 6–8 in. (15–20 cm) high.
Leaves 3–6 in. (7.5–15.0 cm) wide,
heart-shaped, deciduous. Flowers purplish
green outside, deep maroon inside. Zone 4.

caudatum p. 122
British Columbia Wild Ginger. To 6 in.
(15 cm) high. Leaves 3–6 in. (7.5–15.0 cm)
wide, heart-shaped, glossy, evergreen. Flowers
reddish brown. Better ground cover than
A. canadense because it is evergreen. Spreads
moderately by rhizomes. Zone 6.

europaeum p. 123
European Wild Ginger. A refined evergreen
ground cover, to 7 in. (17.5 cm) high.
Similar to *A. caudatum* but hardier. Zone 5.

shuttleworthii p. 122
Southern Wild Ginger. To 5 in. (12.5 cm)
high. Leaves deep green, glossy, leathery, to
5 in. (12.5 cm) wide, mottled with silvery
markings. Evergreen in southern part of its
range. 'Callaway' is a small-leaved cultivar
selected for its distinctive silver markings
and vigorous growth. Zone 6.

Aspidistra
Lily family
Liliaceae

As-pi-dis'tra. About 8 species of evergreen
perennial herbs native in mild areas of Asia.
One species is grown as ground cover in
similar climates of the western and Gulf
states.

Description
Leaves numerous, basal, tough, arising from
a mat of shallow rootstocks. Flowers
inconspicuous, borne singly at ground level.

How to Grow
Aspidistra is valuable for its ability to thrive
under adverse conditions where little else
will grow due to poor soil or low light. It
grows best in humus-enriched porous soil
and light shade. Leaves will scorch in direct
sun. Increase by dividing rootstock.

elatior p. 138
Cast-Iron Plant. To 2 ft. (60 cm) high. Leaf
blades 1–2 ft. (30–60 cm) long, 3–4 in.
(7.5–10.0 cm) wide, shiny, leathery, with a
stout, channeled stalk about a third the
length of the blade. Flowers brown-purple.
Grown as a houseplant in colder areas. Often
sold as *A. lurida.* The common name alludes
to the plant's ability to withstand abuse.
Zone 8.

Astilbe
Saxifrage family
Saxifragaceae

As-til′be. A genus of spirea-like herbs, widely
grown as handsome border perennials.
Sometimes confused with *Aruncus.*

Description
Leaves simple, or twice- or thrice-compound.
Flowers borne in profuse, spirelike panicles
6–12 in. (15–30 cm) long, mostly unisexual,
white, pink, or reddish.

How to Grow
Astilbes are easy to grow in partial shade in
any ordinary moist soil. These heavy feeders
benefit from extra fertilizer during the
summer. The plants reproduce quickly;
divide them about every 4 years for
continued vigor.

chinensis **'Pumila'** *p. 187*
Chinese Astilbe. 8–12 in. (20–30 cm) high.
Leaves compound, fernlike. Flowers mauve-
pink, minute. Panicles create dense, erect
plumes in late summer. China and Japan.
Can tolerate drier soils than other *Astilbe*s.
Excellent for rock gardens and border fronts.
Zone 5.

Baccharis
Daisy family
Compositae

Bak´kar-is. About 350 species of dioecious
shrubs, sometimes evergreen. Their habitats
are diverse, from marshes to deserts.

Description
Shrubs erect or trailing. Leaves alternate,
thick, more or less fleshy. Flowers small,
off-white, tubular, crowded in small heads.
Fruit a conspicuous cottony seed.

How to Grow
Culture varies with species, the one listed
below adapting to various soil conditions.
It will tolerate drought, but grows best in
moderately rich, moisture-retentive soil in
full sun. Prune annually in early spring to
remove old arching branches and maintain
density. To avoid mess and seeding problems
of female plants, choose male plants grown
from cuttings.

pilularis pp. 73, 109

Dwarf Coyote Brush. Forms dense evergreen
mat 1–2 ft. (30–60 cm) high, spreading to
6 ft. (1.8 m). Leaves nearly stalkless,
broadest toward tip, to 1 in. (2.5 cm) long,
toothed. Flowers inconspicuous, blooming in
fall. Coastal bluffs of Calif. Very reliable
ground cover in the West and Southwest,
but susceptible to spider mites. The species is
not planted as often as 'Twin Peaks', a
lower, denser, all-male cultivar with small,
dark green leaves, and 'Pigeon Point', which
is faster growing and mound-forming.
Zone 7.

Berberis
Barberry family
Berberidaceae

Ber´ber-iss. Barberry. A horticulturally
important genus of over 400 species of
evergreen or deciduous shrubs, all more or
less spiny. Most are native to the north
temperate zone.

Description
Although species vary widely, most are
grown for their foliage, which may be
evergreen or brightly colored in autumn.
Many are also grown for their fruit, which

may persist in winter. Leaves simple, in short clusters at ends of short spurs. Usually 3-branched spines in leaf axils. Flowers yellow, in clusters, in spring.

How to Grow
Easy to grow in ordinary, well-drained garden soil. Can be raised from seed sown in autumn, or from cuttings rooted in moist sand. To prevent ranginess, cut plants back selectively but do not shear.

verruculosa p. 97

Warty Barberry. Mounded evergreen shrub to 3 ft. (90 cm) high, with warty branches. Leaves oval, 1 in. (2.5 cm) long, glossy-green, spiny-toothed and pale beneath. Flowers small, golden-yellow. Fruit bluish black, glaucous. Zone 6.

Bergenia
Saxifrage family
Saxifragaceae

Ber-gen'i-a. About 12 Asiatic perennial herbs, several grown in borders for their ornamental foliage and early-blooming flowers. The genus is sometimes known as *Megasea*.

Description
Grows in dense clumps or colonies from thickened rootstocks. Leaves mostly basal, thick, fleshy, half-evergreen. Flowers large, in nodding panicles or racemes. Many hybrids and cultivars available.

How to Grow
Grows in any soil, but prefers humus-enriched soil. Plant in light shade, or in full sun if some moisture is provided. Increase by division of established clumps. Species can also be grown from seeds.

ciliata pp. 135, 136
A choice, showy plant to 12 in. (30 cm) high. Leaves nearly round, tapering toward base, to 12 in. (30 cm) long, edges scalloped, hairy. Flowers white or rose-purple, in clusters 9 in. (22.5 cm) long, blooming in late spring. Zone 6.

cordifolia pp. 134, 136

Heartleaf Bergenia. To 18 in. (45 cm) high. Leaves 12–18 in. (30–45 cm) long, leathery,

with wavy margins. Flowers pink, small. Prey
to slugs. Most widely grown species on the
East Coast. 'Profusion' has large clusters of
pinkish-white flowers. Zone 3.

crassifolia p. 137
Siberian Tea. To 18 in. (45 cm) high.
Similar to *B. cordifolia* but with leaf blade
extending down the stalk. Flowers rose-pink
or lilac, clusters well above the foliage. Well
known on the West Coast. Zone 3.

Bruckenthalia
Heath family
Ericaceae

Brook-en-thay'li-a. A single species of
creeping evergreen shrubs native to se.
Europe and Asia Minor.

Description
Leaves simple, small, dense on stems. Flowers
bell-shaped, deeply 4-lobed, in short, dense
spikes.

How to Grow
Adaptable in any well-drained acid soil,
flowering best in full sun. Stems root down
as plant spreads; to propagate, cut off rooted
divisions in spring. Can also be propagated
by seeds.

spiculifolia p. 187
Spike-Heath. Evergreen shrub to 10 in.
(25 cm) high, spreading to 18 in. (45 cm)
wide. Flowers pink, profuse, about ¼ in.
(6 mm) long, on stems ¾ in. (19 mm) long
in summer. May perform better than related
heaths and heathers in some climates.
Zone 5.

Brunnera
Borage family
Boraginaceae

Brun'er-ra. An anchusa-like herb of the
Caucasus and Siberia, commonly cultivated
as *Anchusa myosotidiflora*.

Description
Leaves large, heart-shaped, basal, on erect,
hairy stems. Flowers in clusters.

How to Grow
Tolerates many soils. Performs best in partial shade and moist soil, but can survive drier, shady sites.

macrophylla pp. 132, 207
Siberian Bugloss. 12–18 in. (30–45 cm) high. Flowers blue, small, starlike, in loosely branched racemes; spring-blooming. Several cultivars have variegated leaves. Zone 4.

Calluna
Heath family
Ericaceae

Ka-loo'na. Heather. A single evergreen species of great variability, native to Europe and Asia Minor. Most forms are spreading mounds suitable for ground cover.

Description
Leaves small, opposite, densely covering twigs. Flowers bell-shaped, white to purple, in dense terminal spikes.

How to Grow
*Calluna*s prefer well-drained, but moisture-retentive, acid soil that is not too rich. They flower best in a sunny location. Protect plants from winter winds. Prune hard in early spring to remove tip injury and promote compact growth. Propagate from summer cuttings or by removing stems showing root development at the base.

vulgaris pp. 168, 169, 188, 189
Heather. To 18 in. (45 cm) high. Hundreds of named varieties are available in many sizes and shapes, with single or double flowers and a range of foliage textures and colors. Long-flowering, some from midsummer into autumn. A few good cultivars for ground cover are 'County Wicklow', with double pale pink flowers and bright green foliage; 'J. H. Hamilton', a late-flowering, low-growing plant with double pink flowers and dark foliage; 'Kinlochruel', with double white flowers in late summer and bright green foliage; 'Silver Knight', with pale lavender flowers in late summer and silvery-gray foliage; and 'Tib', with double deep lilac-pink flowers and dark green foliage. Zone 5, with protection.

Campanula
Bellflower family
Campanulaceae

Kam-pan'you-la. Bellflower. A genus of
about 300 species, more than 2 dozen grown
for their handsome blooms. Those below
from s. Europe. This important group of
garden plants offers the greatest variety of
blue hues.

Description
Basal leaves often unlike the stem leaves.
Flowers typically bell-shaped, often very
showy, mostly blue or white. The species are
very diverse in size and form.

How to Grow
The species below are easy to grow in
ordinary garden soil. Most prefer sunny sites,
but will tolerate light shade. Foliage is
susceptible to slugs. Propagate by division,
cuttings, or seeds.

carpatica pp. 167, 198
Carpathian Harebell. 6–12 in. (15–30 cm)
high. Leaves deeply serrate. Flowers solitary,
erect, blue, nearly 2 in. (5 cm) wide. Prefers
fertile, moist soil with good drainage. Many
white and sky-blue varieties exist; 'Alba' has
white flowers. Long-flowering plant good for
edging. Zone 4.

elatines garganica p. 200
Bellflower. Somewhat sprawling, 6–10 in.
(15–25 cm) high. Basal leaves with small
hairs. Flowers wheel-shaped, solitary, blue,
½ in. (13 mm) wide. Blooms early in
season, with sporadic flowering until fall.
Zone 5.

portenschlagiana p. 204
Dalmatian Bellflower. 6–8 in. (15–20 cm)
high. Leaves heart-shaped or oval, toothed.
Flowers profuse, bluish purple, ¾–1 in.
(2.0–2.5 cm) wide. Prefers well-drained,
gritty soil. Zone 5.

poscharskyana p. 201
Serbian Bellflower. Weak-stemmed or
sprawling plant, 4–6 in. (10–15 cm) high.
Leaves heart-shaped or oval. Flowers
numerous, lilac, 1 in. (2.5 cm) wide.
Adriatic region. Drought-resistant and
vigorous. Zone 4.

Ceanothus
Buckthorn family
Rhamnaceae

See-a-no'thus. About 55 species of deciduous
or evergreen shrubs or small trees, mostly
native to Calif., where they are called wild
lilacs. Many are ornamental. Numerous
hybrids and named cultivars exist.

Description
Leaves alternate or opposite, stem growth
upright or spreading. Flowers small, white or
blue, borne in showy clusters. Sepals often
colored.

How to Grow
Prefers open sunlight and a light, porous
soil. Some species are less tolerant of
moisture than others and are subject to root
rot. Aphids and whiteflies are occasional
pests; spray to control. Propagate species
from seeds, cultivars by cuttings or
layering.

gloriosus p. 206
Point Reyes Ceanothus. Low, dense, growing
to 18 in. (45 cm) high, spreading to 10 ft.
(3 m) wide. Leaves small, leathery, persistent
but not evergreen. Flowers light blue,
blooming in spring. Vigorous ground cover
best suited for large areas in western coastal
conditions. Zone 7.

griseus horizontalis p. 207

Carmel Creeper. 1½–2½ ft. (45–75 cm)
high. Leaves deep green, glossy, oval. Flowers
deep blue, in clusters, blooming in spring. It
is wise to choose named cultivars, because
they have more predictable growth habits.
'Yankee Point' has profuse bright blue
flowers. Will cover a large area. Zone 7.

Cerastium
Pink family
Caryophyllaceae

See-ras'tee-um. The 60 or so species of
chickweed or mouse-ear chickweed are
mostly weedy herbs (sometimes pests),
but a few of them are attractive garden
plants.

Description
Leaves opposite, often hairy. Flowers small,

white, relatively showy in cultivated species due to the profuse, forked clusters.

How to Grow
The species below is very easy to grow in full sun in well-drained soil; increase by division.

tomentosum *p. 81*
Snow-in-Summer. Popular prostrate rock-garden or border plant, to 6 in. (15 cm) high, forming large patches. Leaves numerous, mat-forming, conspicuously white-woolly. Flowers white, to ½ in. (13 mm) wide. Europe. Invasive and persistent. Will grow in pure sand. Zone 4.

Ceratostigma
Plumbago family
Plumbaginaceae

Ser-rat-o-stig′ma. Small genus of perennial herbs or low shrubs from China and Africa, 2 grown as border plants for their blue flowers.

Description
Leaves alternate, hairy on the margins. Flowers in loose, headlike clusters with stiff bracts; corolla tubular.

How to Grow
Does best in moderately fertile, loose soil in full sun, but will tolerate some shade. Propagate by spring division or cuttings. Late to emerge in spring, so take care not to damage dormant plants.

plumbaginoides *p. 199*
Leadwort. Low or semi-prostrate, to 12 in. (30 cm) high. Flowers deep blue, to ½ in. (13 mm) wide. Valuable for its flowers and reddish foliage in autumn. Formerly known as *Plumbago larpentae*. Zone 5, with winter protection.

Chamaemelum
Daisy family
Compositae

Kam-ee-meel′um. Three species of perennial herbs native to w. Europe and Mediterranean

region. Formerly classified under the genus
Anthemis.

Description
Stems leafy, leaves alternate, dissected,
generally pungent. Flowerheads with yellow
or white rays and yellow disk flowers, not
particularly showy.

How to Grow
Easy to grow in ordinary garden soil. Prefers
full sun but will tolerate partial shade.
Increase by seeds, cuttings, or division.

nobile p. 85
Chamomile. Plants form soft-textured, finely
cut clumps, 6–12 in. (15–30 cm) high.
Leaves aromatic, to 2 in. (5 cm) long.
Flowers usually golden-yellow, small,
button-shaped, blooming in summer.
Frequent mowing makes plant clumps form
a tight carpet that can substitute for lawn.
Zone 6.

Chrysogonum
Daisy family
Compositae

Kris-sog′o-num. A single species of perennial
herbs of the e. U.S.

Description
Leaves opposite, long-stalked, bluntly
toothed. Flowerheads yellow.

How to Grow
Grows well in partial shade in moderately
rich soil with good drainage. Not
dependable in all northern areas; will
probably be damaged in zone 4 if there is no
snow cover. Propagate by seeds or division.

virginianum p. 154
Green-and-Gold; Golden Star. 4–10 in.
(10–25 cm) high. Flowerheads solitary or
few, 1½ in. (4 cm) wide, yellow. Plants
flower for a long period in spring and
summer, especially where summers are cool.
Zone 5.

Convallaria
Lily family
Liliaceae

Kon-va-lair'ee-a. About 3 species of
rhizomatous perennial herbs native in
Eurasia and naturalized in e. North America.

Description
Leaves basal. Flowers bell-shaped, borne in a
one-sided raceme.

How to Grow
Does best in full to partial shade and moist,
fertile soil enriched annually with organic
matter. Propagate by division. Thin plantings
when flowering becomes sparse.

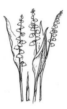

majalis pp. *138, 172*
Lily-of-the-Valley. 6–12 in. (15–30 cm) high.
Leaves 4–8 in. (10–20 cm) long, 2–3 in.
(5.0–7.5 cm) wide. Flowers white, ⅜ in.
(9 mm) wide, waxy, very fragrant, in a
terminal raceme. Blooms in late spring.
Cultivars include 'Rosea', with pink flowers,
and 'Aureo-variegata', with yellow-striped
leaves. Zone 4.

Cornus
Dogwood family
Cornaceae

Kor'nus. Dogwood. A genus of about 45
species, all trees and shrubs except the
species listed below. They are much grown
for their handsome flowers, often brightly
colored fruit, and, in some species, the
winter color of their twigs. Native to Old
World and New World north temperate
zones.

Description
Leaves simple, opposite, without marginal
teeth. Flowers small, petals 4. In a few
species flowers are inconspicuous, set in the
middle of several colored bracts. Fruit fleshy,
sometimes showy.

How to Grow
Most dogwoods are easy to grow in any
good garden soil in sun or light shade.
Usually propagated by seeds or cuttings.

canadensis pp. 112, 113, 166

Bunchberry. Stems to 6 in. (15 cm) high, above the creeping, woody rootstock. Leaves pointed, 2 in. (5 cm) long, whorled. Stems topped by small greenish flowers surrounded by 4–6 showy white bracts in late spring. Shiny red berries follow. A woodland plant requiring humus-rich, moist soil. Zone 2.

Coronilla
Bean family
Leguminosae

Kor-ro-nil'la. A genus of about 20 species of herbs or shrubs scattered from the Canary Islands to w. Asia.

Description
Leaves compound, the leaflets arranged feather-fashion. Flowers pealike, in long-stalked umbels growing from the leaf axils.

How to Grow
The species below is invasive and is best used as deciduous ground cover on steep, sunny banks. Propagate by seeds or division. Mow or trim annually to improve appearance.

varia p. 183

Crown Vetch. Sprawling vinelike herb, to 18 in. (45 cm) high. Leaflets oblong. Flowers ½ in. (13 mm) long, pink, rose, and white, in dense clusters, blooming in summer. Grows best in dry soil. Zone 4.

Cotoneaster
Rose family
Rosaceae

Ko-to'nee-as-ter. About 50 species of shrubs or small trees, many widely planted for their attractive habit and showy fruit. Native to Old World temperate zones.

Description
Leaves alternate, stalked, without marginal teeth; some species evergreen. Flowers small, white or pinkish, blooming in early summer. Fruit small, fleshy, applelike.

How to Grow
Cotoneasters prefer a sunny location and

well-drained soil that is not overly acid.
Prune lightly to maintain shape. Subject to
fire blight and, in dry summers, to lace bug
and spider mites. While these conditions
may be controlled by spraying, use caution
when considering mass plantings. Propagate
by summer cuttings or layering.

adpressus p. 101
Creeping Cotoneaster. Slow-growing
deciduous shrub to 12 in. (30 cm) high,
with rooting stems. Leaves ½ in. (13 mm)
long, wavy-margined. Flowers pinkish, in
spring. Fruit red. The var. *praecox* is more
vigorous, a little taller, with larger fruit.
Zone 5.

apiculatus p. 100
Cranberry Cotoneaster. Deciduous shrub to
3 ft. (90 cm) high and spreading wider.
Leaves nearly round, shiny, about ¾ in.
(19 mm) wide. Flowers pink. Fruit scarlet,
showy. Zone 5.

dammeri p. 103
Bearberry Cotoneaster. Prostrate evergreen
shrub to 12 in. (30 cm) high, with trailing
branches often rooting at the joints. Leaves
1 in. (2.5 cm) long, pale beneath. Flowers
white, berries bright red. Sometimes sold as
C. humifusa. The cultivar 'Skogsholm'
spreads steadily and flowers profusely.
Zone 5.

horizontalis pp. 100, 101

Rock Cotoneaster. Spreading shrub 2–3 ft.
(60–90 cm) high, admired for its fan-shaped
branching habit. Leaves nearly round, ½ in.
(13 mm) long, semi-evergreen in the South,
hardy deciduous in the North. Orange-red
autumn color. Flowers pinkish, fruit red.
'Little Gem' is more compact, does not fruit
freely, but has brilliant autumn color.
'Variegatus' has white-edged leaves and is less
vigorous. Zone 5.

Daboecia
Heath family
Ericaceae

Dab-ee′shi-a. A small genus of low, heathlike
shrubs, native to w. Europe.

Description
Upright evergreen shrubs. Leaves alternate,
simple. Flowers bell-shaped, nodding, in
terminal clusters.

How to Grow
Culture is the same as for *Calluna* (heather).
Propagate from late summer cuttings or
seeds sown on moist peat moss.

cantabrica pp. 171, 190
Irish Heath. Erect, slightly spreading stems
1½–2 ft. (45–60 cm) high. Leaves flat,
glossy, about ½ in. (13 mm) long, white
beneath. Flowers purple in the species, but
several distinct color forms are available,
including 'Alba', with white flowers, and
'County Buchanan', with bright pink
flowers. Blooms from summer to fall.
Sometimes listed as *D. polifolia* or
Menziesia polifolia. Zone 5, with protection.

Daphne
Mezereon family
Thymelaeaceae

Daf'nee. About 50 species of deciduous or
evergreen shrubs native to Europe and Asia,
a few widely grown for their fragrant
flowers.

Description
Spreading or upright shrubs. Leaves mostly
alternate, simple. Flowers in small clusters;
some bloom before leaves unfold. Calyx
corolla-like, usually bell-shaped. Fruit leathery
or fleshy, sometimes showy.

How to Grow
Prefers loose, fertile soil, but some will grow
in ordinary garden soil with lime added.
Excellent drainage will ensure success.
Daphnes flower best in full sun, though
many will tolerate partial shade. In winter,
evergreen kinds may suffer foliage burn; trim
off in early spring. Propagate from fresh
seeds or summer cuttings, or, in low-growing
types, by rooted side-shoots.

cneorum p. 182
Rose Daphne; Garland Flower. Spreading
evergreen shrub to 12 in. (30 cm) high and
3 ft. (90 cm) wide. Leaves small, oblong.
Flowers fragrant, pink, ⅓ in. (8 mm) wide,

in terminal clusters, blooming in spring.
'Ruby Glow' has deep pink flowers. Zone 5.

Dianthus
Pink family
Caryophyllaceae

Dy-an'thus. About 300 species of annual or
perennial herbs, mostly Eurasian. Some are
important garden plants.

Description
Leaves opposite, usually narrow. Joints
swollen. Flowers terminal, usually in small,
often dense cymes or panicles. Petals 5
(much doubled in some horticultural
forms), fringed or toothed in some species.
Most flower in spring.

How to Grow
Most prefer full sun and well-drained soil. In
soil with very low pH, add a bit of lime. For
tidiness in mat-forming sorts, remove spent
flower-stalks to base of plant. Increase by
cuttings, seeds, division, or, in some types,
by layering.

gratianopolitanus *pp. 84, 193*
Cheddar Pink. 6–8 in. (15–20 cm) high.
Flowers solitary, ½–¾ in. (13–19 mm)
wide, pink. Leaves form a gray-green grassy
mat. Cultivars have flowers ranging from
white to carmine. 'Tiny Rubies' has ruby-red
flowers. Sometimes sold as *D. caesius*. Zone 5.

Disporum
Lily family
Liliaceae

Dy-spor'um. A genus of perennial woodland
herbs with creeping rootstocks. Sometimes
called Fairy-Bells.

Description
Leaves somewhat downy, nearly stalkless,
alternate. Flowers bell-shaped.

How to Grow
The species below performs best in dry,
well-drained, humus-rich soil in partial shade.
Propagate by seeds or spring division.

sessile '**Variegatum**' *p. 141*
Variegated Japanese Fairy-Bells. 1¼–2 ft.
(38–60 cm) high. Leaves white-striped,
oblong, to 4 in. (10 cm) long. Flowers
creamy white, small, usually solitary or in
groups of 2 or 3, in spring. Japan. Zone 5.

Duchesnea
Rose family
Rosaceae

Doo-shay´nee-a. Two Asiatic species of herbs
related to *Fragaria*.

Description
Leaves similar to those of wild strawberry,
trifoliate, oval, short-stalked, toothed, with
silky hair on lower surface. Flowers yellow.

How to Grow
Thrives in most soils, but should have rich
soil and sun for best flowers and fruit.
Propagate by division or detaching runners.

indica pp. 110, 161
Mock Strawberry. 2–3 in. (5.0–7.5 cm) high,
trailing with runners. Leaves remain green
well into winter. Flowers tiny, yellow,
solitary, blooming in summer. Fruit red,
surrounded by the persistent calyx,
strawberrylike, but with little flavor. Can
become weedy. Zone 4.

Epimedium
Barberry family
Berberidaceae

Ep-i-mee´di-um. Barrenwort. Rather woody
perennial herbs, the 20 known species all
from the north temperate zone.

Description
Leaves compound, the leaflets finely toothed,
generally heart-shaped, arranged feather-
fashion, forming dense clumps. New leaves
light green, tinged red in some species.
Flowers bloom in spring in clusters.

How to Grow
Barrenworts tolerate sun but prefer partial
shade. With a little protection, foliage may
stay green in winter. They prefer moist soil,
but tolerate dry shade. Propagate by division.

alpinum p. 127
Alpine Epimedium. To 10 in. (25 cm) high. Leaves dense, more or less evergreen. Flowers with red sepals and yellow petals. Zone 4.

grandiflorum p. 126
Longspur Epimedium. Stems to 12 in. (30 cm) high. Flowers 1–2 in. (2.5–5.0 cm) wide, pink with white-tipped spurs. 'Rose Queen' has large flowers; 'White Queen' has white flowers. Also sold as *E. macranthum*. Zone 5.

× *rubrum* p. 126
Red Epimedium. To 12 in. (30 cm) high. Flowers small, bright pink to crimson with white spurs. Bronze-purple autumn foliage. Sometimes sold incorrectly as *E. alpinum*. Zone 5.

× *versicolor* p. 125
Robust, to 12 in. (30 cm) high. Flowers small, petals yellow, spurs red-tinged. 'Sulphureum' is an excellent cultivar with yellow flowers. Foliage persistent but not evergreen in the North. Zone 5.

× *warleyense* p. 127
Warley Epimedium. 9–12 in. (22.5–30.0 cm) high. Flowers small, with 8 orange sepals and 4 spurlike yellow petals. Zone 5.

× *youngianum* **'Niveum'** p. 175
Snowy Epimedium. 8–10 in. (20–25 cm) high. Flowers tiny, pendulous, held well above foliage, white. Slow-growing, but a beautiful specimen in the border. Zone 5.

Erica
Heath family
Ericaceae

E'ri-ka. The true heaths include more than 500 species of much-branched, evergreen shrubs or small trees, largely from South Africa and the Mediterranean region.

Description
Sometimes treelike, more often low shrubs, some nearly prostrate. Leaves small, needlelike, usually in dense clusters. Flowers sometimes solitary, more often in small clusters; corolla bell-shaped.

How to Grow
Basic culture is the same as for *Calluna*.
Species vary greatly in winter hardiness and
climate adaptability. The one listed below is
probably the hardiest and most widely grown
in the U.S.

carnea *pp. 170, 188*
Spring Heath. To 12 in. (30 cm) high,
usually spreading to about 18 in. (45 cm)
wide. Long flowering period, beginning in
early spring. Species flowers are red, but
many selections have been made for flower
color and growth habit. Two of the best are
'Springwood White', which spreads neatly,
the flowers opening white from creamy buds,
and 'Springwood Pink', with pink flowers
and bronzy spring foliage. Zone 5.

Eriophyllum
Daisy family
Compositae

E-ri-o-fill′um. W. North American herbs,
often called woolly sunflowers because of
their white-woolly foliage and sunflowerlike
heads.

Description
Leaves alternate, entire, lobed or cut.
Flowerheads small, numerous, resembling a
miniature sunflower.

How to Grow
The woolly sunflowers are not happy in
slushy or wet eastern winters. In the Far
West, they do well in open, sandy borders
and rock gardens. Increase by seeds or spring
division.

lanatum *p. 151*
Woolly Eriophyllum. To 2 ft. (60 cm) high.
Flowerheads chiefly solitary, 1 in. (2.5 cm)
wide, golden yellow, blooming in spring.
Needs dry, well-drained soil, especially in
winter. Zone 5.

Euonymus
Bittersweet family
Celastraceae

You-on′i-mus. About 170 mostly Asian
species of deciduous or evergreen trees or

shrubs, including creeping or climbing woody vines. Many are grown for their showy fruits or evergreen leaves.

Description
Upright or sprawling, sometimes clinging. Leaves opposite, usually smooth. Flowers greenish, white, or yellowish, inconspicuous. Fruit a capsule, often lobed or brightly colored, opening to show red or orange seeds.

How to Grow
Grows well in ordinary soil in sun or shade, but not all are hardy in cold climates. Some types are subject to euonymus scale; avoid mass plantings of susceptible types. Increase by stratified seeds, hardwood cuttings, or, in some species, by layered stems.

***fortunei* cultivars** *pp. 104, 105, 118*
Winter Creeper. Species is a trailing or climbing evergreen vine with rooting branches to 12 in. (30 cm) high and 20 ft. (6 m) long. Leaves oval, ¾–2 in. (2–5 cm) long. Fruit nearly round, pale pink. Formerly called *E. radicans*. Several cultivars are grown especially for ground cover: 'Colorata' (Purple Winter Creeper) is a trailing shrub to 18 in. (45 cm) high, with leaves deep purple in autumn and winter. 'Kewensis', more correctly called *E. f.* 'Minima', is a fine-textured trailing form to 2 in. (5 cm) high, with small whitish-veined leaves ¼ in. (6 mm) wide; it seldom fruits. 'Silver Queen' is a more mounding form to 2 ft. (60 cm) high and 3 ft. (90 cm) wide, with green and creamy-white leaves. All zone 4.

Fragaria
Rose family
Rosaceae

Fra-gay'ri-a. Strawberry. About 12 species of perennial herbs, essentially stemless except for long runners.

Description
Leaves compound, with 3 leaflets. Flowers generally white (rarely reddish). Calyx forming the hull of the strawberry. Fruit a much-enlarged, fleshy receptacle, in or upon which are embedded small achenes, commonly (but incorrectly) called the seeds.

How to Grow
Grows well in full sun in most garden soil,
particularly if soil is slightly acid. Propagate
by young plants rooted at ends of runners.

chiloensis p. 113
Beach Strawberry. Low bushy plant, 6–8 in.
(15–20 cm) high, runners usually forming
after fruit is set. Leaflets green and glossy
above, pale bluish white beneath, 1–2 in.
(2.5–5.0 cm) long. Flowers white, in spring.
Fruit edible. Coastal Alaska to Calif.; South
America. Zone 5.

Galax
Galax family
Diapensiaceae

Gay'lacks. A single perennial evergreen herb
from e. North America.

Description
Plant forms a clump of scaly rhizomes, from
which arises the cluster of evergreen leaves.

How to Grow
Needs full to partial shade and moist soil.
Optimum growth requires moderately acid
soil with abundant organic matter; add peat
moss to enrich. Increase by spring or fall
division.

urceolata p. 133
A stemless, slowly spreading herb forming
clumps 6 in. (15 cm) high. Leaves nearly
round, grassy, toothed, bronze with age, to
4 in. (10 cm) wide. Flowers white, minute,
in a spikelike raceme, on a long slender stalk,
in late spring or early summer. Also sold as
G. aphylla. Zone 5.

Galium
Madder family
Rubiaceae

Gay'li-um. Weak, almost weedy perennial
herbs, commonly known as bedstraw or
cleavers. Suitable only for informal plantings
in borders or rock gardens.

Description
Stems often prostrate or arching. Flowers
very numerous, small, white, yellow, or

maroon, the corolla wheel-shaped or deeply
4-parted.

How to Grow
Galium requires shade and moist, well-
drained, slightly acid soil to keep foliage
shiny-green into fall. In sunny, dry soil,
plants become stunted and may die down.
Easy to divide in spring.

odoratum pp. 82, 167
Sweet Woodruff. To 12 in. (30 cm) high.
Leaves lance-shaped, small, fragrant when
dried. Flowers white, tiny, in clusters.
Eurasia. Formerly known as *Asperula odorata*.
Zone 5.

Gaultheria
Blueberry family
Ericaceae

Gaul-theer'ri-a. Beautiful evergreen shrubs
(some herblike), most of the 100 species
from the Andes, a few from e. Asia and
North America.

Description
Low or prostrate plants. Leaves usually
alternate, toothed. Calyx ultimately becomes
fleshy and colored and encloses the berrylike
fruit, a capsule.

How to Grow
Needs acid soil. Best grown in the wild
garden or rock garden; all but *G. shallon*
prefer partial shade. They do not transplant
easily from the wild, so it is better to plant
potted specimens. Propagate by cuttings of
half-ripened wood or by seeds; however,
seeds are extremely minute and seedlings
grow slowly.

procumbens pp. 98, 99
Wintergreen; Teaberry. A prostrate, herblike,
evergreen woody plant, the stems half
underground, the tips upright and to 4 in.
(10 cm) high. Leaves ovalish, purplish when
plant is in fruit, 2 in. (5 cm) long, marginal
teeth often bristly. Flowers tiny, solitary in
leaf axils, nodding, white or pinkish, in late
spring to early summer. Fruit scarlet, pea-
size. Zone 5.

shallon pp. 94, 95
Salal. In poor soil and full sun, a low, dense,

vigorous ground cover to 18 in. (45 cm) high, but in moist shade, an erect evergreen shrub, more or less spreading, to 3 ft. (90 cm) high. Leaves round-oval, to 4 in. (10 cm) long. Flower cluster terminal; corolla tiny, pink or white. Blooms in late spring. Fruit purplish black. Chiefly suited to the rock garden. Zone 6.

Gaylussacia
Blueberry family
Ericaceae

Gay-loo-say'she-a. About 40 species of fruit-bearing or ornamental, North and South American shrubs, sometimes evergreen. The fruiting ones are commonly mistaken for the blueberry (*Vaccinium*).

Description
Leaves alternate, usually without teeth, often resinous-dotted. Flowers in small racemes, corolla bell- or urn-shaped, the 5 shallow lobes usually bent backward. Fruit fleshy, edible, but lacking the fine flavor of the blueberry.

How to Grow
Grows best in moist acid soil and partial shade. Propagate by division of the creeping roots (in some species) or by cuttings.

brachycera p. 96
Box-Huckleberry. A nearly prostrate evergreen shrub, 8–16 in. (20.0–40.5 cm) high, the stems subterranean, with ascending aerial branches. Leaves many, elliptic, to 1½ in. (4 cm) long, smooth. Flowers tiny, white or pink, in spring. Fruit blue. Good in shaded, peaty locations. Zone 5.

Gazania
Daisy family
Compositae

Ga-zay'nia. About 16 species of showy South African herbaceous perennials, a few long cultivated for their flowers. Good ground cover or edging plants. Popular in the Southwest and s. Calif.

Description
Leaves alternate and basal. Flowerheads

solitary, long-stalked, closing at night or in cloudy weather. Rays yellow, golden, or white, often with dark spot at base.

How to Grow
Best adapted to dry desert gardens, where they will endure for months. In hot, humid climates, plants perish soon after first bloom unless given excellent drainage. Start seeds indoors 6–8 weeks before last frost; set out in sunny, dry, well-drained soil after danger of frost is past. Or propagate selected forms by late-summer basal cuttings.

rigens p. 150
Treasure Flower. To 16 in. (40.5 cm) high, trailing, branched. Leaves green above, woolly below, long, narrow. Flowerheads 1½ in. (4 cm) wide, the rays orange, yellow, gold, cream, pink, or bronze-red, with black spot near base. Var. *leucolaena* has unspotted yellow flowers. Newer varieties include multicolored blossoms and dwarf kinds with large flowers. Also sold as *G. splendens*. Zone 9.

Genista
Pea family
Leguminosae

Je-niss′ta. Over 75 species of low, handsome, often evergreen or nearly leafless, shrubs, all from temperate or mild regions of the Old World. A few species are cultivated in this country. Some are called broom, but the common broom is a *Cytisus*.

Description
Spiny, usually green-barked, shrubs. Leaves compound, the leaflets often reduced to 1 (rarely 3). Flowers pealike, yellow or white, in usually terminal racemes or heads. Fruit a longish, flattened pod.

How to Grow
Does well in dry, sunny places. Does not transplant easily, so do not move once established. Increase by seeds or by layering. The vigor of the larger species makes them suitable for dry banks; smaller-growing ones spread moderately.

pilosa p. 155
Broom. Prostrate, warty shrub with ascending branches to 20 in. (50 cm) high.

Leaflets tiny, oblong. Flowers yellow, in
sparse clusters in leaf axils, in late spring to
early summer. Pod to 1½ in. (4 cm) long,
silky. Zone 6.

sagittalis p. 157

Broom. Nearly prostrate shrub forming a
mound to 20 in. (50 cm) high. Branches
2-winged. Leaflets small, ovalish or narrower.
Flowers yellow, in terminal clusters, in late
spring. Chiefly suited to the rock garden.
Zone 6.

Geranium
Geranium family
Geraniaceae

Ger-ray′ni-um. About 300 species of hardy
perennial, biennial, or (rarely) annual herbs,
commonly called cranesbill, and mostly
suited to borders or wild gardens. The
common garden geranium belongs to the
genus *Pelargonium.*

Description
Generally low, often half-prostrate herbs,
with forking stems. Leaves to 3 in. (7.5 cm)
long, dissected or lobed, roundish, divided
finger-fashion. Flowers regular, blooming in
early spring. Fruit a collection of beaked,
persistent carpels.

How to Grow
True geraniums prefer moderately rich,
well-drained soil. They flower well in sun or
light shade, but need protection from hot
afternoon sun. Nearly all are good ground
covers. Easy to increase by division of clumps
in spring or fall; the species can also be
grown from seeds.

'Claridge Druce' p. 196
Vigorous ground cover to 20 in. (50 cm)
high. Leaves deeply cut, hairy. Flowers
trumpet-shaped, pink, with purple veining.
Zone 4.

endressii p. 196
Pyrenean Cranesbill. Perennial to 18 in.
(45 cm) high. Leaves deeply cut. Flowers
1 in. (2.5 cm) wide, rose-pink. Pyrenees.
Requires well-drained soil of average fertility.
Where summers are cool, it will flower most
of the season; in hot areas, flowers only in
late spring and early summer. Cultivars

include 'A. T. Johnson', to 12 in. (30 cm)
high, with light silvery-pink flowers, and
'Wargrave Pink', with salmon-pink flowers.
Zone 4.

'Johnson's Blue' *p. 198*
Johnson's Blue Cranesbill. To 2 ft. (60 cm)
high. Flowers profuse, 1½–2 in. (4–5 cm)
wide, petals blue with darker blue veins.
Long flowering season beginning in early
summer. Where summers are hot and dry,
requires moist soil and partial shade. Zone 4.

macrorrhizum *p. 108*
Bigroot Cranesbill. Aromatic perennial,
12–18 in. (30–45 cm) high. Leaves nearly
evergreen, deeply 5- to 7-parted. Flowers
magenta or pink, 1 in. (2.5 cm) wide, in
early summer. S. Europe. Cultivars include
'Album', with white flowers and red calyxes,
and 'Ingwersen's Variety', with pale pink
flowers. Zone 5.

sanguineum *p. 197*
Blood-red Cranesbill. 12–18 in. (30–45 cm)
high. Leaves dark green, deeply lobed.
Flowers 1 in. (2.5 cm) wide, reddish purple
to pale pink. Good for open borders. Will
tolerate full sun even in hot, dry summers.
Var. *striatum* (*lancastrense*) is lower, with
light pink flowers with crimson veins;
there is also a white-flowered variety.
Zone 4.

Gypsophila
Pink family
Caryophyllaceae

Jip-sof'fill-a. Handsome annual or perennial
herbs, some very popular garden plants.
Generally known as baby's-breath because of
its profusion of flowers.

Description
Leaves small, bluish green, opposite. Joints
slightly swollen. Flowers many, usually in
profuse, branched panicles.

How to Grow
Gypsophila needs full sun and a well-drained,
neutral soil that is not too rich. Sow seeds
directly or propagate by cuttings. Established
plants do not transplant easily.

repens p. 185
Creeping Baby's-Breath. 6 in. (15 cm) high.
Leaves smooth. Flowers white, ¼ in.
(6 mm) wide. Mts. of Europe. Good ground
cover for sunny areas; also thrives in well-
drained rock gardens and walls. 'Rosea' has
pink flowers. Zone 4.

Hebe
Snapdragon family
Scrophulariaceae

He'bee. About 75 species of southern
hemisphere trees and shrubs, most common
in New Zealand. Very closely allied to
Veronica. Needs maritime climate; does well
on the West Coast.

Description
Stems mostly hairy. Leaves evergreen, often
overlapping, leathery. Flowers solitary or in
axillary spikes.

How to Grow
Requires moist but well-drained soil. Flowers
best in full sun, but needs a little shade in
areas with hot summers. Prune after
flowering to maintain compact growth.
Taller sorts may be used for hedges, shorter
ones as ground covers. Propagate by seeds or
cuttings.

menziesii p. 168
Evergreen shrub of spreading habit, to 3 ft.
(90 cm) high. Leaves ¾ in. (19 mm) long,
narrow, dense, shiny, toothed. Flowers in
clusters, white tinged with lilac, blooming in
summer. *Hebe* 'Desilior' is a rounded shrub
with long-blooming blue-purple flowers;
'Reevesii' has maroon-tinged dark green
leaves and reddish-purple flowers. All
zone 8.

Hedera
Aralia family
Araliaceae

Hed'er-ra. Evergreen woody vines from
n. Eurasia and n. Africa, generally called ivy.

Description
They have woody stems and climb by aerial
rootlets that cling very easily to brick or
masonry, but less so to wood. Leaves
alternate, evergreen, stalked, usually lobed or
coarsely toothed. Flowers greenish, not very
conspicuous.

How to Grow
Performs best in rich, moist soil; prefers
some shade, especially where summers are
hot. Easy to grow from cuttings, many of
which already have aerial roots. Start in sand
in the greenhouse in winter, or in cold
frames outdoors in sandy soil almost any
time during the growing season.

canariensis p. 133
Algerian Ivy. Stout, high-climbing vine, to
12 in. (30 cm) high as a ground cover.
Leaves roundish or heart-shaped, usually
5- to 7-lobed, 2–6 in. (5–15 cm) long. Fruit
black. Vigorous ground cover used mostly in
Calif. There are several variegated cultivars.
Zone 8.

Helianthemum
Rock rose family
Cistaceae

He-li-an'thee-mum. Usually prostrate or
sprawling woody plants or herbaceous
perennials, a few cultivated for their
roselike flowers. Usually called frostweed
or sun-rose.

Description
Leaves evergreen or semi-evergreen, narrow,
usually gray-green. Flowers very fleeting,
resembling buttercups, in small clusters.

How to Grow
Grows best in full sun in sandy, alkaline soil
that is well drained. Protect plants in regions
with severe winters. Propagate by division or
cuttings.

nummularium pp. 152, 153, 194, 195
Rock Rose. 9–12 in. (22.5–30.0 cm) high.
Flowers yellow, round, 1 in. (2.5 cm) wide,
with 5 petals and a texture like crepe paper.
Europe. Cut back after first flowering to
promote autumn bloom. Among the many
horticultural varieties are 'Firedragon', with
red-orange flowers, 'Raspberry Ripple', with

white and pink flowers, and 'Wisley Pink', with pale pink flowers. Zone 6.

Hemerocallis
Lily family
Liliaceae

Hem-mer-o-kal'lis. Daylily. About 15 wild species of perennial herbs, found from cen. Europe to Japan. Many hybrid forms exist. The arching habit of the leaves makes daylilies suitable as ground cover.

Description
Roots somewhat fleshy. Leaves basal, narrow, sword-shaped, and keeled. Stem or stalk of flower cluster is often branched and usually exceeds leaves. Flowers funnel- or bell-shaped, widely expanding above.

How to Grow
Daylilies flower freely, are easy to grow, and resist disease. They thrive in sun or partial shade and adapt well to almost any location. Individual flowers last only a day, but others follow on branched stems; some may flower a second time in the season. By selecting different varieties it is possible to have flowers from late spring until fall. Increase by division of clumps. Whenever growth gets too congested, divide and replant in late summer or early spring.

hybrids *pp. 148, 149*
Daylily. Thousands of named garden varieties exist, ranging 1–5 ft. (0.3–1.5 m) high. Flowers to 6 in. (15 cm) wide, with petals single, double, or ruffled. Colors include cream through many shades of yellow, orange, red, pink, lavender, and purple. Blooms late spring to autumn. Old-time favorite 'Hyperion' is still one of the best performers. Zone 3. (Evergreen sorts are hardy to zones 6–7.)

Herniaria
Pink family
Caryophyllaceae

Her-ni-a'ri-a. Herniary. About 35 species of prostrate or trailing herbs, all from the Old World, 2 of garden interest.

Description
The horticultural species are low, short-lived perennial herbs with swollen joints, usually much branched. Leaves stalkless, small, opposite. Flowers inconspicuous, in small clusters in leaf axils. Fruit a small capsule enclosed within the persistent calyx.

How to Grow
Easy to grow in ordinary well-drained soil in full sun, but will tolerate light shade. Fertilize lightly. Good between paving stones, and for carpet bedding or covering rocks. In warm regions, attractive foliage persists through winter and turns bronzy red.

glabra p. 73
Rupturewort. Prostrate herb, usually spreading over the ground, stems to 3 in. (7.5 cm) high. Leaves oblong, smooth, ¼ in. (6 mm) long. Zone 6.

Heuchera
Saxifrage family
Saxifragaceae

Hew'ker-a. Alumroot. About 40 species of attractive North American perennial herbs, chiefly from mountainous regions.

Description
Stout rootstocks. Leaves mostly basal, long-stalked, often roundish or lobed. Stalk of flower cluster arising from rootstock, often leafy, crowned with a narrow panicle or raceme of bell- or saucer-shaped flowers. Most color comes from conspicuous 5-lobed calyx.

How to Grow
Well suited for the open, partly shaded border, blooming most of summer. Requires fertile, well-drained soil with a high humus content. In winter, drainage is important, and mulch may be needed. In hot climates, it grows best in filtered shade. Propagate by division of clumps in spring.

sanguinea p. 130
Coralbells. Clump-forming herbaceous perennial to 12 in. (30 cm) high. Leaves lobed, to 2 in. (5 cm) long, on long petioles. Graceful flowering stalks, to 18 in. (45 cm) high, topped by loose clusters of small red bell-shaped flowers ½ in.

(13 mm) wide. Long flowering period from spring into summer. Popular cultivars include 'Chatterbox', with pink flowers, 'Coral Cloud', with coral-pink flowers, 'Splendens', with deep red flowers, and 'White Cloud', with white flowers. Zone 5.

Hosta
Lily family
Liliaceae

Hos'ta. Plantain-lily. Widely cultivated perennial garden herbs, sometimes known as *Funkia* or *Niobe*. About 40 known species, all from China, Korea, and Japan.

Description
Plants tufted with handsome, conspicuously ribbed basal leaves. Flowers terminal, white, lilac, or blue, in spikes or racemes on a stalk arising from the leaves. Flowers tubular, usually expanded at top.

How to Grow
Very easy to grow, usually in the open border, massed under trees, or as single specimens. Readily increased by spring or fall division of clumps. Hostas prefer partial shade and soil that is moist in summer.

hybrids and cultivars *pp. 139, 140, 141*
Hosta species hybridize and sport readily, and hundreds of fancy-leaf selections have been named. Foliage ranges from 10–24 in. (25–60 cm) high. A few of the best for ground cover are 'Francee', with medium-size dark green, white-margined leaves; 'Ginko Craig', a smaller version with lance-shaped leaves; 'Gold Standard', with large chartreuse leaves with blue-green edges; and 'Golden Tiara', with small heart-shaped green leaves with gold margins. All zone 4.

lancifolia *pp. 139, 206*
Narrow Plantain-lily. To 12 in. (30 cm) high. Leaf blades 4–6 in. (10–15 cm) long, oval lance-shaped or narrower, often with a long point, glossy and dark green. Flowers violet, to 2 in. (5 cm) long. Blooms in late summer. Also called *H. cathayana*. Zone 4.

sieboldiana *pp. 134, 135*
Siebold Plantain-lily. To 2½ ft. (75 cm) high. Leaf blades 10–15 in. (25–38 cm) long, oval heart-shaped, blue-gray, puckered.

Flowers pale lilac, to 1½ in. (4 cm) long, on a stalk generally shorter than the leaves. Blooms in midsummer. Sometimes called *H. glauca.* Cultivar 'Elegans' is a sumptuous plant with larger leaves. Zone 4.

Hypericum
St. John's-wort family
Hypericaceae

Hy-per′i-cum. St. John's-wort. About 300 species of herbs or shrubs, nearly all from the north temperate zone. The 2 described below are popular for the border or rock garden.

Description
Leaves generally opposite, mostly resinous-dotted, without marginal teeth or lobes. Flowers yellow, in cymes or solitary. Fruit a capsule, sometimes showy.

How to Grow
St. John's-worts prefer well-drained, not too fertile soil and sun or partial shade. They will tolerate dry soil but grow best with adequate moisture. Propagate by seeds, cuttings, and, in the low-growing kinds, by divisions and rooting stems.

calycinum p. 161
Aaron's-Beard; Rose-of-Sharon. Evergreen subshrub, to 12 in. (30 cm) high. Leaves oblong, 3–4 in. (7.5–10.0 cm) long, pale beneath. Flowers few or solitary, 2 in. (5 cm) wide, yellow. Se. Europe and Asia Minor. Blooms in summer. A good ground cover in sun or shade, and for sandy soils. Zone 5.

Iberis
Mustard family
Cruciferae

Eye-beer′is. About 30 species of annual or perennial herbs, mostly from the Mediterranean region.

Description
Leaves divided or undivided and alternate. Flowers in flat-topped or finger-shaped clusters, the 4 petals separate.

How to Grow
The perennials are very useful for edgings or rock gardens and prefer a sunny, well-drained spot. They will stop flowering if kept too dry. Cut back after flowering to maintain compact growth. In cold and windy northern climates, mulch lightly to protect foliage from browning.

sempervirens p. 169
Perennial Candytuft. Usually evergreen, to 12 in. (30 cm) high, forming a spreading mound. Foliage dark green, narrow-oblong. Flowers white, 1½ in. (4 cm) wide, in lateral racemes, blooming in spring. Europe. Several cultivars have been selected for compact growth and autumn reflowering. Zone 5, with protection.

Ilex
Holly family
Aquifoliaceae

Eye'lecks. About 400 species of mostly evergreen trees and shrubs, widely scattered in temperate and tropical regions. Some are very valuable broad-leaved evergreens, and a few that drop their leaves are grown for their showy fruits.

Description
Leaves alternate, sometimes spiny-toothed. Flowers inconspicuous, white or greenish, usually in small clusters in leaf axils. Fruit berrylike, often showy.

How to Grow
Grows best in well-drained fertile soil. In northern climates, evergreen hollies need adequate moisture before ground freezes and protection from drying winter winds and sun-scorch. Transplant with a soil ball in spring or autumn, and water generously the first year. Propagate by stratified seeds or by cuttings, hardwood or softwood. Male and female plants are separate; both are needed to ensure a crop of berries.

crenata p. 102
Japanese Holly. Handsome evergreen shrub with boxlike habit. Leaves generally oblong, broadest toward tip, wedge-shaped at base, 1 in. (2.5 cm) long, dark green, finely toothed. Fruit black. Two low-growing cultivars are the mound-forming 'Helleri',

to 3 ft. (90 cm) high and twice as wide, and 'Repandens', a dense, compact shrub to 3 ft. (90 cm) high and spreading wider. Zone 6.

Iris
Iris family
Iridaceae

Eye'ris. Over 150 species of herbs, mostly from the north temperate zone, with thousands of horticultural varieties.

Description
Stout rhizomes or bulbous rootstocks. Leaves narrow, often sword-shaped. Flowers in 6 segments arising from spathelike bracts; 3 outer segments (falls) reflexed, inner 3 (standards) usually smaller and erect.

How to Grow
Culture varies greatly from species to species. Most need sun, but some tolerate shade. Plant rhizomatous irises with rhizome showing and fan of leaves pointing in direction you want plant to grow. Propagate species by seed and hybrids by division.

cristata p. 205
Crested Iris. 4–6 in. (10–15 cm) high. Leaves sword-shaped, light green. Flowers lavender-blue with yellow crest, outer segments 1½ in. (4 cm) long, faintly fragrant. Plant in humus-rich, moist soil in partial shade; can tolerate full sun if soil is moist. Mat-forming; does not require frequent division. White and light blue horticultural varieties available. Prey to slugs. Zone 4.

Juniperus
Cypress family
Cupressaceae

Jew-nip'er-us. Juniper. About 70 species of evergreen trees and shrubs, ranging from low, prostrate shrubs to tall, slender trees. Throughout the northern hemisphere, from the arctic to the subtropics. Their diverse habits make them valuable ornamental plants.

Description
On young plants and vigorous branches, leaves usually needle-shaped, borne in threes;

on adult plants, leaves generally small,
scalelike, opposite, pressed close to twigs.
Flowers inconspicuous. Fruit berrylike.

How to Grow
Prefers moderately moist, loamy soil, though
J. horizontalis thrives in dry, rocky places. All
species perform best in full sun. Propagate
by cuttings, seeds, layering, and grafting.
Low, spreading types are excellent around
buildings and for covering slopes.

chinensis p. 87
Chinese Juniper. Species varies from low,
almost prostrate, shrubs to trees 60 ft.
(18 m) high. Var. *sargentii* (Sargent Juniper)
is a prostrate shrub to 18 in. (45 cm) high
and 8–10 ft. (2.4–3.0 m) wide, main
branches prostrate, twigs ascending. Needles
appressed on the twigs, green above, whitish
beneath. Crushed foliage has odor of
camphor. Fruit purplish brown. Zone 5.

conferta pp. 88, 89
Shore Juniper. Prostrate shrub to 18 in.
(45 cm) high. Leaves sharply pointed,
usually in threes, with narrow white band
and groove on upper surface. New growth
light green, later becoming grayish. Fruit
black, glaucous. Suited to sandy soils. 'Blue
Pacific' is a handsome cultivar with blue-
green foliage. Zone 6.

horizontalis pp. 90, 91

Creeping Juniper. Prostrate shrub with long,
spreading branches. Leaves glandular and
either needlelike and slightly spreading, or,
on mature branches, scaly and overlapping;
bluish green or gray-blue. Fruit on a short
stem, blue, sometimes glaucous. Grows well
in sandy, rocky soil. 'Bar Harbor' forms a
dense mat to 12 in. (30 cm) high and has
steel-blue foliage turning silvery purple in
winter. 'Plumosa' (Andorra Juniper) has
ascending branches to 18 in. (45 cm) high
with feathery light green foliage, tinged
purplish in winter. 'Wiltonii' (Blue Rug
Juniper) has prostrate branches forming a
silver-blue carpet 6 in. (15 cm) high, and
trails nicely over a wall or large rock. All
zone 3.

procumbens p. 89
Japanese Juniper. Low, prostrate plant.
Branches ascending, 1⅔–2½ ft. (50–75 cm)
high, twigs bluish green. Needles in
threes, spiny-tipped, greenish blue above,

paler beneath, with green midrib. Retains good color year-round. 'Nana' is a dwarf form to 18 in. (45 cm) high. Zone 5.

sabina p. 88
Savin. Shrub with spreading or trailing branches, usually 2–10 ft. (0.6–3.0 m) high. Leaves dark green and either needlelike in pairs, concave and glaucous above, or, on mature branches, scalelike, thick, with a gland on the back. Fruit globular, brown, glaucous. Withstands city conditions and limy soil. 'Tamariscifolia' is low, to 2 ft. (60 cm) high, with spreading branches; all its leaves are needlelike and bright green. Zone 4.

Lamiastrum
Mint family
Labiatae

Lay-mee-as′trum. A single European perennial herb, differing from *Lamium* in its yellow flowers.

Description
Leaves opposite, coarsely toothed, with pungent odor when bruised. Flowers hooded, double-lipped, in whorls of 5–15.

How to Grow
This durable, rampant-growing ground cover is easy to grow in almost any average soil in a shady spot. Increase by cuttings or division.

galeobdolon pp. 120, 121
Yellow Archangel. To 12 in. (30 cm) high, frequently with stolons. Leaves heart-shaped to ovate, spotted with silver, 1½ in. (4 cm) long, margins doubly toothed. Flowers yellow, ¾ in. (19 mm) long, in dense clusters in leaf axils. Prey to slugs. Also sold as *Lamium galeobdolon* and *Galeobdolon luteum*. Cultivar 'Variegatum' has leaves that are more silvery. 'Herman's Pride', with silvery leaves veined in green, is more restrained in growth habit and is suited to small or medium-size areas. Zone 4.

Lamium
Mint family
Labiatae

Lay′mi-um. Dead Nettle. About 40 known species of somewhat weedy Old World herbs.

Description
Leaves opposite, stalked, with a square stem. Flowers in close whorls crowded in leaf axils, or terminal. Corolla irregular, 2-lipped.

How to Grow
The species below is easy to grow in ordinary moist garden soil in shade. Propagate by division or cuttings.

maculatum pp. 119, 120, 121
Spotted Dead Nettle. To 12 in. (30 cm) high. Leaves 1½ in. (4 cm) long, with narrow white median stripe. Flowers purple-red, nearly 1 in. (2.5 cm) long. Vigorous cultivars include 'Album', with white flowers; 'Shell Pink', with very pale pink flowers; and 'Variegatum', with silver median leaf stripe. 'Beacon Silver' (pink flowers) and 'White Nancy' (white flowers) reach only 9 in. (22.5 cm) high, have showy silver leaves with green margins, and are more restrained in their spreading growth habit. 'Aureum' has yellow foliage with a white stripe. Zone 4.

Lampranthus
Carpetweed family
Aizoaceae

Lam-pran′thus. About 160 South African species of smooth subshrubs, including several succulents known as "ice plants".

Description
Plants upright or trailing, woody at base. Leaves fleshy, curved, 3-sided or cylindrical. Flowers solitary or in clusters, blooming in late winter or spring.

How to Grow
Ice plants prefer well-drained soil that is not too rich, in full sun. Drought-tolerant once established. Propagate by seeds or cuttings.

species and hybrids *pp. 152, 153, 193*
Ice plants include the species *L. aurantiacus,*
L. aureus, L. filicaulis, L. productus, and
L. spectabilis. Stems erect, to 18 in. (45 cm)
high. Leaves fleshy, mostly gray-green.
Flowers to 2 in. (5 cm) wide, solid or in
combinations of brilliant yellow, orange,
pink, or purple. Cultivar 'Gold Bush' has
yellow flowers. These plants are grown
mostly in Calif., primarily as bedding or
bank cover. Zone 9.

Lantana
Verbena family
Verbenaceae

Lan-ta'na. Very ornamental tropical or
subtropical shrubs, one of the 155 species
grown for its profuse bloom.

Description
Leaves usually opposite. Stem usually hairy,
sometimes prickly. Flowers small, in dense
spikes or heads that may be terminal. Calyx
minute. Corolla tubular, 4- to 5-parted,
slightly irregular.

How to Grow
In the North, start seeds indoors in late
winter; germination takes 8 weeks.
Elsewhere, sow outdoors in a sunny spot.
Softwood cuttings root easily. Lantana
prefers warm weather, and is drought-
tolerant once established. When grown as a
perennial, prune hard in spring to prevent
woodiness.

montevidensis p. 181
Weeping Lantana. Vinelike shrub trailing to
3 ft. (90 cm) long and 18 in. (45 cm) high.
Leaves dark green and purplish, 1 in.
(2.5 cm) long, coarsely toothed. Flowers
pink-lilac, in clusters 1 in. (2.5 cm) wide.
Perennial grown as a half-hardy annual in
the North. Long flowering period in
frost-free areas makes it valuable as a bank
cover or for cascading over a wall. Many
color forms available. Sometimes sold as
L. sellowiana. Zone 9.

Leiophyllum
Heath family
Ericaceae

Ly'o-fil'lum. Low evergreen North American shrubs with a neat, compact growth habit that makes them suitable for rock gardens or evergreen plantings.

Description
Leaves small, glossy, dark green, opposite or alternate. Flowers in clusters, white but pink in bud.

How to Grow
Prefers moist, peaty and acid loam in a sunny site. Propagate by cuttings in midsummer or by layering.

buxifolium p. 163
Sand Myrtle. Compact upright shrub, to 18 in. (45 cm) high, sometimes more. Leaves usually alternate, oval, smooth, to ½ in. (13 mm) long, bronze in winter. Flowers white, in terminal clusters, stalks smooth. Fruit a many-seeded capsule. Blooms in late spring. Grow in soil of pH 4–5. The var. *prostratum* (Allegheny Sand Myrtle) is a creeping, nearly flat form growing to only 4 in. (10 cm) high. Zone 6.

Leucothoe
Heath family
Ericaceae

Lew-koth'o-ee. Ornamental shrubs, only a few of which (from U.S. and Japan) can be considered hardy. Evergreen species are low-growing and especially handsome.

Description
Leaves thick, alternate, deciduous or evergreen, turning red or bronze in winter. Branches arching and graceful. In hardy species (including *L. axillaris*), flowers white, occasionally tinged pink, urn-shaped, toothed at top, borne in clusters along or at branch tips. Fruit a dry, round capsule.

How to Grow
Prefers light shade and moist, peaty soil or sandy loam with plenty of humus. Propagate by division, cuttings, seeds, or underground runners. Protect from drying by winter sun and wind. Valuable in foundation plantings

or borders. Sprays make attractive winter bouquets.

axillaris pp. 92, 174

Coast Leucothoe. Evergreen shrub with minutely hairy, arching branches, growing ultimately to 5 ft. (1.5 m) high. Leaves leathery, oval lance-shaped, 2–4 in. (5–10 cm) long, usually short-pointed. Flowers white, in clusters 1–2 in. (2.5–5.0 cm) long, borne in leaf axils. Blooms in spring. To maintain vigor and plant height at 2 ft. (60 cm), cut oldest branches to the ground occasionally. Zone 6.

Liriope
Lily family
Liliaceae

Li-ri′o-pe. Lily-turf. Asiatic herbs, often grown as ground covers in warm regions.

Description
Leaves thick but grasslike, evergreen, numerous, often forming thick mats. Flowers in spikes or racemes. Corolla small, white, blue, or violet. Fruit berrylike, black, ornamental.

How to Grow
Plant in fertile, moist soil amended with organic matter, in shade or sun. In northern winters, foliage may become tattered or brown, but roots will probably survive. Mow foliage to ground to promote new growth. Increase by division.

muscari p. 142

Blue Lily-Turf. To 18 in. (45 cm) high. Flowers lilac-purple to white, ⅛ in. (3.2 mm) wide. Forms clumps, but arching, straplike leaves make this plant useful as a ground cover. Forms available with white- or yellow-variegated leaves. Prey to slugs and snails. Zone 6.

spicata p. 143

Creeping Lily-Turf. To 10 in. (25 cm) high. Leaves narrow, grasslike, to 18 in. (45 cm) long, with minute teeth on margins. Flowers pale lilac to nearly white, to ¼ in. (6 mm) long, the cluster lax and open. There is a striped-leaf form. Zone 5.

Lysimachia
Primrose family
Primulaceae

Ly-si-mack'i-a. Loosestrife. About 165 species
of widely distributed perennial herbs, a few
grown for ornament. All are erect except
L. nummularia, a good creeping ground
cover.

Description
Leaves without marginal teeth, variously
arranged. Flowers solitary or in clusters,
sometimes in leaf axils but often terminal.
Corolla bell- or wheel-shaped.

How to Grow
Grow in reasonably moist sites in the open
border or in shade. Increase by division in
spring or fall.

nummularia *pp. 72, 108, 158, 159*
Moneywort; Creeping Jennie. Prostrate
perennial to 2 in. (5 cm) high, with trailing
stems that root easily at the joints. Leaves
opposite, nearly round, ¾ in. (19 mm)
wide. Flowers solitary in leaf axils, stalked,
yellow. The golden-leaved cultivar 'Aurea' is
less vigorous and needs protection from full
sun. Zone 4.

Mahonia
Barberry family
Berberidaceae

Ma-ho'ni-a. About 100 species of American
and Asian evergreen, thornless shrubs (rarely,
small trees). Handsome, low-growing plants
suitable for shrubbery borders and
foundation plantings.

Description
Leaves alternate, compound, the leaflets
arranged feather-fashion (rarely, in threes),
spiny, often turning purplish in autumn.
Flowers yellow, fragrant, in terminal racemes
or panicles. Fruit a dark blueberry, usually
glaucous (rarely, red or whitish).

How to Grow
Plant in sheltered positions or protect from
wind and sun in winter. Some western
species do well as far north as Canada where
protected in winter by heavy snow covering.

Increase by seeds and suckers, or by layers or cuttings of half-ripe wood.

repens p. 92

Creeping Mahonia. Shrub with underground rooting stems, rarely more than 12 in. (30 cm) high. Leaflets 3–7, roundish-oval, 1½–2½ in. (4–6 cm) long, dull bluish green above, glaucous below, leathery, with spiny marginal teeth. Flowers in terminal racemes at ends of branches, blooming in spring. Fruit small, black, glaucous. Zone 6, with winter protection.

Mazus
Foxglove family
Scrophulariaceae

May'zus. About 30 species of low, prostrate, perennial herbs from Asia, Indo-Malaya, or Australasia. 3 species grown in rock gardens or as ground cover.

Description
Leaves alternate or opposite (sometimes basal), all stalked, toothed, or cut. Flowers blue or white, sometimes yellow-eyed, in terminal racemes.

How to Grow
Prefers a moist location in sun or partial shade. Easy to increase by division.

reptans pp. 104, 201

A ground-covering perennial, to 2 in. (5 cm) high, rooting at the joints. Leaves lance-shaped or elliptic, 1 in. (2.5 cm) long, coarsely toothed. Flowers small, to ¾ in. (19 mm) long, in 1-sided profuse clusters, lavender or purplish blue. Blooms in summer. Interesting to use between stepping stones. May be invasive in rich soil. Zone 6.

Microbiota
Cypress family
Cupressaceae

Mike-roe-by-oh'ta. A single species of coniferous, evergreen dioecious trees. First seen in the wild in Siberia in 1921, it has come into general distribution only recently.

Description
Leaves opposite, scaly, small, resembling needles within crown of plant. Arching branches give a fanlike appearance. Cones berrylike, tiny, with brown scales covering an oval, glossy nut.

How to Grow
Grows equally well in sun or shade in any well-drained location. Tolerant of drought once established. Propagate by hardwood cuttings or, on older plants, by layering. Use as open-space ground cover or under taller evergreens.

decussata p. 86
Siberian Carpet Cypress. Low, flat-topped tree or shrub to 2 ft. (60 cm) high and spreading 15 ft. (4.5 m) wide. Lacy arching branches with scaly or needlelike leaves. In winter, foliage turns bronzy in full sun. Quite adaptable. Zone 3.

Mitchella
Coffee family
Rubiaceae

Mit-chel′la. A prostrate herb, found in woods over most of e. North America. There is a second species in e. Asia.

Description
Evergreen, rather woody perennial. Leaves opposite. Flowers borne in united pairs at end of a short stalk.

How to Grow
Mitchella is a wild garden plant for shady places and rich woods soil. Increase by division.

repens p. 105
Partridge-Berry. Slender stems, not usually over 15 in. (38 cm) long, rooting easily at the joints and making flat patches, to 2 in. (5 cm) high. Leaves nearly round, ¾ in. (19 mm) wide, green, sometimes with white lines. Flowers white, corolla funnel-shaped, ½ in. (13 mm) long. Fruit showy, scarlet, berrylike. Zone 4.

Myosotis
Borage family
Boraginaceae

My-o-so'tis. Forget-Me-Not. 50 species of
annual or perennial herbs, mostly European,
but a few through the north temperate zone.

Description
Leaves alternate, narrow. Flowers small, in
branched or unbranched clusters. Corolla
tubular and spreading, 5-lobed, the throat
crested and often of a different color.

How to Grow
Most garden forget-me-nots are best treated
as hardy annuals or biennials. *M. scorpioides,* a
true perennial, prefers partial shade and
plenty of moisture; it tolerates full sun if soil
is sufficiently moist. Divide in early spring.
Works well under spring bulbs, and does
better when a bit crowded. Short-lived, but
will spread by self-sowing.

scorpioides *p. 203*
True Forget-Me-Not. Stems more or less
prostrate, 12–18 in. (30–45 cm) long. Leaves
and stems create a mat to 8 in. (20 cm)
high. Flowers blue, with a yellow, pink, or
white eye, ⅓ in. (8 mm) wide, in loose,
1-sided clusters at end of stems. Prey to red
spider mites and mildew. The variety
semperflorens blooms until frost. Sometimes
listed as *M. palustris.* Zone 5.

Nandina
Barberry family
Berberidaceae

Nan-dy'na. A single species of evergreen
shrub, native in China and Japan.

Description
Leaves alternate. Flowers small, white, in
panicles.

How to Grow
Prefers reasonably moist soil. Will tolerate
some shade, but best leaf and fruit colors
occur in a sunny location.

domestica 'Harbor Dwarf' *p. 106*
Heavenly Bamboo. Dwarf form of an
attractive shrub. 1½–2 ft. (45–60 cm)

high, spreading freely by underground rhizomes. Leaves twice- or thrice-compound, the ultimate leaflets narrow, bronzy red in fall. Fruit a red 2-seeded berry, very handsome when ripe, and the chief attraction of the plant. The species, 6–8 ft. (1.8–2.4 m) high, is widely grown in the South and on the West Coast, where many selections have been made. 'Harbor Dwarf' is among the best for ground cover. Zone 7.

Nepeta
Mint family
Labiatae

Nep'ta. About 250 species of perennial and annual herbs, found throughout the northern hemisphere.

Description
Tall and erect or dwarf and trailing, generally aromatic, and more or less hairy. Stems square. Leaves mostly heart-shaped, margins toothed. Flowers in close clusters on stems, often in whorls, blue or white. Corolla 2-lipped; stamens 4. May attract cats.

How to Grow
Easy to grow in ordinary, well-drained soil in full sun. Usually propagated from seeds sown during spring or summer, or by division of roots, but sometimes from runners that creep along the ground.

'Blue Wonder' *p. 208*
Catmint. Stems to 2 ft. (60 cm) high, the whole plant gray-green. Leaves oblong, to 1¼ in. (3 cm) long, the base straight. Flowers in dense whorls, corolla bluish lavender. Trim plants back halfway after early summer flowering to improve appearance and encourage a second bloom in late summer. Good for front of the border. Zone 5.

Oenothera
Evening Primrose family
Onagraceae

Ee-no-thee'ra or ee-noth'er-ra. The evening primroses and the day-blooming sundrops constitute 80 species of American herbs.

Description
Leaves alternate. Flowers very showy, day- or night-blooming, usually yellow, white or rose-color in some species, generally 1 or 2 in the leaf axils. Calyx tubular, usually 4-sided, its 4 lobes often bent backward and soon to fall. Petals 4, broad.

How to Grow
Easy to grow in an open, sandy or loamy site. All bloom in summer, and many are weedy. Increase perennial kinds by division.

tetragona p. 155
Sundrops. Perennial herb 1–2 ft. (30–60 cm) high, usually woody at base, the stems reddish. Leaves lance-shaped, oblong, usually short-stalked, 1–2 in. (2.5–5.0 cm) long. Flowers yellow, nearly 2 in. (5 cm) wide. Very similar to *O. fruticosa,* and synonymous with *O. fruticosa* var. *youngii.* Zone 5.

Omphalodes
Borage family
Boraginaceae

Om-fal-lo´dez. Navelwort. About 25 species of low annual or perennial herbs, native to Europe and Asia.

Description
Stems smooth or slightly hairy. Basal leaves long-stalked, lance- or heart-shaped; stem leaves smaller, fewer, alternate. Flowers blue, sometimes pinkish, in loose 1-sided racemes. Corolla a short tube, usually white, with veinlike markings radiating from the center, starlike.

How to Grow
Grows best in a cool, partially shaded position where soil pH is neutral. Sow seeds in spring or propagate by division of roots in spring or fall.

verna p. 129
Blue-Eyed Mary; Creeping Forget-Me-Not. Perennial, to 8 in. (20 cm) high, main stems prostrate but with erect flowering stems. Leaves pointed, ovalish; on flowering stems, short-stalked and spearlike. Flowers blue, ½ in. (13 mm) wide, in pairs in loose racemes. Blooms in spring. Zone 5.

Ophiopogon
Lily family
Liliaceae

O-fi-o-po′gon. Lily-turf. A few species, all
natives of e. Asia. Sometimes known by the
name *Mondo*. Similar to *Liriope*, but has blue
instead of black fruit.

Description
Leaves basal, grasslike but thick, growing
turflike in masses. Flowers small, nodding,
usually borne in small clusters that do not
extend above the foliage. Fruit blue,
berrylike.

How to Grow
Grows well in ordinary garden soil in sun
or shade. Propagate by division. If foliage
becomes shabby in winter, cut back hard in
early spring. Best used under trees or as
border edging. Slugs can be a problem.

japonicus p. 142
Mondo Grass. A good sod-forming ground
cover, to 12 in. (30 cm) high. Leaves dark
green, 8–16 in. (20.0–40.5 cm) long, arising
from underground stolons, the roots bearing
small tubers. Flowers light lilac, ¼ in.
(6 mm) long. Fruit pea-size, blue. Popular
in the South. Zone 7.

planiscapus 'Arabicus' p. 143
Black Monda Grass. Distinctive,
stoloniferous plant, to 10 in. (25 cm) high,
with arching purple-black leaves. Flowers
pink or purple-black, on scapes. Prefers
partial shade. May be listed as *O. planiscapus*
'Nigrescens'. Zone 7.

Opuntia
Cactus family
Cactaceae

O-pun′ti-a; also o-pun′she-a. Prickly Pear;
some also called tuna or cholla. 300 species
of cacti, from New England to Tierra del
Fuego.

Description
Two general types are cultivated: those with
flat or broad joints, and those with
cylindrical or roundish joints. Some are
prostrate or clambering, without a trunk;
others, mostly tropical, are treelike; some

have small spines. Leaves small, usually
deciduous. Flowers generally solitary. Fruit
usually a juicy berry, edible in some.

How to Grow
Full sun and well-drained, sandy soil are ideal
for _O. humifusa._ Moist soil may cause root
rot. Very drought-tolerant. Small red-brown
hairs on surface of joints lodge easily under
the skin, so handle carefully and avoid
planting near walkways. Increase by breaking
off pads and rooting in sandy soil.

humifusa pp. 72, 160
Prickly Pear. Joints flat, oblong, or ovalish,
2–6 in. (5–15 cm) long, the whole plant
prostrate. Depressions (areoles) sparse, spines
1–2 at each cluster, ¾ in. (19 mm) long.
Flowers yellow, 2–3 in. (5.0–7.5 cm) wide.
Fruit fleshy, purplish, edible but not
palatable. Also known as _O. compressa_ and
O. vulgaris. Zone 5.

Osteospermum
Daisy family
Compositae

Os-tee-oh-sper´mum. About 70 species of
annual or perennial herbs or shrubs, mostly
native to South Africa, a few popular in the
Southwest and Calif.

Description
Evergreen, spreading, shrubby. Leaves
alternate, with or without teeth or lobes,
2–4 in. (5–10 cm) long. Daisylike flowers in
a variety of colors, on long stems, opening
only in sunlight.

How to Grow
Plant in spring or fall in sun in any good
garden soil except heavy clay. Cut back old
sprawling branches to encourage flowering
and keep plants tidy. Performs best with
moderate water but will tolerate drought.
Increase by seeds (species only), cuttings, or,
in some types, by layering. Use in borders or
on slopes.

fruticosum p. 192
Trailing African Daisy; Freeway Daisy.
Trailing plant to 12 in. (30 cm) high and
3 ft. (90 cm) wide. Stems root as they
spread. Leaves variable, usually oval with a
few teeth. Flowers 2 in. (5 cm) wide, lilac

fading to white, blooming profusely in late winter and early spring, with sporadic flowering throughout the year. Several forms have purple, pink, or white flowers. Zone 9.

Pachysandra
Box family
Buxaceae

Pack-i-san′dra. 5 species of low-growing perennial herbs or subshrubs native to North America and e. Asia.

Description
Stems fleshy. Leaves spoon-shaped, the upper half with teethlike margins. Flowers greenish white, in spikes. Fruit a small, whitish, oval berry.

How to Grow
Easy to grow in moist, ordinary soil. Widely used for partly shady places; foliage yellows in full sun. Propagate by cuttings taken in summer and planted in an equal mixture of sand and soil. Water well and keep shaded until rooted. For a quick ground covering, plant them 8 in. (20 cm) apart.

procumbens p. 112
Alleghany Spurge. Evergreen in the South, deciduous in the North. Stems trailing at first, then becoming erect, 8–10 in. (20–25 cm) high. Flowers white or purplish. Leaves attractively mottled with gray. Needs humus-enriched soil. Zone 5.

terminalis pp. 114, 115
Japanese Spurge. To 9 in. (22.5 cm) high, stems beneath surface sending out runners. Leaves thick, dark, glossy-green, spoon-shaped, alternate. Flowers white. Makes a thick ground cover and will survive in dense shade where little else will succeed. Cultivar 'Silver Edge', with white-edged leaves, is less somber and less vigorous. Zone 5.

Paxistima
Spindle-tree family
Celastraceae

Pax-is′ti-ma. A genus of 2 North American low evergreen shrubs grown primarily for their foliage. They form neat evergreen tufts and are adapted to rock gardens or low borders.

Description
Leaves small, opposite. Flowers inconspicuous, borne in leaf axils.

How to Grow
Grows in sun or shade and prefers sandy, somewhat peaty soil, but is not particular as long as site is well drained. Propagate by seeds, cuttings, or layers.

canbyi p. 83
Rat-Stripper. Low shrub, to 12 in. (30 cm) high, with trailing, rooting branches. Leaves ½–1 in. (1.3–2.5 cm) long, linear or narrowly oblong, toothed toward tip, margins turned under, turning bronzy in fall. Flowers tiny, reddish, on slender stems, blooming in spring. Zone 5.

myrsinites p. 97
Oregon Boxwood. Spreading shrub with stiff branches, to 2 ft. (60 cm) high. Leaves narrow-oblong or elliptic, to 1¼ in. (3 cm) long, toothed toward tip, margins slightly turned under. Flowers white to reddish, blooming in summer. Growth is more compact in full sun. Zone 5.

Phlox
Phlox family
Polemoniaceae

Flocks. About 60 species of perennial and annual herbs, usually hardy, found mostly in North America, one in Siberia.

Description
Some species strong and erect, others trailing. Leaves lance-shaped, opposite and in pairs, or alternate. Flowers showy, in loose terminal or closely packed clusters, usually with a conspicuous eyelike marking. Corolla of 5 united petals.

How to Grow
Easy to grow and flowers for a long time. All but *P. subulata* benefit from humus-enriched, moist soil. Most prefer sun or partial shade. Propagate from seeds, cuttings, or division. Control powdery mildew with fungicide.

divaricata p. 202

Wild Sweet William. To 12 in. (30 cm) high, with creeping, flowerless, rooting stems. Leaves opposite, narrow. Flowers lavender-blue, to 1 in. (2.5 cm) wide, in loose clusters that bloom in spring. Needs full or partial shade and moist soil. 'Fuller's White' has white flowers. Zone 4.

nivalis p. 163

Trailing Phlox. A low, prostrate perennial forming a cushion to 6 in. (15 cm) high. Leaves to ¾ in. (19 mm) long. Flowers 1 in. (2.5 cm) wide, ranging from white to pink and purple. Many color selections are available. Blooms in spring. Prefers full sun. Zone 6.

stolonifera p. 203

Creeping Phlox. To 10 in. (25 cm) high, spreading with creeping stems that root. Leaves opposite, oval. Flowers purple or violet, ¾ in. (19 mm) wide, in dense clusters that bloom in spring. Needs partial shade. 'Blue Ridge' (blue flowers) and 'Pink Ridge' (pink flowers) are popular; white-flowered selections also exist. Zone 4.

subulata pp. 162, 194, 195

Moss Pink; Ground Pink. Evergreen creeper to 6 in. (15 cm) high, forming a dense mat. Leaves small, crowded, needlelike. Flowers bright purple, pink, or white, ¾ in. (19 mm) wide, in dense clusters. Prefers average, well-drained soil and full sun. For denser plants, shear stems back halfway after flowering. Divide older plants if center dies out. Good for rock gardens, walls, or borders. Many color forms exist, including 'Millstream Laura' (pale pink), 'Millstream Daphne' (rosy pink), 'Millstream Jupiter' (blue), and 'Millstream Coral-eye' (white with a red center). Zone 4.

Polygonum
Knotweed family
Polygonaceae

Pol-lig′o-num. Smartweed; Knotweed. About 150 species of erect, trailing, or climbing annual or perennial herbs, found throughout the world.

Description
Stems angled, swollen at leaf joints,
sometimes spotted or streaked brown. Leaves
alternate, simple. Flowers small, in terminal
spikes or loose racemes. Calyx of 5 sepals
generally pink or white.

How to Grow
Prefers moist soil in sun. Propagate by
division of rootstocks in early spring.
Attracts bees.

cuspidatum compactum pp. 190, 191
Dwarf Japanese Fleece-Flower. Strong-
growing herbaceous perennial to 3 ft.
(90 cm) high. Leaves oval. Flowers pink,
¼ in. (6 mm) wide, numerous, in loose
axillary clusters, blooming in late summer.
Ornamental pink seed pods in autumn.
Invasive and tenacious when established,
suitable only for dry banks and other large
areas. *P. reynoutria* is considered a form of
this variety. Zone 4.

Potentilla
Rose family
Rosaceae

Po-ten-till′a. Cinquefoil. Over 500 species of
mostly perennial herbs or small shrubs,
mainly in northern temperate and arctic
regions.

Description
Stems creeping or erect. Leaves compound,
pinnate or palmate. Leaflets 3 or many, hairy.
Flowers in numerous small, loose clusters.
Corolla of 5 petals growing on calyx rim.
Stamens numerous.

How to Grow
Most species need full sun and dry,
well-drained soil. Propagate by dividing
rootstocks in spring or fall or by sowing
seeds in sandy soil.

tabernaemontani pp. 111, 154
Spring Cinquefoil. Horizontal rooting
branches form mats 4 in. (10 cm) high.
Basal leaves palmate, toothed, with 5 leaflets.
Flowers golden yellow, ½ in. (13 mm)
wide, in loose clusters in spring. Good carpet
over spring bulbs. Also known as *P. verna*.
Zone 4.

tridentata pp. 109, 164
Three-toothed Cinquefoil. To 9 in. (22.5 cm)
high. Leaflets dark shiny green on upper side,
stems woody, forming a mat by creeping
stolons. Autumn foliage maroon. Flowers
small, ¼ in. (6 mm) wide, white, in loose
clusters. Grow in sandy loam. Does not
make a dense cover. 'Minima' is 3 in.
(7.5 cm) high. Zone 3.

Primula
Primrose family
Primulaceae

Prim'you-la. Primrose. Over 400 species of
low-growing, herbaceous perennials, some
short-lived, chiefly natives of the northern
temperate zones.

Description
Stems short, or none. Leaves crowded,
stalked, long and narrow, or roundish, or
tufted, midrib generally prominent on
underside. Flowers on leafless stalks,
sometimes with leafy bracts; solitary, in loose
umbels, whorled in tiers, or in rounded
heads; yellow, white, red, blue, pink, or
purple. Most flower in spring.

How to Grow
Primroses grow best in rich, moist soil in
light shade. Protect from direct sun. The
species below prefer moist, well-drained soil.
Seeds sown in spring germinate easily.
Increase by dividing clumps every 3–4 years
to improve vigor and flowering. Species
below are suitable for borders or rock
gardens, or for naturalizing under trees and
shrubs.

× *polyantha* pp. 146, 147
Primrose. A group of garden hybrid
primroses, derived from *P. elatior, P. veris,*
and *P. vulgaris.* To 12 in. (30 cm) high.
Leaves oblong. Flowers in a variety of colors,
in profuse clusters. Blooms in spring. Easiest
primrose to grow, but short-lived unless
divided often. 'Pacific Giant' has flowers to
2 in. (5 cm) wide. Zone 5.

veris p. 147
Cowslip. Hardy perennial, to 8 in. (20 cm)
high. Leaves basal, wrinkled, broadly
lance-shaped, slightly hairy on underside.
Flowers yellow, to ½ in. (13 mm) wide,

fragrant, in nodding umbels. Calyx pale
green. Blooms in spring. Double-flowered
forms exist. Zone 5.

vulgaris p. 192
English Primrose. Hardy perennial, to 6 in.
(15 cm) high. Leaves basal, broadly lance-
shaped, wrinkled, the margins crinkled.
Flowers numerous or solitary, usually yellow,
on slender, slightly hairy stalks. Blooms in
spring. Often called *P. acaulis*. Many colors
and double-flowered forms exist. Barnhaven
hybrids are vigorous, hardier plants with
pastel flowers. Zone 5.

Pulmonaria
Borage family
Boraginaceae

Pul-mo-nay'ri-a. Lungwort. About 10 species
of low-growing European perennial herbs.

Description
Creeping rootstocks. Basal leaves long-
stalked, broadly lance-shaped, sometimes
mottled. Flowers in terminal, coiled clusters
that straighten as flowers open. Corolla
funnel-shaped, sometimes with a hairy
throat. Stamens 5.

How to Grow
The species below are easy to grow in moist,
ordinary garden soil in full to partial shade.
Propagate by division in fall or early spring.

angustifolia p. 199
Blue Lungwort; Cowslip Lungwort. 6–9 in.
(15.0–22.5 cm) high. Stems lax. Leaves dark
green, narrow, hairy. Flowers blue, ¾–1 in.
(2.0–2.5 cm) long, in nodding heads.
Blooms in early spring. A useful border
plant or cover over spring bulbs. The
cultivar 'Johnson's Blue' has vivid blue
flowers. Zone 4.

montana p. 191
Mountain Lungwort. Leaves basal, hairy,
coarse, broadly oval, to 15 in. (38 cm) high,
forming a mound to 12 in. (30 cm) wide.
Flowering stems emerge before leaves.
Flowers funnel-shaped, violet, in clusters.
Often listed as *P. rubra*. 'Salmon Glow' has
deep coral-red flowers. Attractive to
hummingbirds. Zone 4.

saccharata *p. 118*
Bethlehem Sage. 8–14 in. (20–35 cm) high.
Basal leaves elliptic, mottled white. Flowers
white or reddish purple, ¾–1 in. (2.0–
2.5 cm) long, emerging before basal leaves.
Prefers full shade. Excellent foliage plant.
'Mrs. Moon' is the most widely distributed
cultivar. Zone 4.

Rhododendron
Heath Family
Ericaceae

Ro-doe-den´dron. A very large genus of
evergreen or deciduous shrubs (rarely trees),
chiefly from the north temperate zone, a few
on the high mts. of the Old World tropics.
This genus includes the group of species and
hybrids known as Azaleas. The evergreen
azaleas, which include plants appropriate as
ground cover, are essentially Oriental, though
most interbreeding has been done in Europe
and the U.S. All those below are azaleas.

Description
Small, almost prostrate shrubs to tall,
slender, treelike forms. Leaves opposite,
mostly oval or elliptical, without teeth.
Flower buds form in late summer and early
autumn, blooming in spring unless otherwise
noted. Flowers showy, usually tubular or
funnel-shaped, usually in terminal clusters;
many have conspicuous stamens and pistils.
Two color series: white through pink to
deep rose-pink; and white through yellow
and orange to deep brick-red or darker. Many
have a contrasting color blotch.

How to Grow
Deciduous types tolerate full sun, but most
azaleas perform best with light shade,
especially in the afternoon. All need acid
soil, particularly the deciduous species. All
require considerable, evenly supplied
moisture. Reduce watering outdoor plants as
summer advances to check new growth and
ensure that wood ripens so bark will not
split in winter. Azaleas have shallow, fibrous
roots; do not cultivate soil around
established plants, but provide mulch
year-round to help retain moisture and
minimize cold injury. Prune to check
irregular growth just after blooming, to
ensure formation of new shoots with flower
buds, and to ensure ripening of the wood.

Add humus every year, as leaf mulch or compost; soil should be rich and moist but never sodden. All azaleas can be raised from seed or from branch or mound layers. The evergreens can also be grown from cuttings of half-ripe wood in sand or a sand-and-peat mixture.

indicum hybrids *pp. 177, 178*
Indicum Dwarf Azaleas. A group of evergreen azaleas valued for their late flowering. These include some dwarf forms to 18 in. (45 cm) high, with spreading growth habit, and some with double flowers. 'Balsaminiflorum' (sometimes called 'Rosiflorum'), to 18 in. (45 cm) high, has double salmon-pink flowers; 'Flame Creeper', a semi-prostrate shrub usually to 10 in. (25 cm) high, has orange-red flowers and small leaves; 'Kozan', a ground-hugging trailer, has delicate shell-pink flowers. All zone 6.

kiusianum hybrids *pp. 174, 175, 177, 178, 179*
Kurume Azaleas. To 3 ft. (90 cm) high. Compact, dense plants with small, dark evergreen leaves. Small, profuse, single or double flowers, mostly in intense colors from white to pink to red. Among the most popular cultivars are 'Coral Bells' (double pink), 'Hino-crimson' (bright red), 'Hinodegiri' (cerise red), and 'Snow' and 'Album' (white). Zone 7.

North Tisbury hybrids *p. 179*
North Tisbury Azaleas. Mostly hybrids of *R. rakaharai,* a small-leaved prostrate evergreen species. Branches spread horizontally to 4 ft. (120 cm) wide, mounding to 15 in. (38 cm) high in 10 years. Give them room to spread or they will mound excessively. 'Alexander' has bright red flowers and fine-textured foliage turning bronzy in winter. 'Joseph Hill' has creeping branches and rich red flowers in early summer. 'Pink Pancake', 10 in. (25 cm) high, has bright pink ruffled flowers. 'Late Love', the latest-flowering, has rosy-pink flowers in summer. All zone 6.

Robin Hill hybrids *p. 176*
Robin Hill Azaleas. Evergreen, with large, beautiful flowers in predominantly soft pastel colors. Growing ultimately to about 12-15 in. (30-38 cm) high and spreading 1½-2½ ft. (45-75 cm) wide. Leaves to

2½ in. (6 cm) long. 'Betty Ann Voss' has pale pink, double hose-in-hose flowers and dark green foliage. 'Mrs. Hagar' has vibrant pink double flowers resembling miniature camellias. 'Hilda Niblett' has soft pink flowers with deep rose markings. 'Sir Robert' has large ruffled flowers ranging from white to pale salmon-pink and forms a mound 2 ft. (60 cm) high. All zone 6.

Rhus
Sumac family
Anacardiaceae

Rus. Sumac. A large genus of deciduous or evergreen shrubs and trees, the 150 species widely scattered. Several plants, notably Poison Ivy and Poison Sumac, are poisonous to the touch, but the cultivated species are not.

Description
Leaves usually compound, leaflets arranged feather-fashion with an odd one at the end. Flowers small, greenish, usually with male and female on separate plants. Petals, sepals, and stamens 5 each. Fruit a small drupe, clustered, red, hairy.

How to Grow
Easy to grow in full sun in any garden soil, or even in dry sand or on rocky hillsides. The species below can be increased by seeds or separation of underground runners.

aromatica p. 93
Fragrant Sumac. Sprawling shrub, 1–5 ft. (0.3–1.5 m) high. Leaflets 3, ovalish, 2–3 in. (5.0–7.5 cm) long, coarsely toothed, aromatic. Flowers greenish yellow, in small spikes, blooming in spring before leaves expand. Fruit clusters and brilliant orange or red foliage in autumn. Valuable cover for dry banks. Selected form 'Gro-Low' grows to 2 ft. (60 cm) high. Also known as *R. canadensis*. Zone 3.

Robinia
Pea family
Leguminosae

Ro-bin'ee-a. Locust. A small group of North and Central American deciduous trees

and shrubs, ornamental both in leaf and
flower.

Description
Leaves alternate, compound, the leaflets
arranged feather-fashion with an odd one at
the tip. Flowers pea-shaped, white, pink, or
purple, in pendulous racemes. Fruit a flat,
many-seeded pod.

How to Grow
Prefers soil of moderate fertility, but often
thrives in poor, sandy soil. Propagation is
mainly by seed, though some can be
multiplied by stolons.

hispida p. 176
Rose Acacia; Pink Locust. Spreading shrub,
usually 3–4 ft. (90–120 cm) high. Branches
brittle, covered with red bristles. Leaflets
7–13, oval or rounded, 1 in. (2.5 cm) long.
Flowers pink or rose-colored, in few-flowered
clusters in early summer. Its vigorous,
stoloniferous habit makes this handsome
locust good for dry bank erosion control.
Zone 5.

Rosmarinus
Mint family
Labiatae

Ros-ma-ry'nus. Rosemary. A few species
of evergreen shrubs, native in the
Mediterranean region, one widely cultivated
as a culinary and sweet herb.

Description
Leaves small, lance-shaped, dark green above,
woolly below. Flowers in clusters growing
from leaf axils.

How to Grow
Tolerates hot sun and poor soil, but good
drainage is essential; grows best in soil that
is not too rich. Prune after flowering to
improve tidiness and prevent excess
woodiness. Propagate in early fall from
cuttings of young shoots 6 in. (15 cm) long;
insert in an equal mixture of sand and soil
in a cool greenhouse or cold frame. After
rooting, plant them and leave in cold frame
during winter.

officinalis 'Prostratus' p. 82
Trailing Rosemary. Prostrate form with

trailing branches spreading to 4 ft. (120 cm) wide and mounding to 2 ft. (60 cm) high. Leaves aromatic, grayish green on upper side, white beneath. Flowers light blue, to ½ in. (13 mm) long. Species grows upright to 6 ft. (1.8 m) high. Low-growing cultivars are popular in the Southwest and Calif. as ground cover or for cascading over walls. Zone 7.

Rubus
Rose family
Rosaceae

Roo'bus. An immense genus of shrubby, usually prickly plants, including the wild brambles, several cultivated for berries, and a few others grown for ornament. Nearly all from the north temperate zone.

Description
Plants erect or trailing. Leaves usually compound with leaflets arranged finger-fashion (rarely feather-fashion), or occasionally alternate, simple, and lobed. Flowers usually white, purplish pink in a few, the 5 petals often rounded, sometimes small or even missing. Stamens numerous. Fruit edible in some species.

How to Grow
Ornamental brambles grow best in well-drained soil of average fertility. They prefer full sun or light shade. Somewhat drought-tolerant. Increase by division or by layering where stems touch the ground.

calycinoides p. 124
Bramble. An evergreen, trailing subshrub, the creeping stems forming a rooting carpet 2 in. (5 cm) high. Leaves dark green, puckered, rounded, 1½ in. (4 cm) wide, glossy above and white felted beneath. Flowers small, white. Sometimes listed as *R. jockeanus.* Zone 7.

Sagina
Pink family
Caryophyllaceae

Sa-jy'na. Pearlwort. Slender annual or perennial herbs, often tufted or matted, all

25 species from the north temperate zone.
Related to *Arenaria*.

Description
Leaves opposite, often united at base,
needlelike. Flowers tiny, terminal, solitary or
in clusters.

How to Grow
Though it looks like moss, *Sagina* will not
thrive in the damp shade preferred by true
mosses. Plant in moderately fertile, moist,
but well-drained soil. In hot climates it
prefers partial shade to full sun. Useful for
ground cover in small areas or between
paving stones. Propagate by division or
seeds.

subulata p. 78
Irish Moss. Tufted perennial evergreen herb,
to 4 in. (10 cm) high. Leaves very small,
numerous, prostrate, mosslike. Flowers
profuse, tiny, white, on short stalks,
blooming in summer. The cultivar 'Aurea'
(Scotch Moss) has golden-green leaves.
Zone 5.

Santolina
Daisy family
Compositae

San-to-ly′na. 8 species of evergreen, aromatic
subshrubs, most from the Mediterranean
region.

Description
Leaves alternate, finely divided. Flowerheads
solitary, globe-shaped, without ray flowers.

How to Grow
Grows best in full sun and well-drained soil.
Where winters are cold, they require mulch.
Propagate by summer stem cuttings, which
root easily in sand.

chamaecyparissus pp. 84, 156
Lavender Cotton. Silvery-gray evergreen,
1–2 ft. (30–60 cm) high. Leaves aromatic,
cut into very narrow segments. Flowerheads
¾ in. (19 mm) wide, yellow, the stalks 6 in.
(15 cm) long. Blooms in summer. Prune
after flowering to prevent plants from
becoming ragged. Also sold as *S. incana*.
Zone 6.

virens pp. 85, 157

Green Lavender Cotton. Evergreen, 10–18 in.
(25–45 cm) high. Leaves smooth, dark
green, very narrow, nearly 2 in. (5 cm) long,
the margins toothed, creating an airy
appearance. Flowerheads ½ in. (13 mm)
wide, creamy yellow, on stout stalks 6–10 in.
(15–25 cm) long, blooming in summer.
Sometimes sold as *S. viridis*. Zone 6.

Sarcococca
Box family
Buxaceae

Sar-ko-kok′a. Sweet box. A small group of
Asiatic and Malayan evergreen shrubs, 4 of
the 14 known species planted for ornament.

Description
Leaves stalked, without marginal teeth,
rather leathery. Flowers small, whitish,
without petals, the male and female separate
on the same plant. Fruit black or dark red,
fleshy, berrylike.

How to Grow
Grows best in moist, humus-enriched soil.
Maintains foliage appearance even in deep
shade, but best flower and fruit production
occurs in light shade. Protect from winter
sun. Propagate by cuttings or seeds.

hookerana humilis p. 107

Sweet Box. Low-growing form of a
rhizomatous shrub, with stems ½–2 ft.
(15–60 cm) high. Twigs hairy when young.
Leaves elliptic to lance-shaped, 1–3 in.
(2.5–7.5 cm) long, shiny, dark green.
Flowers white, fragrant, in short racemes
from leaf axils in spring. Fruit fleshy, to
⅜ in. (9 mm) long, purple to black. Useful
on the West Coast and in the South.
Zone 6.

Saxifraga
Saxifrage family
Saxifragaceae

Sacks-iff′ra-ga. Saxifrage; Rockfoil. About 300
species of mostly perennial herbs, found
chiefly in temperate regions of Europe and
America.

Description
Usually low-growing and spreading or
creeping; rootstocks spread by offsets or
runners. Leaves thick and fleshy or soft and
mosslike, sometimes in a rosette, roundish or
spoon-shaped to ovalish, margins often
silvery. Flowers pink, white, purple, or
yellow, in clusters.

How to Grow
Plant in light shade or where shaded from
midday sun, in gritty soil with lime.
Propagate from seeds in early spring, division
of rootstocks in spring or summer, or by
runners and bulblets, the latter found in
some species. Useful in rock gardens or
borders, since they seldom run over other
plants. Foliage changes color with the
seasons.

***stolonifera** pp. 124, 173*
Strawberry Geranium. To 5 in. (12.5 cm)
high and sending out rooting runners like a
strawberry. Leaves hairy, dark green, marked
with white on upper side, reddish on
underside. Flowers white, ¾ in. (19 mm)
wide, in loose racemes. Blooms in early
summer. Good evergreen ground cover,
and a useful basket or pot plant. Prefers
some moisture. Also sold as *S. sarmentosa*.
Zone 7.

× ***urbium** pp. 75, 184*
London Pride. To 6 in. (15 cm) high.
Toothed leaves form carpets of shiny, dark
green rosettes; leaves light green in spring,
turning blue-green, then dark. Flowers
pink, ¼ in. (6 mm) wide, in airy clusters
8–10 in. (20–25 cm) above the foliage. Not
suited to hot, dry climates. Also sold as *S.
umbrosa*. Zone 5.

Sedum
Stonecrop family
Crassulaceae

See′dum. Stonecrop. About 600 species of
chiefly perennial, fleshy herbs found through
the temperate and colder regions of the
northern hemisphere.

Description
Diverse in habit, some creeping, with the
stems rooting or trailing, some tufted, others
in rosettes, still others upright. Leaves

alternate, opposite, or in whorls, margins sometimes cut. Flowers white, yellow, pink, red, or blue, in terminal clusters.

How to Grow
Easy to grow in well-drained garden soil in sun or light shade. Adequate drainage is especially important in winter. Propagate by seeds, division of roots, cuttings, or leaves set into sandy soil. Sedums are particularly adapted to the rock garden; a few species can be used in the flower border. Some are too vigorous for small areas. The species below are especially suitable for ground cover in sunny areas or good in rock wall crevices.

anglicum p. 74
English Stonecrop. Stoloniferous evergreen, forming a carpet to 2 in. (5 cm) high. Leaves alternate, fleshy, cylindrical, crowded along stem, to ¼ in. (6 mm) long. Flowering stems to 6 in. (15 cm) high. Flowers white, star-shaped, to ½ in. (13 mm) wide, in summer. Zone 4.

brevifolium p. 75
Shortleaf Stonecrop. Stoloniferous evergreen with stems to 3 in. (7.5 cm) high. Leaves to ⅛ in. (3.2 mm) long, grayish, flushed red, tightly packed on upright branches. Flowers white, ¼ in. (6 mm) wide, in summer. Zone 4.

cauticola p. 74
Shortleaf Stonecrop. Deciduous trailing stems about 8 in. (20 cm) long and 3 in. (7.5 cm) high, arising from a central crown. Leaves rounded, opposite, gray, scattered along stems. Flowers ½ in. (13 mm) wide, bright pink, in terminal clusters, in late summer. Zone 5.

kamtschaticum pp. 77, 158
Stonecrop. Erect perennial, 6–9 in. (15.0–22.5 cm) high. Leaves alternate, ovalish, to 2 in. (5 cm) long, margins toothed. Flowers star-shaped, yellow, to ¾ in. (19 mm) wide, in summer. There is a form with white-variegated leaves. Zone 4.

lineare p. 80
Stringy Stonecrop. A vigorous spreader, to 6 in. (15 cm) high, with trailing, rooting stems. Leaves narrow, light green, deciduous, 1 in. (2.5 cm) long. Flowers abundant, yellow, star-shaped, in early summer. Also

called *S. sarmentosum*. 'Variegatum', with
white-edged leaves, is more compact and less
aggressive. Zone 5.

reflexum p. 79
Yellow Stonecrop. Creeping evergreen,
forming a carpet to 3 in. (7.5 cm) high.
Leaves crowded on stem, gray-green, fleshy,
narrow, cylindrical, to ½ in. (13 mm) long.
Flower-stalks to 12 in. (30 cm) long.
Flowers golden yellow, to ½ in. (13 mm)
wide, in summer. Zone 5.

× *rubrotinctum* p. 77
Pork and Beans. A slow-growing, creeping or
procumbent evergreen perennial, to 8 in.
(20 cm) high, rooting at joints. Leaves fat,
cylindrical, ½ in. (13 mm) long, resembling
jelly beans, turning bronzy-red in full sun.
Flowers ⅓ in. (8 mm) wide, yellowish red,
blooming in spring. Sometimes incorrectly
sold as *S. guatemalense*. Zone 8.

spurium pp. 76, 180
Two-row Stonecrop. Strong-growing creeper,
to 6 in. (15 cm) high. Leaves semi-
evergreen, 1 in. (2.5 cm) long or more,
opposite, ovalish, coarsely toothed, the
surface roughened. Flowers pink, to ½ in.
(13 mm) wide, in flat clusters, in late
summer. Often called *S. stoloniferum*.
'Dragon's Blood' has deep rose-red flowers
and mature foliage tinged bronzy-purple
on the margins. 'Splendens' has deep
carmine flowers larger than in the species.
There is also a white-flowered form. All
zone 3.

'Weihenstephaner Gold' pp. 76, 159
Deciduous perennial, a procumbent cluster
to 6 in. (15 cm) high. Leaves to 1 in.
(2.5 cm) long, shiny, dark green, toothed,
densely covering rooting stems. Flowers
bright yellow, star-shaped, to 1 in. (2.5 cm)
wide, in early summer, followed by showy,
rusty-red seed capsules. Long season. Zone 4.

Skimmia
Citrus family
Rutaceae

Skim′i-a. Nine known species of somewhat
tender Asiatic evergreen shrubs.

364

Description
Leaves alternate, short-stalked, dotted,
without marginal teeth, aromatic when
crushed. Flowers small, white, some species
having both male and female parts, others
unisexual. Male flowers larger, very fragrant,
in larger panicles; females usually with 4–5
sterile stamens. Fruit red, berrylike, showy in
autumn.

How to Grow
Grows best in humus-rich soil in a lightly
shaded location with protection from winter
sun. Propagate by seeds or by cuttings set
in a flat or frame over a heating cable.
Dioecious species need both male and female
plants for fruit to set. Subject to spider mites
and thrips.

reevesiana p. 102
Reeves Skimmia. Low, densely branching
shrub, to 2 ft. (60 cm) high. Leaves dark
green, lance-shaped, to 4 in. (10 cm) long.
Flowers small, white, in terminal panicles in
spring, followed by fruit that is yellow when
unripe, dull red when ripe, retained into
winter. Self-fertile. Zone 7.

Stachys
Mint family
Labiatae

Stack'iss. Betony; Woundwort. About 300
species of annual or perennial herbs
distributed throughout the world, but
chiefly in the temperate zones.

Description
Leaves opposite, ovalish or broadly lance-
shaped. Flowers purple, scarlet, yellow, or
white, in 2- to many-flowered whorls, in
terminal spikes. Corolla tubular, opening
into 2 lips. Stamens 4.

How to Grow
Easy to grow in average well-drained soil in
full sun. Propagate by seeds in early spring
or by division in early spring or fall. Useful
in flower borders.

byzantina pp. 128, 129
Lamb's-Ears. Forms mats to 8 in. (20 cm)
high. Leaves soft, white-woolly, growing
densely on lax, spreading stems. Flowers
purple, in whorls, on stems 18 in. (45 cm)

high. 'Silver Carpet' is nonflowering and
makes a denser, more compact ground cover.
Good edging plant. Cut back winter-
damaged leaves in early spring. Also sold as
S. lanata and *S. olympica.* Zone 5.

Symphytum
Forget-me-not family
Boraginaceae

Sim-fy'tum. Comfrey. About 25 species of
hardy perennial herbs, natives of Europe, n.
Africa, and w. Asia.

Description
Stem and leaves covered with bristly hairs.
Basal leaves large, stem leaves alternate or
opposite. Flowers yellowish, blue, white,
rose, or purple, in branching clusters. Corolla
tubular. Stamens 5.

How to Grow
Easy to grow in sun or partial shade in
average well-drained soil. Propagate by seed
or division in autumn or spring.

grandiflorum *p. 170*
8–12 in. (20–30 cm) high. Leaves oblong or
oval, hairy. Flowers pale yellow, ¾ in.
(19 mm) wide, tubular, in curved panicles.
One of the best ground covers for dry shade.
Usually offered as *Pulmonaria lutea.* Zone 5.

Taxus
Yew family
Taxaceae

Tacks'us. Yew. About 8 closely related
species of beautiful, slow-growing evergreen
shrubs and trees with fine dark foliage and
comparative freedom from disease.

Description
In age, bark is scaly, reddish brown. Leaves
spirally arranged, 2-ranked, narrow, typically
dark green with 2 yellowish or grayish-green
bands on underside. Male and female flowers
on different plants, without sepals or petals,
only the female producing the scarlet or
brownish berrylike fruit, a modified cone.
Juice of foliage and seed are poisonous.

How to Grow
Tolerates a wide range of conditions, so long as soil is well drained and not too acid; subject to root rot in poorly drained soil. Grows well in sun or shade and tolerates pruning or shearing. Protect the tender bark from damage by lawn mowers and ice storms.

baccata 'Repandens' *p. 86*
Spreading English Yew. Spreading shrub to 2 ft. (60 cm) high and 6 ft. (1.8 m) wide with long, horizontal branches that sweep the ground. Leaves to 1¼ in. (3 cm) long, gradually tapering to a slender point. Fruit berrylike, olive-brown. Does not thrive in dry, hot summers. Many horticultural varieties exist. Attractive foundation plant or shady bank cover. Zone 5.

cuspidata 'Densa' *p. 87*
Cushion Japanese Yew. Dense, spreading round-top shrub, to 18 in. (45 cm) high, wider than tall, with short side branches. Leaves 1 in. (2.5 cm) long, tapering to a short, dark green point. Berrylike fruit scarlet. Many other horticultural forms exist. Zone 5.

Tellima
Saxifrage family
Saxifragaceae

Tell-ly′ma. A single species, native in w. North America.

Description
Creeping rootstocks. Leaves chiefly basal, hairy. Flowers nodding, bell-shaped.

How to Grow
Grows well in woodland conditions with light shade and moist, well-drained soil. Increase by division of clumps.

grandiflora *p. 132*
Fringe-Cups; False Alum-Root. A slender herb, to 12 in. (30 cm) high. Leaves stalked, roundish or heart-shaped, toothed, 4 in. (10 cm) wide. Flowers greenish at first, ultimately pink or reddish, on graceful stems 2 ft. (60 cm) high, corolla of fringed petals, blooming in late spring. Cultivar 'Rubra' has attractive maroon foliage. Evergreen in mild

climates, deciduous at northern edge of its
range. Zone 5.

Teucrium
Mint family
Labiatae

Too'kri-um. Germander. About 300 species
of perennial herbs or subshrubs, some grown
for ornament or fragrance.

Description
Leaves opposite, becoming small and
bractlike near the flower clusters. Flowers in
small whorls, mostly in racemes or spikes.
Corolla 2-lipped, the lower lip much larger
than the upper.

How to Grow
The species below will grow in average to
poor soil in a sunny, well-drained spot.
Drought-tolerant once established. Needs
protection in northern winters. Prune
winter-damaged top growth in early spring.
Propagate by division or summer cuttings.

chamaedrys pp. 81, 186
Wall Germander. Prostrate evergreen
subshrub, to 12 in. (30 cm) high. Leaves
glossy, small, dark green. Flowers small, red-
purple or rose, in loose spikes. Europe. A
good bedding or edging plant. Prefers full
sun. 'Prostratum' grows to 6 in. (15 cm)
high, spreading to 2 ft. (60 cm) wide.
Zones 5–6.

Thymus
Mint family
Labiatae

Ty'mus. Thyme. Pleasantly aromatic woody
perennials or subshrubs, about 100 species,
most from the Mediterranean region. Several
are widely grown for ornament or for their
fragrant leaves, which are used as seasoning.

Description
Erect or nearly prostrate plants. Leaves
small, opposite, without marginal teeth,
diminishing in the flower cluster to tiny
leaflike bracts. Flowers lilac, or purplish in
cultivated species, small.

How to Grow
Prefers a sunny location in well-drained soil
that is not too rich. Easy to increase by
cuttings or division. The species below are
suitable for ground cover between paving
stones or in other small areas, and will
tolerate some foot traffic.

pseudolanuginosus pp. 78, 184
Woolly Thyme. Creeping, mat-forming,
rooting perennial or subshrub, to 1 in.
(2.5 cm) high. Leaves and stems densely
gray-hairy. Leaves tiny, elliptic. Flowers few,
pink. Frequently offered erroneously as
T. lanuginosus. Zone 4.

serpyllum pp. 83, 185
Creeping Thyme; Mother-of-Thyme.
Creeping, mat-forming perennial, woody at
the base, with erect flowering stems to 4 in.
(10 cm) high. Leaves tiny, linear to elliptic.
Flowerheads nearly globular, flowers purple.
Can be used as a lawn substitute, but the
flowers are attractive to bees. There are
different color forms. Zone 4.

Tiarella
Saxifrage family
Saxifragaceae

Ty-a-rell´a. A small group of chiefly
woodland perennial herbs, found in North
America and e. Asia.

Description
Rhizomatous or stoloniferous stems. Tuft of
basal leaves from which arises one or more
flowering stems. Flowers small, whitish or
reddish.

How to Grow
Grows best in woodland conditions with
moist, but well-drained, humus-rich soil in a
lightly shaded location. Will not make a
dense cover in deep shade.

cordifolia p. 172
Foamflower; False Mitrewort. Deciduous
perennial (more or less evergreen in the
South), to 6 in. (15 cm) high. Leaves
broadly heart-shaped, 3–4 in. (7.5–10.0 cm)
wide, the margins lobed and toothed.
Flowers small, white, in a dense finger-
shaped raceme on a slender stem 8 in.

(20 cm) high, in spring. Petals 5, with a claw. Zone 5.

Tolmiea
Saxifrage family
Saxifragaceae

Toll′me-a. A single species of perennial herbs, native from Alaska to Calif.

Description
Closely related to *Tiarella,* differing by having only 2 or 3 stamens.

How to Grow
Grows best in cool woodland conditions, with shade and moist soil. Easy to increase by removing a mature leaf and placing only its base in moist soil, where it will root to form a plantlet. Grown as a houseplant in cold climates.

menziesii *p. 131*
Piggyback Plant; Mother-of-Thousands. Flowering stems to 2 ft. (60 cm) long, growing from a basal rosette of leaves. Leaves heart-shaped, to 4 in. (10 cm) wide, lobed or bluntly round-toothed, hairy, abundantly produced, forming a mound 9 in. (22.5 cm) high. Young plantlets form at junction of mature leafstalk and blade (hence the common name). Flowers greenish, inconspicuous, in summer. Zone 8.

Vaccinium
Heath family
Ericaceae

Vak-sin′i-um. Over 150 species of erect or prostrate shrubs, ranging from the arctic circle to the summits of tropical mountains. Some are grown for ornament, but others, such as the blueberry and cranberry, are of agricultural interest.

Description
Leaves alternate, short-stalked, often minutely hairy on the margins. Flowers generally small, not showy, in terminal clusters. Fruit a true, many-seeded berry, crowned with the often persistent lobes of the calyx, all edible, some palatable.

How to Grow
Growing requirements vary from species to species. Those listed below grow best in rocky, peaty, acid soils. They tolerate light shade, but full sun is needed for best flower and fruit production. Increase by cuttings and, for low-growing species, by division.

angustifolium p. 95
Low-Bush Blueberry. A twiggy deciduous shrub, 1–2 ft. (30–60 cm) high. Leaves small, narrowly elliptic. Flowers tiny, urn-shaped, white, often with reddish lines, in spring. Fruit blue-black, glaucous, edible, ½ in. (13 mm) in diameter. Tolerates heat and dryness. Can be kept low and dense by occasional shearing. Brilliant autumn foliage. Zone 3.

vitis-idaea p. 103
Cowberry; Foxberry; Lingonberry. A prostrate evergreen plant, the rootstocks creeping, but stems erect, to 12 in. (30 cm) high. Leaves small, ovalish, shiny green. Flowers tiny, bell- or urn-shaped, pink, in nodding racemes. Fruit bright red, edible but sour. Prefers moist soil. Zone 5. The North American variety *V. vitis-idaea minus* (Mountain Cranberry) is hardier and forms dense mats to 6 in. (15 cm) high. Zone 3.

Vancouveria
Barberry family
Berberidaceae

Van-koo-veer′ia. 3 species of low-growing herbs, natives of the woods of nw. America, similar to *Epimedium*.

Description
Rootstocks thick and creeping. Leaves alternate, compound, the 3 leaflets ovalish, bright glossy-green. Flowers small, white or yellow, in drooping terminal clusters.

How to Grow
Makes an excellent ground cover and can also be used in borders. Requires deep, rich soil and shade. Propagate by division of the rootstocks.

hexandra p. 125
American Barrenwort. To 18 in. (45 cm) high. Flowers white, to ½ in. (13 mm)

long. Hardiest species of *Vancouveria,* but
deciduous. Has a dense, fernlike appearance.
Zone 5.

Verbena
Verbena family
Verbenaceae

Ver-bee'na. Vervain. About 200 species of
tender or hardy annual or perennial herbs,
mostly natives of North and South America.

Description
Leaves generally opposite, lobed or toothed.
Flowers small, white, lilac, red, or purple,
sometimes stalked, in terminal spikes or
roundish clusters.

How to Grow
Verbenas are useful plants for sunny, well-
drained borders, dry banks, or cascading over
walls. Drought-tolerant once established.
Grown as an annual in cold climates.
Propagate by seeds in early spring or by
cuttings taken in early fall.

peruviana pp. 180, 181
3–4 in. (7.5–10.0 cm) high. Stems prostrate,
rooting at the nodes, forming dense mats.
Leaves oblong, dark, with toothed margins,
rough to the touch. Flowers bright red,
⅔ in. (17 mm) wide, tubular. Hybrids and
cultivars are available in white, pink, rose,
and purple. Popular bank cover in the
Southwest. Prune in fall to promote dense
growth. Zone 8.

Veronica
Snapdragon family
Scrophulariaceae

Ver-on'i-ka. Speedwell. Over 250 species of
herbs for borders or rock gardens. Some are
attractive, flowering, prostrate plants, good
for ground cover or edging.

Description
Stem leaves usually opposite, upper ones
nearly always alternate. Flowers mostly in
terminal spikes or racemes. Corolla with a
short tube.

How to Grow
Most are easy to grow in average to rich,
well-drained soil, in sun or partial shade.
Increase by division after flowering is
finished. Some species can also be grown
from seeds, cultivars from cuttings.

incana p. 209
Woolly Speedwell. A white-hairy herb, to
15 in. (38 cm) high. Leaves oblongish,
toothed, 2–3 in. (5.0–7.5 cm) long, forming
mats 6 in. (15 cm) high. Flowers blue, in
spikes nearly 6 in. (15 cm) long, blooming
in midsummer. Eurasia. A good edging
plant. Zone 4.

prostrata pp. 186, 209
Rock Speedwell. A prostrate perennial with
erect branches, to 10 in. (25 cm) high.
Leaves small, linear to egg-shaped. Flowers
blue, pink, or white, in terminal racemes.
Europe. In full sun, it forms a dense mat.
Also known as *V. rupestris*. Several color
forms exist; 'Rosea' has purplish-pink
flowers. Zone 4.

repens p. 200
Creeping Speedwell. A mosslike, prostrate
perennial, the leaves tiny, shiny, forming
mats to 4 in. (10 cm) high. Flowers small,
rose-pink or bluish, in few-flowered clusters.
Corsica and Spain. There is also a white-
flowered form. Good cover for bulbs or
between paving stones; will tolerate some
foot traffic. Zone 5.

Viburnum
Honeysuckle family
Caprifoliaceae

Vy-bur'num. About 225 species of upright,
chiefly deciduous shrubs and small trees of
the northern temperate zone. Many are
cultivated for their flowers or fruit.

Description
Leaves opposite. Flowers small, often
fragrant, usually white, in showy clusters.
Fruit often showy, persistent, and a favorite
food of birds. All but the few evergreen
species have fine autumn color.

How to Grow
Adaptable, but grows best in moderately
rich, well-drained, neutral soil in sun or light

shade. Protect evergreen types from hot sun
and winter winds. Prune shrubs to prevent
legginess. Propagate by stratified seeds,
hardwood cuttings, or layers.

davidii p. 128

David Viburnum. Handsome, compact
evergreen shrub, 1–2½ ft. (30–75 cm) high
and 3–4 ft. (90–120 cm) wide. Leaves glossy,
elliptical, to 6 in. (15 cm) long, the veins
giving the leaves a pleated appearance.
Flowers white, not showy, in summer. Fruit
light blue. Zone 8.

Vinca
Dogbane family
Apocynaceae

Vin′ka. About 12 species of evergreen, erect
or trailing perennial herbs or vinelike shrubs,
natives of the Old World.

Description
Leaves opposite, simple, ovalish, shiny green,
leathery. Flowers blue or white, solitary,
stalked, growing in leaf axils.

How to Grow
Vinca will make a thick carpet in moderately
fertile garden soil. Tolerates full sun but
grows best in light shade. May be sheared
annually to encourage dense growth. Easy to
propagate by cuttings or division.

major p. 107

Big Periwinkle. Trailing, the stems thin and
wiry, mounding to 18 in. (45 cm) high,
usually less. Leaves heart-shaped at base, dark
green. Flowers blue, 1–2 in. (2.5–5.0 cm)
wide. Cultivar 'Variegata' has yellowish-
white leaf margins. Much used as an annual
in window boxes in cold climates, and as
ground cover in the South and West. Less
cold-hardy and more open in growth habit
than *V. minor.* Zone 7.

minor pp. 106, 202

Periwinkle; Creeping Myrtle. Trailing, hardy,
to 10 in. (25 cm) high, the rooting stems
thin and wiry. Leaves broadly lance-shaped,
to 2 in. (5 cm) long, dark green. Flowers
small, light blue. Forms selected for flower
color, double flowers, or variegated foliage.
Good plant for shady places. Zone 5.

Viola
Violet family
Violaceae

Vy-o'la. Violet. About 500 species of hardy
perennial herbs, a few annual, distributed
throughout temperate regions and including
the violet and the pansy.

Description
Low-growing, generally tufted plants, some
species producing runners. Basal leaves
simple, heart-shaped or oval, sometimes
lobed, slightly wrinkled, stalked, coarsely
toothed. Stem leaves alternate, simple,
ovalish, usually stalked, with rounded teeth.
Flowers stalked, solitary, sometimes nodding,
violet, blue, reddish purple, lilac, yellow, or
white. Petals 5, 4 arranged in pairs.

How to Grow
Pansies and violas, usually grown as annual
bedding plants, prefer full sun, but the
perennial species (violets) perform equally
well in light shade. Violets grow best in
rich, moist soil. The species below are
usually short-lived perennials maintained by
self-seeding. They may also be increased by
division or by separation of rooted runners.
Suitable for border edgings or naturalizing.

labradorica p. 204
Labrador Violet. Tufted perennial with erect
leafy stems to 4 in. (10 cm) high. Leaves
heart-shaped, 1 in. (2.5 cm) wide and long,
dark purplish, coloring less intense in deep
shade. Flowers purple. Zone 5.

odorata p. 171
Sweet Violet; Florists' Violet. Tufted
perennial, to 6 in. (15 cm) high, with long
runners. Leaves basal, broadly heart-shaped,
to 3 in. (7.5 cm) long. Flowers deep violet
or white, sweet-scented. Popular cultivars
include 'Royal Robe', with purple flowers,
'White Czar', with white flowers, and
'Rosina', with pink flowers. Zone 6.

sororia p. 205
Woolly Blue Violet; Meadow Violet.
Perennial to 6 in. (15 cm) high, with a stout,
branching rootstock. Leaves smooth or hairy,
long-stalked, shallowly heart-shaped, 3–6 in.
(7.5–15.0 cm) wide. Flowers long-stalked,
blue, with a light center, ½ in. (13 mm)
long, in spring. Self-sows readily. Zone 5.

Waldsteinia
Rose family
Rosaceae

Wald-sty′ni-a. A small genus of
strawberrylike herbs closely related to the
strawberry but with dry, hairy fruits.

Description
Creeping rhizomes. Most leaves basal, 3–5,
lobed or divided, with toothed or notched
tips. Flowers small, yellow.

How to Grow
Barren Strawberries grow best in humus-rich,
moist soil. They prefer light shade but will
tolerate full sun if adequate soil moisture is
maintained. Propagate by division.

fragarioides pp. 111, 160
Barren Strawberry. Evergreen, 4–6 in.
(10–15 cm) high. Leaves basal, glossy,
consisting of 3 wedge-shaped leaflets. Flowers
in small clusters in late spring. Zone 5.

ternata p. 110
Barren Strawberry. Evergreen, carpet-forming
perennial to 6 in. (15 cm) high. Leaves
glossy, with 3 oval leaflets. Flowers in small
clusters on 8-in. (20-cm) stems in spring.
Occasionally listed as *W. sibirica*. Zone 4.

Xanthorhiza
Buttercup family
Ranunculaceae

Zan-tho-ry′za. A single species of low shrubs,
a native of the e. U.S.

Description
Stoloniferous. Leaves deciduous, compound,
long-stalked. Flowers in drooping racemes.

How to Grow
Grows well in sun or shade in thoroughly
moist soil. Tolerates wet soil. Propagate by
division of stolons.

simplicissima p. 93
Yellowroot. To 2 ft. (60 cm) high, with
yellow, bitter roots. Stems upright. Leaflets
ovalish, deeply cut, 2–4 in. (5–10 cm) long.
Flowers tiny, brownish purple, in spring
before the leaves. Orange or reddish autumn
foliage. Zone 5.

Vines

A vine is any plant that requires some support for its proper development. This category includes trailing woody shrubs, herbaceous perennials, and annuals with long stems that are so weak they must either trail along the ground or depend on an object, such as a trellis or fence, for climbing support. Unlike trees or shrubs, vines do not constitute a separate botanical class, but are grouped by virtue of their vining growth habit.

Vines in the Garden
The great advantage vines offer to gardeners is their flexible stems, which can be bent and trained to grow in almost any manner to cover a particular area. Even the smallest garden can accommodate vines, for they take up little ground space if trained vertically. Because most gardens are planned on the horizontal, vines can add a new, vertical dimension of interest to the more usual plantings of ground covers, foundation shrubs, or herbaceous borders.

Accents and Screens
As accent plants, vines can be used to highlight an attractive ornamental feature; for example, a small-leaved vine trained up a pillar or fieldstone chimney will call attention to the architectural features of a building. They are also utilitarian plants, excellent for screening undesirable views or providing privacy. A large-leaved, vigorous climber will cover an ugly cement block wall or chain link fence in a very short time. You can also train vines to climb on an arbor or some other framework; they create a solid screen that will hide a neighbor's dog pen or offer overhead protection from hot summer sun. For either of these purposes, choose a large-leaved, dense vine such as Porcelain Vine or grape. If your objective is filtered shade or a light screen that does not obstruct summer breezes, choose an open-textured vine such as Trumpet Honeysuckle or the annual Cardinal Climber.

Annual vines can be used as a quick cover while a perennial vine is getting established. For camouflage operations it is best to use evergreen vines whenever possible, since most unsightly objects do not improve in wintertime. Keep in mind, however, that evergreen vines may dry out in winter sun and are thus best used on a north or east wall, where they will have some shade.

Flowers, Foliage, and Fruit
Quite apart from their utilitarian roles, vines offer a special beauty to the garden. Climbing roses and many clematis are grown for their exceptionally lovely flowers, and wisterias and jasmines are valued for the fragrance of their blooms. Many vines, such as euonymus and the variegated ivies, have attractive foliage; others are noted especially for their brilliant fall leaf colors or for their edible or ornamental fruit.

Vines as Ground Covers

Without supports on which to climb, many vines trail along the ground and become suitable ground covers. Even twining vines can be encouraged to creep horizontally if you cover the area with twiggy branches secured in place. Use vines as ground cover only where there are no shrubs or small trees nearby to serve as supports, though, because vigorous vines will quickly climb and cover them. For steep banks choose vines that root along the stems where they touch the ground, such as the Memorial Rose. Plants with this feature help considerably in controlling soil erosion.

Climbing Habit

Some vines climb by stems or tendrils that twine around available supports; others have aerial roots or adhesive disks that cling to various surfaces. It is important to know a plant's climbing habit so that you can provide a suitable support and avoid potential problems. Do not, for instance, plant clinging vines such as ivy or Virginia Creeper against a wooden house, because the rootlets can damage the finish and work their way under the clapboards. Likewise, a wisteria that grows large and heavy can weigh down and dislodge the drainpipe that supports it.

Selecting Vines

To choose the right vine for a particular spot, always consider the plant's growth habit—how fast it grows, how tall it gets, how it climbs, what kind of support it needs, whether it remains green all year. Equally important are the plant's hardiness and cultural requirements. Some vines need full sun, others require shade, and a number are adapted to both; some vines prefer moist soil, while others thrive on dry, sandy banks. Gardeners in mild climates have the widest range of vines to select from, but even those in the frozen northern reaches have a few choices. Keep in mind, however, that many vines, such as Japanese Honeysuckle, that are well behaved or do little more than just survive in far northern gardens can become extremely vigorous menaces in more benign climates. The text accounts that follow will help you choose vines to suit almost any purpose and add beauty to your garden.

Actinidia
Silver Vine family
Dilleniaceae

Ak-ti-nid´i-a. 40 species of quickly climbing woody vines from Asia, most grown for their dense, handsome foliage, a few for their edible fruit.

Description
Leaves alternate, simple, margins toothed; leafstalks cover succeeding winter bud. Flowers inconspicuous, cup-shaped, often dioecious. Fruit a many-seeded berry.

How to Grow
Grow in ordinary garden soil in full sun or partial shade. Propagate by spring-sown seeds, cuttings of partly ripened wood in summer, or matured wood under glass in winter. Layering is also effective. Seed should be stratified.

arguta p. 223
Bower Actinidia; Tara Vine. Densely leafy, woody vine, to 50 ft. (15 m) high. Leaves broadly oval, 5 in. (12.5 cm) long, lustrous green, the stalks 2 in. (5 cm) long, reddish. Flower cluster shorter than leafstalk, usually of 3 small brownish-white flowers. Fruit elliptic, 1 in. (2.5 cm) long, yellowish or green, sweet, edible. Zone 5.

kolomikta p. 213
Kolomikta Vine. Rarely over 20 ft. (6 m) high. Leaves with white or pink blotches at end, oblong, 5 in. (12.5 cm) long. Flowers small, white, fragrant. Fruit oblong or ovoid, 1 in. (2.5 cm) long, greenish yellow. Blooms in spring. Zone 5.

Adlumia
Bleeding-heart family
Fumariaceae

Ad-loom´i-a. A climbing, delicate, herblike biennial vine, native to rich woods in e. North America. Sometimes grown in wild gardens for its flowers, which resemble bleeding hearts.

Description
Leaves alternate, thrice-compound, ultimate leaflets fragile, fernlike. Flowers white or

purple, irregular, spurred, drooping in a loose cluster. Fruit a several-seeded pod.

How to Grow
Easy to grow in partial shade and rich, but not overly acid, humus. Protect from wind. Propagate by self-sown seeds.

fungosa p. 212
Climbing Fumitory; Allegheny Vine; Mountain Fringe. Often climbing to 25 ft. (7.5 m) high by its slender tendrils. Flowers ¾ in. (19 mm) long. Blooms in summer. Zone 5.

Akebia
Akebia family
Lardizabalaceae

A-kee′bi-a. Four species of Asiatic woody vines, the one below cultivated for shade and for covering walls and arbors.

Description
Leaves almost evergreen, palmately compound, leaflets 3 or 5. Male and female flowers separate, spring-blooming, in loose clusters, male flowers small, purplish brown, females larger, pale fawn. Fruit a black-seeded pod.

How to Grow
Grows best in well-drained soil in sun, but will tolerate partial shade. Propagate by division, hardwood or softwood cuttings, or seeds.

quinata p. 221
Fiveleaf Akebia. A stout, twining climber, to 30 ft. (9 m) high. Leaflets 5. Flowers fragrant, inconspicuous. Fruit (often absent in cultivation) a purple pod. Can grow out of control in warm climates, but recovers quickly if cut to the ground in late winter. Zone 5.

Ampelopsis
Grape family
Vitaceae

Am-pe-lop′sis. A genus of woody, tendril-bearing vines, a few species commonly grown for covering walls.

Inedible fruit and nonshredding bark differentiate these North American or Asiatic vines from the closely related grape vines.

Description
Leaves simple or compound, the tendrils forking and without sucking-disks. Flowers small, greenish or yellowish. Fruit a 1- to 4-seeded berry.

How to Grow
Grows well in sun or light shade and tolerates a wide range of soil types. Propagate by seeds or by hardwood or softwood cuttings.

brevipedunculata p. 222
Porcelain Vine. Stout, vigorous vine to 25 ft. (7.5 m) high. Leaves simple, 5 in. (12.5 cm) wide, with 3 coarsely toothed lobes. Fruit pale blue at first, turquoise when ripe, ¼ in. (6 mm) in diameter. Not a dense cover, but grown for its distinctive fruit. Sometimes known as *A. heterophylla.* Zone 5.

Antigonon
Rhubarb family
Polygonaceae

An-tig′o-non. A small group of showy, tropical American, tendril-climbing vines, one widely grown for its profuse bloom in warm regions.

Description
Leaves alternate, without marginal teeth. Flowers numerous, in drooping racemes from leaf axils, ending in a tendril.

How to Grow
Thrives in full sun and tolerates a wide range of soils. May go dormant in summer without adequate moisture. Increase by seeds or cuttings. In zones 8–9, the species below is commonly grown over porches, fences, and walls. Elsewhere, but rarely, it is a greenhouse plant.

leptopus p. 232
Coral Vine; Mountain Rose; Confederate Vine. To 30 ft. (9 m) high or more. Leaves arrow- or heart-shaped, 1–3 in. (2.5–7.5 cm) long, the lower leaves larger. Flowers tiny, pink or white, in trailing sprays. Blooms midsummer to autumn. Zone 8.

Aristolochia
Birthwort family
Aristolochiaceae

A-ris-toe-loe´ki-a. A genus of 180 species of
mostly tropical, woody vines and a few
temperate species of vines and perennial
herbs. Widely grown for their distinctive
flowers, fine, rich foliage, and ability to cover
unsightly objects quickly.

Description
Leaves alternate, often evergreen. Flowers
solitary or in clusters, tubular, usually
peculiarly shaped and irregular. Fruit a
capsule.

How to Grow
Thrives in sun or shade and prefers fertile
soil and adequate moisture, but tolerates less
favorable conditions. Easy to grow from
seeds. Can also be increased by cuttings of
ripened wood.

durior p. 218

Dutchman's-Pipe; Pipevine. To 30 ft. (9 m)
high. Leaves roundish or kidney-shaped,
6–14 in. (15–35 cm) wide, stalked. Flowers
1½ in. (4 cm) long, U-shaped, yellowish
brown, in summer. The coarse leaves overlap
like shingles, creating a dense cover ideal for
shading porches. Formerly known as
A. macrophylla. Zone 5.

Bignonia
Trumpet-creeper family
Bignoniaceae

Big-known´i-a. A single species of evergreen
or partly evergreen woody vines native in the
se. U.S. At one time the name was applied
to more than 150 species.

Description
Leaves compound, with 2 stalked leaflets and
a terminal tendril. Flowers funnel-shaped,
slightly irregular, in cymes in leaf axils.

How to Grow
Prefers rich, moist, well-drained soil in sun
or partial shade. Propagate by cuttings or
seeds, if available.

capreolata p. 227
Cross Vine. Climbing woody vine, to 50 ft. (15 m) high. Leaflets 4–6 in. (10–15 cm) long, without marginal teeth. Flowers 2 in. (5 cm) long, reddish orange. Fruit a long, narrow, slightly flattened pod. Zone 7.

Bougainvillea
Four o'clock family
Nyctaginaceae

Boo-gen-vill-ee′a. The 10 known species, all South American, are perhaps the most handsome, and certainly the most widely planted, ornamental vines of the tropics, and great favorites in s. U.S. and Calif.

Description
Tall-growing, woody vines. Leaves alternate, stalked. Flowers small, not showy, the color coming from 3 of the large, showy bracts surrounding each flower.

How to Grow
Grows easily in any well-drained soil in sun, but benefits from some afternoon shade in hottest areas. Limit watering in midsummer to encourage flowering. Withstands drought. Propagate by cuttings. These vines are among the finest creepers for covering an arbor, porch, or corner of a house.

spectabilis p. 238
Vigorous climber with spiny stems. Leaves oval, hairy. Flower bracts reddish in the species. 'Texas Dawn' has pink flower bracts and grows to 30 ft. (9 m) high. 'Temple Fire' is more shrubby, to 6 ft. (1.8 m) high, with bronzy-red bracts. The related *B. glabra* 'Sanderana' flowers almost continually. Zone 9.

Campsis
Trumpet-creeper family
Bignoniaceae

Kamp′sis. Two species of handsome, rampant-growing, woody vines cultivated for ornament.

Description
Tall-growing, climbing by aerial rootlets. Leaves opposite, compound, leaflets arranged

feather-fashion with an odd one at the end.
Flowers showy, slightly irregular, orange or
scarlet, in terminal cymes or panicles, calyx
tubular or bell-shaped, corolla funnel-shaped.
Fruit a long-stalked capsule.

How to Grow
Grows best in full sun in any well-drained
soil. Propagate by seeds, layering, or cuttings.
Useful for quick cover because of its
vigorous, rapid growth. Can become top-
heavy and pull away from its support unless
thinned or fastened in place.

radicans p. 228
Trumpet Creeper; Trumpet Vine. Stout,
woody vine to 30 ft. (9 m) high. Aerial
rootlets numerous. Leaflets 9–11, elliptic or
ovalish, 2–3 in. (5.0–7.5 cm) long. Flowers
orange-scarlet, 2 in. (5 cm) wide, 3½ in.
(9 cm) long, in late summer. Excellent for
smoke-ridden cities or for the country.
Invasive and next to impossible to eradicate
in southern part of its range. Long known as
Tecoma radicans and *Bignonia radicans*. The
hybrid 'Mme. Galen' has larger, showier,
salmon-red flowers. Zone 4.

Celastrus
Staff-tree family
Celastraceae

See-las′trus. Bittersweet. More than 30 species
of primarily woody vines, mostly Asiatic,
American, or Australian; 3 are cultivated for
ornament.

Description
Leaves alternate, stalked. Flowers small,
greenish, mostly unisexual. Fruit a usually
yellow capsule that, upon splitting, discloses
the fleshy crimson aril of the seeds.

How to Grow
Thrives in ordinary soil. Tolerates shade, but
best fruiting occurs in full sun. Both male
and female plants are required. Propagate by
stratified seeds, suckers, or cuttings. Requires
heavy pruning to keep it under control.
These vines have handsome foliage and
brilliant autumn fruit and are useful for
walls, trellises, or arbors.

orbiculatus p. 223

Oriental Bittersweet. Handsome, twining
vine to 30 ft. (9 m) high. Leaves nearly
round or oblongish, 3–5 in. (7.5–12.5 cm)
long. Flowering and fruiting clusters often
partly hidden in leaf axils. Fruit orange-
yellow, persistent. Can become rampant
and smother smaller vines and shrubs.
C. rosthornianus (Chinese Bittersweet)
is a similar species but less hardy.
Zone 5.

scandens p. 222

American Bittersweet; Waxwork; Fever
Twig. A rampant but not tall-growing
woody vine, to 20 ft. (6 m) high. Leaves
oblong-oval, 2½–5 in. (6.0–12.5 cm) long,
tapering at tip. Flower and fruit clusters
mostly terminal. Fruit yellow, the aril a
brilliant crimson. Suitable for covering low
wall tops. Zone 3.

Clematis
Buttercup family
Ranunculaceae

Klem′a-tis. About 270 species of herbs or
shrubby or woody vines, widely distributed,
mostly in e. Asia, the Himalayas, and North
America.

Description
Leaves opposite, mostly compound,
sometimes simple, but usually with 3–5 or
more leaflets, the leafstalk often curling like
a tendril. Flowers often very showy, without
petals, but with 4 (sometimes 5–8) petal-
like sepals, in white, yellow, pink, red,
purple, and intermediate shades. 3 general
forms: small white flowers in panicles or
loose and irregular spreading clusters; bell-
or urn-shaped flowers; and flat or open
flowers. Fruit a collection of achenes, some
with a plumed, often showy, tail-like
appendage.

How to Grow
Grows on trellises, fences, arbors, walls, tree
stumps, and other surfaces. Most species will
scramble through loose shrubs and small
trees into sunlight. Clematis prefers cool,
rich, moist, well-drained soil. Add dolomitic
lime, leaf mold, and sand when planting;
never allow plants to become too dry.
Provide a stable support when plants are set

out, since stems are brittle and break easily
in the wind. Clematis grows best with leaves
and flowers in full sun but with roots in
shade. To accomplish this, mulch and
underplant with a shallow-rooted ground
cover, or plant on north side of a low wall.
Spring-blooming types flower on previous
year's growth; prune after flowering to
preserve plant's general shape and remove
dead wood and tangled stems. Summer-
flowering kinds, including large-flowered
hybrids, produce flowers on current year's
wood, so prune in late winter or early spring.
Young plants may be cut back to within
a few inches of the ground or to 2–3 buds;
established plants, to 12–18 in. (30–45 cm).
Propagate hybrid clematis by layering or by
softwood cuttings. The species can also be
increased by seeds. To control stem rot,
remove affected parts of plant below ground
level, then spray vine and planting area
repeatedly with fungicide.

armandii p. 250
Armand Clematis. The only evergreen vining
clematis, 15–20 ft. (4.5–6.0 m) high. Leaflets
3, on twisted stalks, oblongish, 3–5 in. (7.5–
12.5 cm) long. Flowers white, 1½–2½ in.
(4–6 cm) wide, in leafless clusters in spring.
Fruit long-plumed. Prune after flowering.
Grown mostly in Calif. and the Pacific
Northwest. Zone 7.

Large-flowered cultivars and hybrids
pp. 240, 241, 250

Showy, colorful plants of garden origin, the
most popular hardy vines grown in the U.S.
To 15 ft. (4.5 m) high. Flowering times
vary, but all produce flat sprays of colored
petal-like sepals around a central cluster of
stamens and pistils, creating "flowers"
4–8 in. (10–20 cm) wide, often in profusion.
Colors range from white through pink and
red to blue and purple. Prune in late winter.
Well-known 'Jackmanii' has profuse, deep
velvety purple blooms in early summer; its
cultivar 'Rubra' has pink flowers. 'Henryi',
widely grown, has large, pure white flowers
8 in. (20 cm) wide with dark stamens. 'Mrs.
Cholmondeley' has pale lavender-blue
flowers. 'The President' has purple flowers.
All zone 5.

macropetala p. 240
Downy Clematis; Bigpetal Clematis. Climbs
to 10 ft. (3 m) high. Leaves 2–3 times
compound, the leaflets cut or lobed. Flowers

solitary, nodding, 3–4 in. (7.5–10.0 cm)
wide, pink or lavender. Showy silvery seed
heads follow. Zone 5.

montana pp. 234, 235
Anemone Clematis. Vigorous woody vine
to 25 ft. (7.5 m) high. Leaflets 3, oblong
or ovalish, short-stalked, 1½–4½ in.
(4.0–11.5 cm) long, usually deeply toothed.
Flowers slender-stalked, white, 1½–3½ in.
(4–9 cm) wide, in spring. The var. *rubens,*
more popular than the species, has purplish
foliage when young, and pink flowers. Both
forms are free-flowering and charming when
allowed to cascade. Prune after flowering, if
needed. 'Tetrarose' has larger, mauve-pink
flowers. Zone 5.

paniculata p. 251
Sweet Autumn Clematis. To 30 ft. (9 m)
high. Leaves compound, leaflets 3, egg-
shaped, 1–4 in. (2.5–10.0 cm) long, leathery.
Flowers 1–1½ in. (2.5–4 cm) wide, white,
freely produced in panicles in late summer.
Fluffy seed heads in autumn. Correctly
named *C. dioscoreifolia robusta* but usually
sold as *C. paniculata.* Zone 5.

tangutica p. 224
Golden Clematis. Woody vine 6–10 ft.
(1.8–3.0 m) high. Leaves compound, leaflets
oblongish, 1½–2½ in. (4–6 cm) long.
Flowers solitary, nodding, yellow, blooming
in late spring and often again in fall. Fruits
plumed. Zone 4.

texensis pp. 230, 237
Scarlet Clematis. Slightly woody vine 5–8 ft.
(1.5–2.4 m) high. Leaflets 4–8, the
uppermost often replaced by a tendril,
broadly oval, 2–3½ in. (5–9 cm) long,
bluish green. Flowers solitary, stalked,
distinctively bell- or urn-shaped, scarlet to
rose-pink, 1½ in. (4 cm) long, in late
summer. May die to ground in winter but
recovers and blooms on current year's
growth. Best-known hybrid is 'Duchess of
Albany'. Zone 5.

virginiana p. 249
Virgin's Bower; Old-Man's-Beard. Climbing
to 18 ft. (5.5 m) high, or sprawling as a
wild plant. Dioecious. Leaflets ovalish,
2½–4 in. (6–10 cm) long, coarsely toothed.
Flowers white, ¾–1½ in. (2–4 cm) wide, in
panicles in leaf axils, in late summer to fall.
Fruits cluster nearly 2½ in. (6 cm) wide.

Less ornamental than other clematis but
suitable for wild gardens. Zone 4.

Clerodendrum
Verbena family
Verbenaceae

Kler-ro-den'drum. About 450 species of
chiefly tropical shrubs, vines, or trees.

Description
Leaves opposite or whorled, often lobed but
not compound, malodorous when crushed.
Flowers showy, in clusters (often panicles or
racemes). Calyx often colored, bell-shaped,
corolla tubular. Fruit fleshy, enclosed by the
withered calyx.

How to Grow
Grows best in fertile, moist but well-drained
soil. Needs a support for twining. Flowers
on new wood, so prune at winter's end.

× *speciosum* p. 231
Pagoda Flower. To 8 ft. (2.4 m) high.
Similar to *C. thomsoniae,* one of its parents,
but with pink papery calyx and red corolla.
Leaves handsome, dark green, deeply veined.
Grown outdoors in the South and Calif.
Elsewhere grown as a pot plant and
overwintered in a greenhouse. Zone 10.

thomsoniae p. 246

Glory Bower. Handsome woody vine to 8 ft.
(2.4 m) high. Leaves ovalish, 3–5 in.
(7.5–12.5 cm) long. Flowers very showy, in
branching clusters in late summer; calyx
ivory-white, corolla crimson. Much grown in
greenhouses and outdoors on Gulf Coast and
in Calif. Top can be winter-killed, but
blooms on new wood next season.
Sometimes listed as *C. balfouri.* Zone 10.

Clytostoma
Trumpet-creeper family
Bignoniaceae

Kly-tos'to-ma. Eight species of South
American evergreen woody vines, one
cultivated outdoors in mild climates for its
showy bloom.

Description
Leaves compound, with 2 leaflets; end of main leafstalk prolonged into a slender unbranched tendril. Flowers in clusters of 2, calyx bell-shaped, corolla funnel-shaped, its lobes wavy.

How to Grow
An attractive, medium-size vine for Fla., Calif., and other mild-climate regions, the species below grows in any garden soil in sun or light shade. Slow-growing until thoroughly established. Propagate by cuttings of last season's wood.

callistegioides p. 235
Violet Trumpet Vine. To 8 ft. (2.4 m) high. Leaflets 2, evergreen, glossy, oblongish, to 4 in. (10 cm) long. Flowers in terminal pairs, 3 in. (7.5 cm) long, light purple or very pale lavender, streaked darker purple inside. Blooms in spring. Sometimes known as *Bignonia speciosa* or *B. violacea*. Zone 8.

Cobaea
Phlox family
Polemoniaceae

Ko-bee'a. Tendril-climbing, tropical American woody vines.

Description
Leaves alternate, compound, leaflets arranged feather-fashion, the terminal one a branched tendril. Flowers solitary, on long stalks from leaf axils; corolla bell-shaped or cylindrical.

How to Grow
Start seeds indoors 8 weeks before last frost. Set out when danger of frost is past. Provide tall, strong supports to prevent wind damage. Where summers are cool, plant facing west or south; where summers are warm, plant in area with afternoon shade. Prefers warm weather.

scandens p. 243
Cup-and-Saucer Vine; Mexican Ivy. Quick-growing, showy, 10–25 ft. (3.0–7.5 m) high. Flowers violet, greenish purple, or white, 2 in. (5 cm) long, 1½ in. (4 cm) wide; calyx inflated, leaflike, stamens protruding, curved. There is a white-flowered form. Tender perennial grown as an annual

in the North. Long flowering period.
Zone 9.

Decumaria
Saxifrage family
Saxifragaceae

De-koo-mare'ee-a. 2 known species of woody
vines related to *Hydrangea,* the one described
below native in se. U.S.

Description
Leaves opposite, entire, oval. Flowers small,
white, all fertile, in clusters.

How to Grow
Prefers fertile, moist soil and partial shade.
Propagate by cuttings in late summer.

barbara *p. 245*
Climbing Hydrangea; Wood Vamp. Stems
climbing by aerial roots, to 30 ft. (9 m)
high, covered with peeling, shreddy bark.
Leaves glossy, half-evergreen. Flowers small,
white, in terminal corymbs. Calyx turban-
shaped. Fruit a small ribbed capsule, splitting
between the ribs. Suitable as a wall cover.
Zone 7.

Distictis
Trumpet-vine family
Bignoniaceae

Dis-tick'tis. A small genus of tropical
American woody vines native to the West
Indies and tropical America.

Description
Leaves have 3 leaflets, or 2 leaflets and a
terminal tendril. Flowers tubular, in terminal
clusters.

How to Grow
Grows best in full sun or light shade in
fertile soil. Increase by cuttings from side
shoots in early summer.

buccinatoria *p. 229*
Blood-red Trumpet Vine. Handsome
evergreen vine to 18 ft. (5.5 m) high. Leaves
opposite, compound, leaflets 2, usually with
a terminal branched tendril. Flowers in
drooping terminal racemes; corolla tubular or

funnel-shaped, nearly 4 in. (10 cm) long,
bright red, yellow at base and inside.
Sometimes known as *Bignonia buccinatoria*.
Prized for its foliage and long flowering
period. Zone 9.

Euonymus
Bittersweet family
Celastraceae

You-on'i-mus. Spindle-tree. About 170
mostly Asian species of shrubs, vines, or
trees, more than a dozen grown for their
showy fruits or evergreen foliage.

Description
Leaves opposite, stalked, usually smooth.
Flowers inconspicuous, greenish, white,
or yellowish, in small cymes in leaf axils.
Fruit a capsule, often lobed, with a showy,
fleshy, orange or red aril. All flower in late
spring and set fruit from midsummer
to frost.

How to Grow
This species is not particular about soil
and grows equally well in sun or shade.
Propagate by stratified seeds, or by cuttings
from the old wood.

fortunei radicans p. 214
Winter Creeper. Trailing or climbing
evergreen vine to 12 ft. (3.5 m) high. Leaves
ovalish or broadly elliptic, glossy, to 1 in.
(2.5 cm) long. Flowers greenish white. Fruit
nearly round, pale pink. Will climb and
cling if supported, or it can be used as
ground cover. Best evergreen vine for the
North. There is a variegated form. Often
listed as *E. radicans*. Zone 5.

Ficus
Mulberry family
Moraceae

Fy'kus. Over 800 species of chiefly tropical
trees, shrubs, and vines, including the
Common Fig and many ornamentals.

Description
Nearly all have milky juice. Leaves alternate.
Flowers and fruit (achenes) minute, borne

inside a closed, fleshy receptacle edible in the
Common Fig but in few others.

How to Grow
The species below grows best in fertile soil
in sun or shade. Will not climb a hot south
or west wall satisfactorily. Propagate by
cuttings.

pumila p. 213
Creeping Fig; Climbing Fig. Popular
greenhouse vine to 40 ft. (12 m) high.
Leaves dense, very numerous, oval heart-
shaped, ¾ in. (19 mm) long, but larger on
fruiting branches. Fruit pear-shaped,
yellowish, 2 in. (5 cm) long, not edible.
Where hardy it grows neatly and flat against
walls, except for the fruiting branches. Prune
to keep young growth vigorous and to
prevent development of mature leaves and
branches, which are coarse and detract from
the trim effect. Incorrectly known as *F.
repens.* Zone 9.

Gelsemium
Buddleia family
Loganiaceae

Gel-see′mi-um. Two or three evergreen
woody vines native in e. Asia and e. North
America.

Description
Leaves opposite. Flowers funnel-shaped,
borne singly or in clusters in leaf axils.

How to Grow
Needs fertile, well-drained soil in sun or
light shade. Propagate by seeds or cuttings.
Attractive on a trellis, fence, or lamppost, or
as a ground cover.

sempervirens p. 226
Carolina, or Yellow, Jessamine or Jasmine.
Not a true jasmine (*Jasminum*). Climbing
10–20 ft. (3–6 m) high. Leaves oblongish,
2–4 in. (5–10 cm) long, shining. Flowers
bright yellow, very fragrant, in a dense cyme,
usually in leaf axils, in spring. Corolla
funnel-shaped, 1 in. (2.5 cm) long. Fruit a
small, flattened, short-beaked capsule. All
parts of the plant are toxic. There is a
double-flowered form. Zone 7.

Hedera
Aralia family
Araliaceae

Hed′er-ra. Evergreen woody vines from n.
Eurasia and n. Africa, generally called ivy.

Description
They climb by aerial rootlets that cling easily
to brick or masonry, less so to wood. Leaves
alternate, evergreen, stalked, usually lobed or
coarsely toothed. Flowers produced only on
mature specimens of English Ivy; greenish,
not very conspicuous.

How to Grow
Ivy thrives in rich, moist soil. Grows well in
shade; full sun will scorch some varieties.
Propagate ivy from cuttings of young
growth rooted in sand, a light soil mix, or
water, or from layers. Prune heavily or shear
for desired habit and compact growth. It
readily covers any rough surface, and will
hide a chain link fence, but does not twine
and must be woven into the links. Makes a
good ground cover under trees where grass
cannot be maintained. Its deep roots help
control soil erosion on banks.

colchica pp. 216, 217
Persian Ivy. Climbing vine to 50 ft. (15 m)
high. Leaves broadly oval or heart-shaped,
5–10 in. (12.5–25.0 cm) long, usually not
lobed, dark green, leathery. Fruit black.
Largest-leaved ivy, popular on the West
Coast. Covers large areas. Best-known
varieties are 'Dentata', with slightly toothed
leaves, and 'Dentato-variegata', with cream
and gray-green marbling on dark green
leaves. Zone 8.

helix pp. 215, 216, 217

English Ivy; Evergreen Ivy. Creeping or
climbing, to 50 ft. (15 m) high, often
completely covering walls. Ordinary leaves
3- to 5-lobed, 2–5 in. (5.0–12.5 cm) long,
dark green above, yellowish green beneath.
Leaves on flowering branches of mature
plants larger, squarish, not lobed. Flowers
green, inconspicuous, umbels globe-shaped.
Fruit tiny, nearly round, black. Popular
horticultural varieties include 'Baltica', a
hardy form with medium-size triangular
leaves and prominent white veins;
'Buttercup', with brighter, less somber, green
leaves; 'Glacier' and 'Gold Heart', both
variegated forms; the widely planted,

vigorous 'Hibernica', with glossy leaves; 'Ivalace', a bushy spreader for small areas; and 'Thorndale', said to be hardy to −20°F (−29°C). All zone 6.

Humulus
Hemp family
Cannabinaceae

Hew'mew-lus. Hop. Rough-stemmed annual or perennial vines, all natives of the north temperate zone. Valuable commercial plants, of garden interest as fast-growing vines.

Description
Leaves opposite, lobed. Male and female flowers green, on separate plants. Male flowers in catkinlike racemes; female flowers in pairs, each pair beneath a large bract forming the conelike "hop," valued in beer-making. Fruit a small achene surrounded by the persistent calyx.

How to Grow
Requires full sun, rich soil, and ample moisture throughout growing season.

lupulus p. 220

Common Hop. Perennial, to 25 ft. (7.5 m) high. Leaves heart-shaped, 3-lobed, rough above, less so beneath. Male flowers in a cluster. Female flowers between bracts that are much enlarged in fruit (the hop). The common green form has little decorative interest, but the yellow-leaved form 'Aureus' is grown for ornament. Can become a nuisance. Useful for rapid summer screening on porches and arbors. Zone 6.

Hydrangea
Saxifrage family
Saxifragaceae

Hy-dran'jee-a. Important garden shrubs and woody vines, many of the 23 species grown for their showy flower clusters. Most garden sorts are Asiatic or North American.

Description
Leaves opposite, stalked, usually toothed. Flowers small, prevailingly white, blue, or pink, in dense, flat-topped or globe-shaped clusters. Fruit a 2- to 5-valved capsule.

How to Grow
Prefers partial shade but will tolerate full sun
if rich, moist, well-drained soil is provided. If
vine is planted against a tree, feed and water
it often until well established. Prune only to
retain desired shape. Propagate by layers or
heel cuttings.

anomala petiolaris p. 246
Climbing Hydrangea. Woody vine climbing
by aerial rootlets, to 50–60 ft. (15–18 m)
high. Leaves broadly oval, rounded or
heart-shaped at base, 2–5 in. (5.0–12.5 cm)
long. Flower clusters loose, white, 6–12 in.
(15–30 cm) wide, in summer. Clings well to
brick or masonry walls or tree trunks. Nice
golden autumn foliage color. Sometimes sold
as *H. petiolaris.* Zone 4.

Ipomoea
Morning-glory family
Convolvulaceae

Ip-po-mee′a. Morning Glory. About 500
species of mostly annual or perennial twining
vines, many of tropical origin, and a few of
much garden importance.

Description
Vines often milky-juiced, the perennials
frequently with enormous roots. Leaves
alternate, generally stalked, simple, or
compound and with several leaflets. Flowers
large, showy, usually solitary or a few in leaf
axils. Calyx lobed or parted. Corolla chiefly
funnel-shaped. Blooms in summer or early
autumn.

How to Grow
Needs well-drained soil of moderate fertility
and a warm, sunny location. Propagate by
seeds. To hasten germination, notch the hard
seeds with a file or soak in tepid water for 8
hours before sowing. The species below are
especially useful for quick cover and color on
trellises, fences, or porches.

alba p. 251
Moon-Flower. Milky-juiced tender perennial
with somewhat prickly stems, to 8 ft.
(2.4 m) high. Leaves large, broadly oval,
sometimes 3-lobed. Flowers white,
sometimes green-banded, fragrant, 5–6 in.
(12.5–15.0 cm) wide, opening in the
evening. Occasionally listed as *Calonyction*

aculeatum. Grown as an annual to the north.
Zone 9.

× *multifida* p. 230
Cardinal Climber. Tender annual, 8–10 ft.
(2.4–3.0 m) high. Leaves fine, in threadlike
segments. Flowers to 2 in. (5 cm) long,
corolla crimson or scarlet, with white to
cream-colored eye. Annual.

quamoclit p. 231
Cypress Vine. To 20 ft. (6 m) high. Foliage
fernlike. Flowers scarlet, funnel-shaped,
5-lobed, to 1½ in. (4 cm) long. Naturalized
in the South and planted in Calif. Also sold
as *Quamoclit pennata.* Zone 8.

tricolor p. 242
Morning Glory. To 10 ft. (3 m) high.
Leaves large, heart-shaped. Flowers purplish
blue, 4–5 in. (10.0–12.5 cm) long, corolla
with white tube and red tip before opening.
Cultivars with white, lavender, or blue
flowers. Will tolerate poor, dry soil. Tender
perennial grown as a tender annual.
Zone 8.

Jasminum
Olive family
Oleaceae

Jas'mi-num. Jasmine; jessamine. 200 species
of chiefly tropical and subtropical shrubs or
vines found in Eurasia and Africa, one in the
New World. They are widely cultivated for
their attractive, fragrant flowers.

Description
Climbing or spreading shrubs. Leaves
compound, opposite or alternate, sometimes
with only 1 leaflet; stems angled, often
green. Flowers about 1 in. (2.5 cm) wide, in
many-flowered clusters, yellow, pink, or
white in cultivated species. Calyx bell-shaped.
Corolla tubular, with 4–9 spreading lobes.
Fruit a small berry.

How to Grow
Jasmines prefer sun and loamy soil.
Propagate by layers and cuttings of nearly
ripe wood.

polyanthum p. 234
Pink Jasmine. Deciduous or evergreen
scrambling shrub to 20 ft. (6 m) high.

Flowers pink outside, white inside, fragrant,
in axillary panicles in spring and summer.
Similar to *J. officinale,* the common white
jasmine, but less hardy. In greenhouse
or outdoors, secure it to its support.
Zone 9.

Kadsura
Schizandra family
Schizandraceae

Kad-soor'a. A small genus of woody
climbers, mostly from tropical Asia. Only
the species below is hardy.

Description
Leaves oblong or lance-shaped. Flowers
inconspicuous. Striking scarlet fruits in fall.

How to Grow
Prefers a sunny position and evenly moist,
loamy soil. Propagate by cuttings. Can be
trained on a pillar, fence, or trellis or grown
in containers if supported.

japonica p. 214

Scarlet Kadsura. To 15 ft. (4.5 m) high or
more. Leaves handsome, alternate, thick,
toothed, 2–4 in. (5–10 cm) long. Flowers
tiny, yellow-white, dioecious, usually borne
singly in leaf axils, in summer. Fruit
clustered, scarlet, showy. Evergreen in the
South but loses its leaves in northern
winters. Zone 7.

Lathyrus
Pea family
Leguminosae

La'thi-russ. An important group of over 100
species, chiefly from the north temperate
zone, several widely grown for ornament.

Description
Most cultivated species tendril-bearing,
vinelike, with winged or angled stems.
Leaves alternate, compound, leaflets usually
few. Flowers typically pealike, often showy.
Fruit a flattish pod.

How to Grow
Grow in full sun in any well-drained soil.
Pick flowers to encourage extended bloom

and prevent seed-pod formation. Sweet peas perform best in cool weather and benefit from mulching. Propagate annual sorts by seeds sown indoors or on site in early spring, or in autumn in mildest climates. Increase perennial kinds, by spring-sown seeds or division.

latifolius p. 237
Perennial Sweet Pea; Everlasting Pea. Tendril-climbing, to 10 ft. (3 m) or more. Flowers several in long-stalked cluster, rose-pink, red, or white, 1–1½ in. (2.5–4.0 cm) wide. Can become a nuisance. Use as a bank cover or let clamber over shrubs. Zone 5.

odoratus p. 236

Sweet Pea. Vinelike annual, 4–6 ft. (1.2–1.8 m) high. Leaflets gray-green. Flowers fragrant, 3–5 (rarely 7), 2 in. (5 cm) wide, in clusters; many colors now cultivated, perhaps originally only purple. Pod 2 in. (5 cm) long, hairy. Keep evenly moist and provide support for vining types. Afternoon shade in hot climates extends flowering time. Cultivars include nonclimbing dwarfs and heat-resistant varieties. Annual.

Lonicera
Honeysuckle family
Caprifoliaceae

Lon-iss´er-ra. Honeysuckle. About 180 species of shrubs and woody climbers found throughout the northern hemisphere.

Description
Leaves opposite, usually entire, sometimes evergreen. Flowers showy, abundant, tubular or bell-shaped, sometimes sweetly scented, 5-lobed or (more often) 2-lipped, borne in pairs in leaf axils or in clusters at ends of branches. Fruit an ornamental, fleshy berry, white, yellow, orange, red, blue, or black.

How to Grow
Easy to grow. Loamy, reasonably moist soil is best. Propagate by seeds, cuttings of ripe wood, or layers.

× *heckrottii* p. 232
Goldflame Honeysuckle. Attractive shrub to 12 ft. (3.5 m) high, with spreading,

sometimes twining branches. Leaves oblong or oval, 1–2½ in. (2.5–6.0 cm) long, whitish beneath, blue-green above. Flowers 1½ in. (4 cm) long, in terminal clusters, purple outside, yellow within, tube slender. Long-blooming, in late spring and summer. Zone 4.

japonica p. 224

Japanese Honeysuckle. Vigorous, half-evergreen climber 20–30 ft. (6–9 m) high, with slender, hairy branches. Leaves ovate to oblong, 1–3 in. (2.5–7.5 cm) long, pointed, usually downy on undersides. Flowers white tinged with purple, fading to yellow, sweetly scented, 1–1½ in. (2.5–4.0 cm) long, blooming in late spring. Fruit black. Can become a nuisance in e. U.S.; less rampant northward, but prune hard if necessary. The cultivar 'Halliana' (Hall's Honeysuckle) has white flowers that fade to yellow and are not tinged purple. A useful bank or fence cover when controlled. Drought-tolerant. Zone 5.

periclymenum p. 233

Woodbine. Woody climber to 15 ft. (4.5 m) high. Leaves ovate to oblong, bluish green on undersides, upper pairs almost stalkless but not fused. Flowers in clusters, yellowish white, often tinged red, fragrant, 2 in. (5 cm) long, blooming in summer. Fruit red, appearing in early fall. Var. *belgica* has flowers with purple outside. Equally hardy is *L. henryi* (Henry Honeysuckle), with purple-red flowers in summer and black fruit. Zone 5.

sempervirens pp. 225, 233

Trumpet Honeysuckle; Coral Honeysuckle. Climbing vine to 50 ft. (15 m) high. Evergreen in mild climates. Leaves oval to oblong, bluish green beneath, slightly downy, upper pairs united to form a disk. Flowers in terminal clusters, bright orange or red outside, yellow within, 2 in. (5 cm) long, corolla lobes of almost equal length; late spring through summer. Fruit orange to scarlet. Not fragrant, but attracts hummingbirds. 'Sulphurea' is a choice cultivar with clear yellow flowers. Zone 4.

Mandevilla
Dogbane family
Apocynaceae

Man-de-vil′la. About 100 species of tropical
American woody vines, a few cultivated in
the greenhouse or outdoors in mild
climates.

Description
Leaves opposite, without marginal teeth,
milky-juiced. Flowers large, showy, in
few-flowered racemes. Corolla funnel-shaped,
slightly twisted, stamens 5. Fruit a pair of
follicles.

How to Grow
Requires rich soil, full sun, and ample water
when in active growth. Propagate from
cuttings.

'Alice du Pont' *p. 236*
Woody, twining evergreen vine to 20 ft.
(6 m) high, less when grown in pots. Leaves
glossy, oval. Flowers pink, flared, trumpet-
shaped, 2–4 in. (5–10 cm) wide, spring
through autumn. Often a greenhouse plant;
good in tubs or hanging baskets. Pinch off
tips of new stems to induce dense growth.
Zone 10.

laxa p. *247*
Chilean Jasmine (but native to Argentina).
Climbing woody vine to 15 ft. (4.5 m) high.
Leaves opposite, oblong or heart-shaped,
1–3 in. (2.5–7.5 cm) long, pale bluish green
beneath. Flowers fragrant, showy, white,
funnel-shaped, to 2 in. (5 cm) wide, mostly
in loose racemes. Widely grown outdoors in
mild climates, and in warm greenhouses
elsewhere. Cut to the ground in late winter
if it gets overgrown. Often listed as
M. suaveolens. Zone 8.

Menispermum
Moonseed family
Menispermaceae

Men-i-spur′mum. Moonseed. Only 2 species
of twining, woody vines with attractive
foliage, from North America and Asia.

Description
Leaves alternate, shield-shaped, 3- to 7-lobed.
Flowers small, white or yellow, in terminal

racemes or compound terminal panicles.
Fruit berrylike.

How to Grow
Grows best in partial shade and average soil.
Easy to grow from seeds or cuttings of
ripened wood. Only female plants produce
fruit.

canadense p. 219
Moonseed; Yellow Parilla. Herbaceous vine
climbing to 12 ft. (3.5 m) high. Leaves
round-oval, 4–8 in. (10–20 cm) long, not
toothed, sometimes lobed, soft-hairy beneath
when young. Flowers small, white, dioecious,
blooming in late spring. Fruit black,
resembling grapes. Spreads by underground
stems and can become invasive. Suitable for
ground cover. Zone 5.

Muehlenbeckia
Rhubarb family
Polygonaceae

Mew-len-beck'i-a. Somewhat woody, vinelike
plants, the 20 known species all from the
south temperate zone.

Description
Stems wirelike, usually greenish. Leaves
alternate, small, with sheathing stipules.
Flowers small, inconspicuous, in clusters in
leaf axils. Fruit an achene.

How to Grow
Grows well in ordinary soil in sun or light
shade. Propagate by summer cuttings or
seed, if available. In the greenhouse they
need cool, dry conditions. Rarely cultivated
except for the species below, which is
occasionally used for hanging baskets.

complexa p. 212
Wire-Vine; Maidenhair-Vine. Twining,
dark-stemmed vine to 20 ft. (6 m) high.
Stems wirelike, forming a dense mat if not
supported. Leaves nearly circular, or fiddle-
shaped. Flowers greenish, inconspicuous,
dioecious. Often planted in Calif.; good for
covering rocks and old stumps. Zone 6.

Parthenocissus
Grape family
Vitaceae

Par-then-o-sis'sus. Woody climbers from e.
Asia and North America, grown chiefly for
their foliage, some brilliantly colored in
autumn. Sometimes called *Psedera*.

Description
Tendrils disk-tipped. Leaves alternate, leaflets
3–5. Flowers small, inconspicuous, in clusters
opposite the leaves. Fruit small, dark blue or
almost black.

How to Grow
Not particular about soil, but grows more
vigorously in fairly moist loam in sun or
light shade. Propagate by seeds, cuttings,
or layers.

henryana p. 220
Silver-vein Creeper. To 20 ft. (6 m) high.
Leaflets 1½–3 in. (4.0–7.5 cm) long,
narrowly ovate, sometimes broader, toothed
toward tip, velvety or bronze above with
silvery markings, reddish beneath. Red
autumn color. Flowers in summer. Fruit
blue. Foliage highly ornamental, with best
color developed in lightly shady locations.
Zone 8.

quinquefolia p. 221
Virginia Creeper; Woodbine; American Ivy.
Vigorous, to 50 ft. (15 m) high. Leaflets 5,
elliptic to oblong, 2–5 in. (5.0–12.5 cm)
long, pointed, toothed. Flowers in summer.
Fruit blue-black, glaucous. Leaves scarlet in
autumn. Not dense but suitable for a fence,
wall, or trellis, or as ground cover. Zone 4.

tricuspidata p. 219
Boston Ivy; Japanese Ivy. Climbs to 60 ft.
(18 m) high and clings firmly. Leaves either
of 3 leaflets or simple and 3-lobed, to 10 in.
(25 cm) long, usually shiny on both sides.
Flowers in summer. Fruit blue-black,
glaucous. Foliage brilliant scarlet in autumn.
Outstanding wall cover, the leaves
overlapping like shingles. Formerly known as
Ampelopsis tricuspidata. Cultivar 'Veitchii' has
smaller leaves that are purple when young.
Zone 5.

Passiflora
Passion-flower family
Passifloraceae

Pass-i-flow′ra. Passion-flower. Tendril-
climbing vines, most of the 400 species
natives of the New World, several cultivated
for ornament.

Description
Leaves alternate, stalked, lobed or undivided.
Flowers often showy, regular, the 3–5 sepals
often petal-like, sometimes tubular. Petals
3–5, sometimes none. Within the flower is a
usually fringed corona composed of many
free filaments; corona is sometimes tubular
and fringed at the top.

How to Grow
Passion-flowers grow best in light, evenly
moist soil and full sun. Increase by cuttings
of ripe wood. May die to the ground in
winter, but will resprout if roots live. Useful
for a fence or trellis, or rambling over
shrubs. Also suited to greenhouse pot
culture.

caerulea p. 238
Blue Passion-Flower. To 20 ft. (6 m) high.
Leaves 5-lobed, the lobes narrow. Flowers in
summer, to 4 in. (10 cm) wide, fragrant,
white or pinkish, the corona white and
purple. Fruit 1½ in. (4 cm) long, yellow.
Some hybrids have even larger flowers.
Zone 8.

incarnata p. 239
Maypop; Wild Passion-Flower. To 20 ft.
(6 cm) high. Hardiest of the cultivated
species, but less showy. Leaves 3-lobed, the
lobes toothed. Flowers 2 in. (5 cm) wide,
white, the corona purplish pink, in summer.
Fruit edible, yellow, 2 in. (5 cm) long. Can
be grown from seed. Zone 7.

Plumbago
Plumbago family
Plumbaginaceae

Plum-bay′go. Leadwort. About 20 species of
mostly perennial subshrubs or herbs,
sometimes climbing or trailing, and natives
of s. Europe, Africa, Asia, and tropical
America.

Description
Stems slender. Leaves alternate, simple, broadly lance-shaped. Flowers in terminal spikes or clusters; blue, white, or red. Individual flower has calyx of 5 sepals, sometimes colored. Corolla long, narrow, tubular, with 5 lobes that open saucerlike.

How to Grow
Grows in any well-drained soil in light or part-day shade; tolerates full sun. An attractive cover for fence or trellis outdoors in zones 9 and 10. Tie plants to a support. Propagate by seeds in spring or by cuttings of side shoots taken in summer. They make excellent pot plants in a cool greenhouse and can be moved to the garden in summer. Allow pot-grown plants to become partially dry in late winter.

auriculata p. 249
Cape Plumbago. Tender, spreading shrub, to 10 ft. high (3 m) or more if supported. Leaves alternate, lance-shaped, smooth, thin, 2–3 in. (5.0–7.5 cm) long. Flowers in terminal clusters, white or azure-blue. Corolla tubular, narrow, to 1½ in. (4 cm) long, petals spreading saucerlike. Will flower spring through autumn if pruned hard at end of previous winter. 'Alba' is a white form. Sometimes listed as *P. capensis.* Zone 9.

Polygonum
Knotweed family
Polygonaceae

Pol-lig'o-num. Smartweed; Knotweed. About 150 species of erect, trailing, or climbing annual or perennial herbs, the climbing species sometimes woody. They are found throughout the world.

Description
Stems angled, swollen at joints where leaf base clasps stem, sometimes spotted or streaked brown. Leaves alternate and simple. Flowers small, in terminal spikes or loose racemes. Sepals 5, pink or white. Stamens 3–9. Fruit dry, triangular.

How to Grow
Easy to grow in average soil in sun. A few species are cultivated for foliage and flowers,

but some are too aggressive for the garden. Propagate the species below from seeds sown in a cool greenhouse or cold frame in early spring; by rootstock division; or by ripe wood cuttings.

aubertii p. 244

Silver-Lace Vine; Fleece-Vine. Hardy, twining, woody perennial with slender stems, to 25 ft. (7.5 m) high. Leaves to 2½ in. (6 cm) long, broadly lance-shaped. Flowers greenish white, airy, fragrant, in long, erect or drooping clusters in leaf axils near top of plant, in late summer. Control vigorous growth by pruning severely in late winter. Zone 5.

Rosa
Rose family
Rosaceae

Ro′za. Rose. About 200 species of shrubs or vines, comprising all the true roses.

Description
Prickly shrubs or vines with alternate, compound leaves, the leaflets arranged feather-fashion, always with an odd one at the end. Prickles hooked or straight. Flowers solitary or in small clusters, with 5 petals in wild, single roses, much doubled in most horticultural forms. The species below all have single flowers. Stamens numerous; pistils numerous, enclosed in a cup-shaped receptacle that becomes fleshy and berrylike (the rose hip).

How to Grow
Roses grow well in fertile, well-drained soil free of tree roots and need at least 6 hours of sunlight daily. Most species roses require no special care and seem to have fewer insect problems than many modern roses, though they can be bothered by aphids, mites, and Japanese beetles. Black spot, powdery mildew, and canker are common diseases. Species roses are good for borders or for naturalizing. When secured, the long canes of some species suit them for fences and trellises. Others left unsupported make good ground covers.

banksiae pp. 252, 253
Lady Banks' Rose; Banksia Rose. Climbing, evergreen, 15–30 ft. (4.5–9.0 m) high, with

a few hooked prickles or none. Leaflets
3–5 (rarely, 7), elliptic-oval, 1–2½ in.
(2.5–6.0 cm) long. Flowers profuse, slightly
fragrant, white or yellow,1–2 in.
(2.5–5.0 cm) wide, in summer. Long,
vigorous canes make this rose outstanding
for fences, arbors, or cascading from trees.
Disease-resistant. Zone 7.

Climbing cultivars *p. 239*
Climbing roses have long, sturdy canes; they
do not actually climb, but can be used as
vines if secured to supports. Several
categories exist; large-flowered kinds are
most popular. Most have flowers 3–4 in.
(7.5–10.0 cm) wide on canes 8–10 ft.
(2.4–3.0 m) high. Best flowering occurs
when canes are supported horizontally. Listed
here are a few good choices for the average-
size garden: 'America' grows upright and has
fragrant, coral-salmon flowers in midseason.
'Blaze' has semidouble, medium red flowers
in midsummer with good repeat flowering.
'Don Juan' has fragrant, double, dark red
flowers, profuse in midsummer with good
repeat bloom, and unlike most climbers bears
flowers well all along canes when supported
vertically. Good pillar or trellis rose, but not
dependably winter-hardy in cold climates.
'New Dawn' has pale pink, semidouble
flowers in midsummer with good repeats.
All zone 6.

laevigata p. 253

Cherokee Rose. Almost evergreen, widely
naturalized in the South. To 15 ft. (4.5 m)
high, with scattered hooked prickles.
Leaflets 3 (rarely, 5), elliptic-oval, 2–3 in.
(5.0–7.5 cm) long, shining. Flowers solitary,
to 3½ in. (9 cm) wide, white, fragrant.
Hips bristly, red, decorative. Disease-
resistant. The parent of the hardier, very
popular climber 'Silver Moon'. Zone 7.

wichuraiana p. 252
Memorial Rose. Prostrate or trailing,
half-evergreen, to 20 ft. (6 m) high, the
strong prickles hooked. Leaflets 7–9,
roundish, blunt, shining, ¾–1 in.
(2.0–2.5 cm) long. Flowers nearly 2 in.
(5 cm) wide, white, fragrant, mostly in
corymbs, midsummer to fall. Disease-
resistant. Its sprawling, stem-rooting habit
makes it a good ground cover. Cultivars
useful for covering walls and banks include
'Dorothy Perkins', 'Dr. Walter Van Fleet',

'May Queen', and Kordesii hybrids
(*R. wichuraiana* × *R. rugosa*). Zone 6.

Schizophragma
Saxifrage family
Saxifragaceae

Sky-zo-frag'ma. Asiatic woody vines related
to *Hydrangea* and *Decumaria*.

Description
Differs from *Hydrangea* in having only a
single enlarged sepal in the sterile flowers.

How to Grow
Grows well in average soil, but benefits from
supplementary fertilizer and water if planted
at base of a large tree. Needs at least a half
day of sun for good flowering. Propagate by
seeds, layers, or cuttings in late summer.
Effective on a low wall, or climbing a tree
from which the lower branches have been
removed.

hydrangeoides p. 247
Japanese Hydrangea Vine. Climbing, clinging
vine to 30 ft. (9 m) high. Leaves opposite,
nearly round, 3–4 in. (7.5–10.0 cm) wide,
pale on underside, toothed. Flowers white,
in loose, terminal, flat-topped corymbs, in
summer. Central flowers fertile, small. Outer
marginal flowers showy, sterile. Climbs
by aerial rootlets, but needs support.
Zone 5.

Stephanotis
Milkweed family
Asclepiadaceae

Steff-a-no'tis. About 15 species of twining
woody vines, native from Madagascar to the
Malay Archipelago, only the species below in
general cultivation. Excellent greenhouse
climber.

Description
Leaves opposite, thick, leathery. Flowers
showy, large, white, in umbel-like clusters
in leaf axils. Corolla 5-lobed, opening
salvar-wise, tube swollen at base and
sometimes at throat. Crown formed by
stamens attached to tube.

How to Grow
Grows best in fertile, well-drained, moist
soil, outdoors only in zones 9–10. Propagate
by cuttings from half-ripened shoots.
Requires filtered or half-day sun and some
shade over roots; apply mulch or overplant
with a shallow-rooted ground cover. Keep
drier in winter.

floribunda p. 248
Madagascar Jasmine; Wax Flower. Stems
twining, to 15 ft. (4.5 m) high. Leaves
ovalish, to 4 in. (10 cm) long, evergreen.
Flowers waxy-white, fragrant, in summer
outdoors, longer in greenhouse if allowed to
rest periodically. Zone 9.

Tecomaria
Trumpet-vine family
Bignoniaceae

Teck-o-mair′i-a. A small genus of African
woody vines or scrambling shrubs.

Description
Leaves opposite or whorled, divided
feather-fashion. Flowers yellow, orange, or
red, funnel-shaped, the tube curved.

How to Grow
Adaptable to most growing conditions
except deep shade, as long as soil is well
drained. Tolerates drought and salt air. Good
cover for hot, dry banks or for a wire fence,
if secured. Increase by cuttings or seeds.

capensis p. 229
Cape Honeysuckle. Handsome evergreen, to
20 ft. (6 m) high as a supported vine or to
6 ft. (1.8 m) high as a scrambling shrub
when pruned. Leaves opposite, compound,
the 7–9 leaflets toothed, ovalish. Flowers
orange-red or scarlet, in showy, terminal,
stalked racemes, blooming most of the year.
Corolla slightly irregular, 2 in. (5 cm) long.
There is a smaller, yellow-flowered form.
Zone 9.

Thunbergia
Acanthus family
Acanthaceae

Thune-ber'ji-a. About 100 species of tender
woody or herbaceous vines or shrubs, mostly
Asiatic or African, the species below grown
for ornament.

Description
Leaves opposite, often arrow-shaped at base.
Flowers showy, solitary in leaf axils, below
them 2 or more leafy bracts. Corolla funnel-
or bell-shaped, sometimes curved.

How to Grow
Prefers warm weather and grows best in
average soil in sun. In mild-winter areas, sow
seeds in garden in early spring. Elsewhere,
start indoors 6–8 weeks before last frost. Set
out hardened-off seedlings when soil is
warm. Provide support. Vigorous, covering a
trellis or porch in a short time; also suitable
for hanging baskets.

alata p. 227
Black-eyed Susan Vine. Twining, to 6 ft.
(1.8 m) high. Flowers long-stalked, 1–2 in.
(2.5–5.0 cm) wide, usually orange-yellow,
with purple throat, but white or creamy
yellow forms are available. Perennial grown
as a tender annual.

Trachelospermum
Dogbane family
Apocynaceae

Tra-kell-o-sper'mum. 20 species of Indo-
Malayan or Chinese woody vines, most with
showy flowers, the species below grown for
ornament.

Description
Leaves opposite, short-stalked. Flowers small,
in loose clusters, the corolla usually white,
salver-shaped.

How to Grow
Grows in a variety of soils with average
watering, but slow to establish. Give
some shade in hot areas. Provide support
beginning at planting time and train it on a
post, wall, or trellis. Prune older plants

occasionally to prevent excess woodiness.
Can also be grown as a ground cover if
growing tips are occasionally pinched out to
encourage branching. Propagate by layers or
summer cuttings. Allow milky sap in stems
to dry before rooting cuttings.

jasminoides p. 248

Star Jasmine; Confederate Jasmine. Twining,
to 30 ft. (9 m) high or more. Slow-growing.
Leaves evergreen, ovalish, narrowed at both
ends, 2–4 in. (5–10 cm) long. Flowers white,
starlike, resembling a pinwheel, to 1 in.
(2.5 cm) wide, sweetly fragrant, in sparse,
long-stalked cymes. A favorite throughout
the South and Calif. Zone 9.

Tropaeolum
Nasturtium family
Tropaeolaceae

Tro-pee'o-lum. About 65 species of mostly
climbing annual or perennial soft-stemmed
herbs, native to cooler parts of South
America.

Description
Leaves alternate, round, light green, with
strongly marked veins radiating from center,
where stalk arises. Leafstalk fleshy, sensitive,
curling around any object it touches. Flowers
showy, solitary, in leaf axils, fragrant. Sepals
5, joined at base, 3 prolonged into a spur at
back of flower. Petals usually 5, broad,
narrowing at base.

How to Grow
Best in full sun and dry soil. Easy to grow
from seeds or cuttings taken in fall. Sow
seeds in garden 2 weeks before last frost. Or
sow indoors in peat pots early and transplant
when danger of frost is past. Soil should not
be too rich or plants will produce lots of
foliage and few flowers. Requires relatively
cool temperatures; does not do well in the
se. U.S. during summer.

majus p. 226
Nasturtium; Indian Cress. Tender annual
climbing 8–12 ft. (2.4–3.5 m) high. Flowers
2½ in. (6 cm) wide, yellow or orange
(sometimes striped and spotted with red),
scarlet, or mahogany. Newer, compact
varieties hold blossoms well above foliage.

Excellent for trellises, posts, rocks, and
hanging baskets. Annual.

peregrinum p. 225
Canary-Bird Vine; Canary Creeper. Tender
annual, climbing to 8 ft. (2.4 m) high.
Leaves deeply lobed, gray-green. Flowers
bright yellow, upper petals fringed, giving
the effect of a small bird. Prefers light shade
and some moisture. Annual.

Vitis
Grape family
Vitaceae

Vy'tis. Grape. About 60 species of woody
vines from the north temperate zone,
climbing by tendrils, the species below
grown for ornament rather than fruit.

Description
Bark usually shreddy, tendrils forked. Leaves
alternate, often lobed finger-fashion, always
toothed. Flowers small, greenish, unisexual
or polygamous, sometimes dioecious; in
small clusters mostly opposite the leaves.
Calyx entire or with small teeth. Petals
separate or united and withering. Stamens 4
or 5, opposite the petals. Fruit the familiar
grape, 2- to 4-seeded.

How to Grow
Grapevines tolerate a variety of growing
conditions but prefer well-drained, fertile soil
in sun or light shade. The species below is
vigorous and should be pruned to desired
size and shape. Propagate by seeds, or by
summer or dormant wood cuttings.

coignetiae p. 218
Crimson Glory Vine. Strong-growing, to
50 ft. (15 m) high. Leaves roundish or
ovalish, 4–12 in. (10–30 cm) wide, deeply
heart-shaped at base, grayish or rusty
beneath. Flower panicle short, blooming in
summer. Fruit glaucous, purplish black,
inedible. Cultivated mostly for foliage, which
turns bright crimson in fall. Attractive on a
trellis or fence, or cascading from a tree.
Zone 5.

Wisteria
Pea family
Leguminosae

Wis-tair'i-a. Wisteria: Beautiful woody vines,
2 species native in the U.S., the other 5
Asiatic, widely grown for their profuse bloom.

Description
Leaves alternate, compound, the leaflets
arranged feather-fashion, with an odd one at
the end, the leaflets also alternate. Flowers
pealike, in showy, drooping racemes. Fruit a
stalked, flattened pod.

How to Grow
Grows best in fertile, well-drained soil.
Tolerates some shade, but flowers best in full
sun. Slow to become established, so provide
extra fertilizer and water when young; older
plants flower better without supplements.
May be trained as a single-stem or multi-
stem vine over a porch, trellis, or dead tree.
May also be grown as a small weeping tree
or as ground cover. Wisterias require several
years to reach blooming stage. Mature plants
can be encouraged to set buds by proper
pruning techniques. Discourage excessive
vegetative growth by pruning roots and
fertilizing with superphosphate to promote
flowering. Propagate by layers or late
summer cuttings. Grafted plants are
available; remove understock suckers.

floribunda p. 242
Japanese Wisteria. To 30 ft. (9 m) high.
Leaflets 13–19, ovalish or oblong, 2–3 in.
(5.0–7.5 cm) long. Flowers violet-blue or
violet, in spring, the cluster nearly 18 in.
(45 cm) long. Selections have been made for
white or pink flowers or for length of flower
clusters. Zone 5.

sinensis pp. 243, 244
Chinese Wisteria. Climbing to 40 ft. (12 m)
high. Leaflets 7–13 (mostly 11), ovalish or
oblong, 2–4 in. (5–10 cm) long. Flowers
bluish violet, fragrant, the cluster 12 in.
(30 cm) long, in spring. Pods densely
velvety. 'Alba' is a white-flowered form.
Zone 5, but not as hardy as *W. floribunda*.

venusta p. 245
Silky Wisteria. To 30 ft. (9 m) high.
Leaflets 9–13, to 4 in. (10 cm) long, hairy,
lance-shaped. Flowers lavender or whitish, in
profuse clusters to 6 in. (15 cm) long. Zone 5.

Grasses

Ornamental grasses are frequently overlooked as garden subjects. Long acclaimed in Europe and the Orient, grasses are just beginning to gain popularity in the United States, where American gardeners are discovering that these plants have unmatched beauty and grace.

Size, Color, and Flowers

Grasses are extremely diverse in size and form, ranging from low-growing tufted mounds, such as Sheep's Fescue, to giants with names like 'Skyracer' that grow taller than a man can reach.

Grasses come in a variety of subtle hues, from the blue-green of Blue Fescue to the bright yellow of Bowles' Golden Grass. Add to that the variegated foliage of some grasses, the bronzy-red autumn tints of others, and the subtle buffs and tans of some species in winter, and the result is a full palette of color offering long-term interest and diversity to the garden.

The flowers of many grasses are attractive too; a number of grasses, such as *Eragrostis,* are grown chiefly for their ornamental blooms, which may be cut for fresh or dried arrangements. If a grass has beautiful flowers but lacks a pleasing form, plant it in a cutting garden or in a spot where more attractive neighboring plants will obscure its base.

Grasses in the Landscape: Borders and Screens

Perennial ornamental grasses have many of the same landscape uses as shrubs. In mixed borders, for example, choices depend on a plant's mature height and basic form—narrow-upright, arching, mounding, or irregular. Tall grasses that tend to lose their lower leaves belong in the background, while small, mounding forms are appropriate for edging the border.

Many tall grasses grow so fast that they are ideal for screening purposes. Within a short time they will be high enough to create a visual barrier that ensures privacy or hides undesirable views.

Specimen Plantings

Grasses with outstanding form, foliage, or flowers deserve a prominent place in the garden and are often shown to best advantage when planted as specimens, either along or with other unusual grasses. Some, like Pampas Grass, are best used as accents because their large size and distinctiveness overwhelm other plants. For accent planting, use grasses that are attractive in the garden for at least six months of the year. Place grasses that are interesting during winter near the house, where they can be seen and enjoyed from indoors.

Naturalized Plantings

Ornamental grasses are a natural in now-popular meadow gardens. They also look at home in the informal transition zones between gardens and woods and are good wildlife cover. Grasses that tolerate moist soil are especially appropriate when incorporated in naturalized settings near ponds and streams.

Woody-stemmed Grasses and Grasslike Herbs

The woody-stemmed grasses—the bamboos and their relatives—constitute a diverse subfamily or tribe within the grass family. (Confusion over the botanical classification of bamboos is reflected in the scientific names of these plants. To simplify matters, we have applied the names currently used by the American Bamboo Society to the listings in this book wherever possible.)

In the tropics, bamboos grow in majestic stands impossible to reproduce in the temperate United States, although you can achieve similar effects on a reduced scale. Bamboos are not winter-hardy in colder climates, so growing them outdoors is mostly confined to zone 8 and southward; a few exceptions survive to zone 6. In warm regions that support bamboos, some gardeners achieve a pretty effect with *Phormium,* a grasslike herb that is actually a member of the agave family.

No other garden plants can duplicate the beautiful effects bamboos create: They may be arching or upright, with striped, spotted, or even "snakeskin" stems. Their leaves range from slender to very broad, and some smaller species have striking, variegated foliage patterns.

Using Bamboos

The bamboos most often grown in American gardens are medium-size plants 10–50 ft. (3–15 m) high. They can be used as screens and hedges or alone as accent plants. Mostly evergreen, they provide winter interest even when the leaves are damaged by cold. Small-growing bamboos can be used as ground covers and look best if cut to the ground in late winter; the new foliage that appears will be fresh and green. Small and medium-size bamboos are also good as pot plants and can be grown successfully in a cool greenhouse.

Controlling Growth

The invasive tendencies of many grasses and bamboos can cause problems in small spaces unless you restrict their growth with a physical barrier. Buildings, paving, or bodies of water are effective restraints, or you can sink metal or concrete enclosures into the ground to curb the plants' exuberance.

The plant accounts that follow offer a wide array of ornamental grasses and grasslike plants to choose from, no matter what climate you live in.

Acorus
Arum family
Araceae

Ak'or-us. Marsh herbs, hardy all over
the U.S.

Description
Leaves long, parallel-sided, thickish but
grasslike, growing from a thick, stout
rootstock. Flowers greenish, minute, on a
stalkless spadix that arises from a leaflike
sheath near end of stalk. Fruit berrylike,
stalkless.

How to Grow
Suitable for bogs, watersides, or marshes.
Easy to grow in moist or wet soil in
sun or light shade. Propagate by dividing
the creeping rootstock in almost any
season.

gramineus p. 274
Japanese Sweet Flag. Tufted herb, the leaves
to 12 in. (30 cm) high. Blooms in summer.
Not a member of the Grass family
(Gramineae), but usually sold and used as
an ornamental grass because of its fine leaf
texture. 'Variegatus' has a creamy stripe
down the leaf and is more widely grown
than the species. Zone 6.

Alopecurus
Grass family
Gramineae

A-low-pee-cure'us. 40 species of meadow
grasses, mostly from the cooler parts of the
north temperate zone.

Description
Medium-size grasses of upright, open habit
with slowly creeping rhizomes. Leaf blades
flat. Panicles dense, spikelike.

How to Grow
Prefers fertile, moist soil in full sun or light
shade. Increase by division. Suitable for
meadow gardens or as ground cover.

pratensis p. 275
Meadow Foxtail. Perennial, the stem
unbranched and growing erect, to 2 ft.
(60 cm) high. Leaves to 6 in. (15 cm) long,
slightly roughish. Spike buff-colored, dense,

1–3 in. (2.5–7.5 cm) long, usually standing above leaves, blooming in spring. 'Aureovariegatus' (Yellow Meadow Foxtail) has leaves with broad gold margins; 'Aureus' has golden leaves and a green midrib. Both variegated forms are more widely cultivated than the species. Zone 5.

Arrhenatherum
Grass family
Gramineae

Ar-re-nath′er-rum. A genus of tall, oatlike perennial grasses of European origin.

Description
Stems tall, to 3½ ft. (105 cm) high. Leaves coarse, rough-edged. Flower cluster a narrow panicle.

How to Grow
Grows best in cool seasons, spring and fall, in any fertile soil in sun or light shade. Increase by division. Drought-tolerant once established.

elatius bulbosum p. 271
Bulbous Oat Grass. A curiosity, producing small bulbils at base of stems. Leaves narrow, 12 in. (30 cm) high, rough, growing from spreading culms. Flowering panicle 12 in. (30 cm) long, its numerous branches erect, purplish green. The species is invasive and seldom cultivated. 'Variegatum' has attractive white-striped leaves. Useful for edging or ground cover. Zone 5.

Arundinaria
Grass family
Gramineae

A-run-di-nay′ri-a. About 30 species of rhizomatous woody grasses (bamboos), mainly from e. and s. Asia.

Description
Canes round, smooth, erect, lacking internodal grooves. Leaves flat, short-stalked, forming persistent sheaths. Upper leaves longer, petioled, crowded, with grooved midrib and overlapping sheaths.

How to Grow

Most require well-drained but moist, fertile soil in sun or, preferably, light shade. Tall species benefit from wind protection. Propagate by dividing off a section of rhizome in early spring just as new growth begins. These aggressive spreaders should be restrained by stout barriers below ground.

pygmaea p. 282

Pygmy Bamboo. Canes to 12 in. (30 cm) high, bright green, round, becoming purplish toward the flattened tip. Nodes prominent, purple. Leaves narrow, to 5 in. (12.5 cm) long, sharp-pointed, bright green and hairy above, silvery green beneath. Extremely invasive. Useful in pots or for ground cover and erosion control. Mow in late winter to encourage density. Frequently offered as *Sasa pygmaea*. Zone 7.

viridistriata p. 283

Running bamboo to 6 ft. (1.8 m) high, usually less. Canes ¾ in. (19 mm) wide, new shoots creamy gold. Leaves narrow, to 8 in. (20 cm) long, tapering to a pointed tip, bright green with broad yellow-gold stripes. Gold coloration pronounced in full sun, muted in partial shade. Distinctive tub or patio plant. Cut to the ground in late autumn to improve following year's display. Zone 7.

Arundo
Grass family
Gramineae

A-run′doe. A genus of ornamental grasses from the Old World.

Description

Stems tall and woody. Leaves long, stiff, 2-ranked on the stems. Flowers grasslike, crowded into a large, silky, plumelike, striking panicle, seldom produced except southward.

How to Grow

Grows best in full sun in moist, well-drained soil. Propagate by division or, with the species, also from seeds.

donax pp. 256, 286

Giant Reed. Stout evergreen plant to 12 ft. (3.5 m) high. Leaves 1–2 ft. (30–60 cm)

long, 2½ in. (6 cm) wide. Flowers persistent into winter, the cluster spirelike. One of the tallest true grasses. 'Variegata' (Striped Giant Reed), a handsome cultivar to 8 ft. (2.4 m) high, has white-striped leaves and is somewhat less hardy. Both are invasive but effective alongside a stream or lawn. Cut old culms to the ground in late winter. Zone 7.

Bambusa
Grass family
Gramineae

Bam-boo′sa. The true bamboos constitute a large genus of often gigantic, woody, hollow-stemmed Old World grasses, grown for ornament and construction in the tropics.

Description
Rhizomes short; plants form dense clumps. Stems usually polished, hollow, interrupted by partitions at joints that conspicuously ring trunk. Leaves short-stalked, parallel- or netted-veined. Flowers (rare in cultivated specimens) in spikes bunched on panicles.

How to Grow
Grows best in rich, moist, well-drained soil that is not too acid. Choose a sunny or lightly shaded location. Propagate by division of clumps or by stem layering in spring.

glaucescens p. 285

Hedge Bamboo. Stems 3–20 ft. (0.9–6.0 m) high, to 1½ in. (4 cm) in diameter, with branches at each node down to ground level. Leaves narrow, lance-shaped, to 6 in. (15 cm) long. Less commonly cultivated than its lower-growing, fancy-leaf forms. Useful for hedges, accents, or tub culture. Various forms are hardy to zone 8.

Bouteloua
Grass family
Gramineae

Boo-tel-oo′ah. About 50 species of annual or perennial grasses from the cen. U.S. through South America.

Description
Clump-forming, leafy at base. Blades flat, smooth, curly at base. Spikes 2 to several. Flowers stalkless, in 2 rows along one side of stem, the florets hanging below the spikelets.

How to Grow
Grows best in light or even dry soil in full sun. Increase by spring division or seed.

gracilis p. 280
Mosquito Grass; Blue Grama. Fine-textured perennial grass of open, upright growth habit, to 2 ft. (60 cm) high. Leaves mostly basal, arching, to 5 in. (12.5 cm) long. Inflorescence a one-sided spike with numerous spikelets, resembling a miniature comb, to 2 in. (5 cm) long, purplish. Prominent on the Great Plains and attractive in a meadow garden. Zone 5.

Briza
Grass family
Gramineae

Bry′za. Slender annual or perennial grasses, cultivated for their graceful nodding, seed-bearing clusters.

Description
Spikelets resemble small, flattened hops, often nodding on their threadlike stalks, hence usually called quaking grass.

How to Grow
Grows best in poor soils in full sun. Increase by seed. Do not transplant annual species. Perennials are easy to propagate by division. The dried panicles are used for winter decoration.

maxima p. 281
Large Quaking Grass. 1–2 ft. (30–60 cm) high. Leaves narrow, 4–6 in. (10–15 cm) long. Flowers in a loose panicle with tiny spikelets, pale yellow or metallic with age. Coarser than *B. media*. Annual.

media p. 280
Quaking Grass. Perennial, 10–18 in. (25–45 cm) high. Leaves narrow, tufted near base. Flower panicle 5–10 in. (12.5–25.0 cm) long, branched, the tiny spikelets broadly

oval, purplish, aging to light beige, the stalks stiffish. Zone 5.

Calamagrostis
Grass family
Gramineae

Cal-a-mah-gros'tis. A genus of annual and deciduous perennial grasses of sporadic distribution in Europe and Africa.

Description
Strong-growing, clump-forming, upright grasses with creeping rhizomes and slender stems. Leaves rough to the touch. Inflorescence a lance-shaped panicle produced in summer.

How to Grow
Grows well in any fertile soil in full sun. Tolerates moist soil and is well suited for pondside plantings. Those listed below are grown mostly for their flowers and are also valuable for background plantings in mixed perennial borders. Propagate by division.

acutiflora stricta p. 261
Feather Reed Grass. To 5 ft. (1.5 m) high. Leaves dull green, to 2 ft. (60 cm) long, arching. Inflorescence a narrow panicle to 12 in. (30 cm) long, turning purplish, produced in early summer, the flowers persistent into winter. Performs well in heavy clay soil, which keeps it under control. Sometimes listed as *C. epigeios* 'Hortorum'. Zone 5.

arundinacea brachytricha p. 264
Feather Reed Grass. Slender deciduous perennial, slowly forming sizable clumps to 3 ft. (90 cm) high. Inflorescence a loose, oblong panicle produced in autumn, white or pale pink, turning brown. Flowers are attractive fresh or dried. Most effective in small groups. Zone 5.

Carex
Sedge family
Cyperaceae

Cay'rex. The sedges are an enormous genus of over 2000 species of grasslike plants, most grown for their ornamental foliage.

Description

Stems solid, 3-angled, lacking joints where leaf blades and leaf sheaths meet. Most are tufted, arching, and of low to medium height. Flowers minute, green, crowded in flattish, spikelike clusters atop slender, grasslike stalks.

How to Grow

The sedges below grow best in fertile, moist garden soil. Some thrive in full sun, others prefer partial shade. Increase by division. Species with long, hairlike leaves are improved by an early spring "combing" to remove dead leaves. Most are suitable for border edging or pondside planting.

buchananii p. 261

Leatherleaf Sedge. Densely tufted, evergreen, to 2 ft. (60 cm) high. Foliage fine-textured, coppery brown, with curled leaf tips. Suitable for water garden or mixed border. Prefers full sun. Zone 6.

conica 'Variegata' p. 270

Miniature Variegated Sedge. Tufted, to 6 in. (15 cm) high. Leaves dark green, silver-edged, to 12 in. (30 cm) long. Flowers yellow. A tidy, compact plant for the rock garden or border edging. Grow in sun or light shade. Zone 5.

grayi p. 269

Gray's Sedge; Morning Star Sedge. Tufted perennial, to 2 ft. (60 cm) high. Leaves narrow, to 18 in. (45 cm) long, bright green. Seed heads unusual, triangular, borne in summer and autumn. Prefers light shade. Zone 3.

morrowii 'Aureo-variegata' p. 275

Variegated Japanese Sedge. Mound-forming, to 12 in. (30 cm) high. Leaves flat, semi-evergreen, grasslike, with central yellow stripe. Basal sheaths around each cluster of leaves reddish brown. Flower-spikes on stalks about as long as the leaves. 'Variegata' has dark green leaves with white margins. Valuable for border edging or damp rock gardens. Zone 6.

pendula p. 268

Drooping Sedge. Mound-forming perennial to 2 ft. (60 cm) high, evergreen except at northern limits of hardiness. Leaves narrow, to 18 in. (45 cm) long, bright green, arching. Flower-spikes terminal, gray-green,

pendulous, on stalks well above foliage.
Graceful for specimen use or woodland
naturalizing. Zone 5.

Chasmanthium
Grass family
Gramineae

Kas-man'the-um. Spike grass. 5 species of
American perennial grasses.

Description
Strong-growing plant. Leaves grasslike,
clasping stem. Flower-spikes in flat, terminal,
loose-branching clusters.

How to Grow
Prefers moist, loamy soil and tolerates shade.
Propagate by division of roots in fall or early
spring, or occasionally by seeds. The species
below is grown for its showy ornamental
spikes, which can be cut and dried in late
summer.

latifolium p. 281
Northern Sea Oats; Wild Oats; Spangle
Grass. To 5 ft. (1.5 m) high. Leaves 9 in.
(22.5 cm) long, 1 in. (2.5 cm) wide.
Flower-spikes on slender, drooping stalks, the
clusters graceful, 8 in. (20 cm) long, in
summer, the flowers persisting. One of the
best native ornamental grasses. Frequently
listed as Uniola latifolia. Zone 5.

Coix
Grass family
Gramineae

Ko'icks. A small genus of leafy-stemmed
grasses of the Indo-Malayan region, one
grown in the Far East for its edible grain,
here for ornament or as a curiosity.

Description
Leaves coarse, stiffly upright. Flower cluster
terminal. Peculiar, ornamental, beadlike
structure develops from the female clusters.

How to Grow
Grown from seeds as an annual. Soak
seeds in water for 24 hours to increase
germination. Plant in moist soil in full sun
or light shade. Grows best in areas with

long, hot summers from zone 8 southward;
may not set fruit in areas with short
summers.

lacryma-jobi p. 285
Job's Tears. To 3 ft. (90 cm) high. Leaves
1–2 ft. (30–60 cm) long, ¾–1½ in.
(2–4 cm) wide, sword-shaped, with
prominent midrib. Beads ¾ in. (19 mm)
wide, very striking, hard, shiny, gray-black at
maturity. Annual.

Cortaderia
Grass family
Gramineae

Kor-ta-deer'i-a. Pampas Grass. 24 species of
tall, reedlike grasses confined to s. South
America and New Zealand.

Description
Clump formers, with leaves clustered at base
of stems. Inflorescence a large, plumelike
panicle.

How to Grow
Grows best in fertile, well-drained soil in full
sun, but will tolerate dryness. Propagate by
division of the woody roots. Plant where it
will not overwhelm smaller plantings.
Occasionally remove dead material by hand
from center of clump to improve appearance,
or cut plant to the ground in late winter;
handle razor-sharp leaf edges carefully.

selloana p. 263
Pampas Grass. Stems 8–12 ft. (2.4–3.5 m)
high. Leaves numerous, rough-margined,
long, narrow. Dioecious, only the female
producing the showy terminal cluster of
graceful, feathery plumed spikes; spikes
1–3 ft. (30–90 cm) long, silvery or pale
pink. One of the finest ornamental grasses,
of year-round interest. Zone 8.

Cyperus
Sedge family
Cyperaceae

Sy-peer'us. About 600 species of annual and
perennial grasslike herbs, a few of garden
interest.

Description
The species below are tall-stemmed, practically aquatic sedges. Flowers inconspicuous, in crowded spikelets.

How to Grow
Most *Cyperus* are from wet habitats and prefer rich, moist soil in sun or light shade. They will also grow in shallow pools or in pots placed on stands in deep water. Propagate by division or by detaching the leaf crown, which, in moist sand or water, will send up new plants from most of the axils.

alternifolius p. 287
Umbrella Plant. Stems usually several, slender, 2–4 ft. (60–120 cm) high, essentially leafless but with brownish sheaths. At top of each stem an umbrella-shaped cluster of leafy bracts gives rise to flower spikelets. Zone 9.

papyrus p. 259
Paper Plant. Rhizomatous, evergreen aquatic sedge, stems 6–8 ft. (1.8–2.4 m) high, essentially leafless but with sheaths. Drooping threadlike leaves to 18 in. (45 cm) long at tip of stem. Terminal cluster of flower spikelets umbel-like, borne in short stems just above the whorl of leaves. The plant from which the Egyptians made paper. It can be potted and submerged in outdoor ponds in summer, then moved to a greenhouse for winter. Zone 10.

Dactylis
Grass family
Gramineae

Dak′til-is. A single species of Old World perennial grass.

Description
Rhizomes short, the cluster of shoots forming a tussock. Leaf blades flat. Few-flowered spikelets.

How to Grow
Easy to grow in well-drained soil that is not too heavy, in sun or partial shade. Increase by division.

glomerata p. 271
Orchard Grass; Cock's-Foot Grass. Stout perennial to 2 ft. (60 cm) high, usually

forming dense, arching clumps. Leaves narrow, flat, rough. Grasslike flowers in a one-sided panicle. The species is a pasture grass, but *D. glomerata* 'Variegata' is an ornamental garden plant to 18 in. (45 cm) high with slender leaves striped green and white. Suitable for ground cover, rock gardens, or specimen use. Zone 5.

Deschampsia
Grass family
Gramineae

Des-kamp′se-a. Hair Grass. 50 species of annual or perennial temperate-zone grasses.

Description
Leaves medium-textured, tufted at base of plant. Inflorescence in narrow or open panicles, well above foliage on erect or arching stems.

How to Grow
Grows well in sun or shade in any moist but well-drained garden soil. Propagate by division or seeds.

caespitosa p. 268
Tufted Hair Grass. Mound-forming evergreen perennial to 2 ft. (60 cm) high. Leaves dark green. Summer inflorescence an open, feathery panicle to 20 in. (50 cm) long, 8 in. (20 cm) wide, very graceful. Color of inflorescence ranges from silvery to gold to green and purple; many color selections have been made. Suited to perennial borders, specimen use, or naturalization. Cut flowerheads before seeds ripen. Zone 5.

Elymus
Grass family
Gramineae

El′i-mus. Over 50 species of perennial grasses, usually known as wild rye or lyme grass, all from temperate regions.

Description
Leaves flat, grasslike. Flowering spike dense, terminal, usually unbranched.

How to Grow
Plant in any well-drained soil in full sun.
Foliage colors are best in dry, hot sites.
Propagate by early spring division.

glaucus p. 266

Blue Lyme Grass; Blue Wild Rye. Strong-
growing, rhizomatous, to 3 ft. (90 cm) high.
Leaves 12 in. (30 cm) long, narrow, bluish
green. Flowering spike 5–7 in. (12.5–17.5 cm)
long, stiff. Valuable for its distinctive foliage
color and for erosion control; also an asset to
border plantings if contained. Zone 4.

Eragrostis
Grass family
Gramineae

E-ra-gros'tis. About 250 species of annual or
perennial grasses, a few grown for their
delicate flower-spikes.

Description
Leaf blades arching, dark green, very narrow,
tapering to a point. Flower-spikes spraylike,
borne in open, lax, branching panicles.

How to Grow
Performs best in light, sandy soil and full
sun. Increase by division or seeds.

trichodes p. 279

Sand Love Grass. Slowly spreading tufted
perennial to 4 ft. (120 cm) high. Leaf blades
to 3 ft. (90 cm) long, erect or arching.
Narrow panicle later spreading to 12 in.
(30 cm) wide, purplish, turning buff-brown
when dry. Admired by flower arrangers but
not distinctive in the garden, since flowers
are not held well above the foliage. Used as
a specimen, in a mixed perennial border, or
for naturalizing. Zone 5.

Erianthus
Grass family
Gramineae

E-ri-an'thus. About 20 species of reedlike,
mostly perennial grasses of tropical and
temperate regions, usually called plume grass.

Description
Leaf blades elongated and flat. Inflorescence terminal, oblong, usually dense, silky.

How to Grow
A sunny location and fertile, well-drained soil are ideal. Propagate by division or seeds. The species below should have a specimen location, but can also be used as a screen.

ravennae p. 259
Ravenna Grass; Plume Grass. Stout, stately, strong-growing grass, to 14 ft. (4.3 m) high, stems smooth and stiff. Leaves to 3 ft. (90 cm) long, narrow, veins roughish, sheath at base hairy and very rough. Flowering plume much-branched, to 2 ft. (60 cm) long, very silky and showy, silvery, turning beige in autumn. Autumn foliage chestnut-brown. Zone 6.

Festuca
Grass family
Gramineae

Fess-too'ka. Fescue. A genus of nearly 100 annual or perennial grasses, usually tufted. Most species are from temperate regions, some found in pasture or lawn mixtures, a few of interest for ornament.

Description
Leaves flat and typically grasslike, but some with rolled or coiled leaves that appear very fine and threadlike. Flowering cluster usually a narrow panicle.

How to Grow
Ornamental fescues prefer light, well-drained soil in full sun. They tolerate a little shade, but blue-gray species have best leaf color in full sun. Evergreen, but may be cut back when foliage becomes shabby. Propagate by division; plants benefit from division every few years. Effective as accents or in border fronts.

amethystina p. 266
Large Blue Fescue. Densely tufted perennial to 18 in. (45 cm) high, with short rhizomes. Leaf blades threadlike, soft, to 10 in. (25 cm) long, glaucous, silvery blue-green. Flowering panicle much-branched, spikelets usually purplish. Selections available with bronzy and olive-green leaf color. Zone 4.

ovina p. 267

Sheep's Fescue. Stems many, very fine, slender, tufted, 8–12 in. (20–30 cm) high, producing no stolons. Leaves rolled, threadlike, to 6 in. (15 cm) long. Flowering panicle often 1-sided. Var. *glauca* (Blue Fescue) has silvery-blue foliage and is widely grown. If plants die out in center, divide, reset, and cut back. Correct botanical name is *F. caesia,* but usually sold as *F. o. glauca.* Zone 4.

Glyceria
Grass family
Gramineae

Gly-seer'i-a. A genus of perennial spring- and summer-flowering grasses native to wet places in the north temperate zones.

Description
Deciduous, stoloniferous, with erect, smooth culms. Leaf sheaths cylindrical, blades rough. Inflorescence a much-branched panicle.

How to Grow
The variety listed below grows well in fertile garden soil in full sun. May also be grown at water's edge or even in shallow water; to restrain aggressive spreading, plant in a submerged container. Increase by division in spring.

maxima 'Variegata' p. 276

Manna Grass; Sweet Grass. Distinctive, to 2½ ft. (75 cm) high. Leaves brilliantly striped with white or creamy yellow, to 2 in. (5 cm) wide, with blades to 20 in. (50 cm) long, pointed. Sometimes offered as *G. aquatilis* 'Variegata'. Zone 5.

Hakonechloa
Grass family
Gramineae

Hack-oh-nee-cloh'a. A genus of low-growing, rhizomatous grasses recently introduced into cultivation from Japan. Only one species has been distributed to any extent in the U.S.

Description
Slowly spreading deciduous perennial grass. Stems smooth, bright green. Leaf blades soft.

Inflorescence a delicate open panicle, blooming in late summer.

How to Grow
Prefers fertile, well-drained garden soil and light shade, since leaf color burns out in direct sun. Propagate by division.

macra 'Aureola' *p. 277*
Golden Variegated Hakonechloa. To 18 in. (45 cm) high. Leaves to 8 in. (20 cm) long, narrow, bright yellow with fine green stripes. Autumn foliage buff-colored, handsome. This plant's graceful arching habit and coloration make it a distinctive accent in the high shade of deciduous trees. Fine for specimen use or as ground cover. The species has bright yellow-green leaves and is also ornamental. Zone 5.

Helictotrichon
Grass family
Gramineae

Hel-lick-toe-try'kon. About 30 species of perennial grasses native in Eurasia and North America, a few grown for ornament.

Description
Tufted perennial without stolons. Leaf sheaths basal, blades stiff, arching. Flowering panicle 1-sided, arching, with few spikelets.

How to Grow
Prefers full sun but tolerates light shade. Soil should be well drained and not too acid. Will tolerate dryness once established. Effective in groups or as a specimen, but the arching leaves need room.

sempervirens *p. 260*
Blue Oat Grass; Avena Grass. To 2 ft. (60 cm) high. Foliage blue, glaucous. Blades narrow, to 12 in. (30 cm) long. Arching stems to 3 ft. (90 cm) long, holding summer flowerheads well above foliage. Evergreen except at northern limits of hardiness. Cut back in late winter, if needed, or "comb" out dead leaves. Frequently listed as *Avena sempervirens*. Zone 4.

Holcus
Grass family
Gramineae

Hol'kus. Perennial grasses native to Eurasia, allied to *Avena* (oats) and *Agrostis* (bent grass).

Description
Stems and leaves hairy. Flowering panicle of flattened spikelets.

How to Grow
Grows well in fertile, moist, well-drained soil. Tolerates full sun, but leaf colors last longer in light shade. Propagate by division.

mollis 'Albo-variegatus' *p. 272*
Variegated Velvet Grass. Moderately creeping rhizomes and spreading stems to 12 in. (30 cm) high. Leaves striped green and white, hairy. Suitable for ground cover or border edging. Will brown out in dry soil. Often listed as *H. mollis* 'Variegatus'. The similar *H. lanatus* 'Variegatus' has erect rather than spreading stems and is suited for specimen use or borders. Zone 5.

Imperata
Grass family
Gramineae

Im-per-a'ta. A genus of ornamental grasses recently introduced into cultivation in the U.S., the species below from Japan.

Description
Leaf sheaths cylindrical, blades flat. Leaves deep red, green at base.

How to Grow
Prefers reasonably fertile, moist, well-drained garden soil. Does equally well in sun and light shade. Increase by division.

cylindrica rubra *p. 276*
Japanese Blood Grass. Tufted perennial grass of upright, open habit, to 12 in. (30 cm) high. Leaves deep red, color remaining intense through growing season. Mass plants in a border, or use mature clumps for accent. Especially striking if planted for backlighting effect. Zone 5, with protection.

Juncus
Rush family
Juncaceae

Jun′kus. A very large genus, known
generally as rushes. Leaves of larger species
have been used for weaving or plaiting mats
and chair seats.

Description
Leaves grasslike, round or 3-sided, often
jointed. Compact clusters of small greenish
or brownish flowers in spikelets.

How to Grow
Best suited for boggy waterside sites in full
sun. Plant in sunken pots on site to control
vigorous growth.

effusus p. 270
Common Rush; Bog Rush. Tufted perennial
2–3 ft. (60–90 cm) high, more or less pliant.
Stems upright, light green, ridged, with
small flower cluster near tip. Grown
primarily in boggy areas where more
desirable plants will not survive. Can be
invasive. Selections have been made for
variegated stem color or stem form and
less aggressive behavior. Most popular is
J. e. spiralis (Corkscrew Rush), with bright
yellow-green spiral stems. Zone 5.

Koeleria
Grass family
Gramineae

Koe-leer-i′a. About 20 species of annual or
perennial grasses, mostly from the northern
temperate zones, a few grown for ornament.

Description
Tufted grass with slim, upright stems and
narrow leaf blades. Flower panicles glossy,
spikelike, sometimes tipped with bristles.

How to Grow
Thrives in full sun in well-drained garden
soil that is not too acid. Propagate by
division in spring or fall, or by seeds.

glauca p. 265
Blue Hair Grass. Stems 18 in. (45 cm) high,
bulbous at base. Leaf blades usually flat,
glaucous above, hairy beneath. Buff-colored
flower panicle is of interest, but plant is

grown chiefly for its blue-green foliage. May
be listed incorrectly as *K. cristata* 'Glauca',
which is a different plant. Zone 5.

Luzula
Rush family
Juncaceae

Looz'you-la. About 80 species of wood
rushes of wide natural distribution, typically
in rich, moist woodlands.

Description
Densely tufted perennials of fine to medium
texture, the species below stoloniferous.
Leaves soft, flat, differing from true rushes in
their hairy leaf margins. Flowers in spikes,
umbels, or heads.

How to Grow
Grows best in shade or part shade in
humus-rich, woodsy soil, but adapts to most
soil types. Increase by seeds or division. Cut
back foliage in late winter if it becomes
unsightly.

nivea p. 267
Snowy Wood Rush. Semi-evergreen, of
upright, arching habit, to 2 ft. (60 cm) high.
Leaves grasslike. Flowers in spring showy,
white, in roundish umbels. Good ground
cover under trees and shrubs where fine
texture is needed. Also suitable for shaded
perennial borders or rock gardens. Zone 4.

sylvatica p. 269
Greater Wood Rush. Strong-growing,
forming bright green mounds to 12 in.
(30 cm) high. Basal leaves narrow, to 12 in.
(30 cm) long. Flowers in spring, rusty
brown, in nodding terminal clusters held
well above foliage. Makes a dense ground
cover in shade. Zone 5.

Milium
Grass family
Gramineae

Mill'i-um. Wood Millet. A small genus of
annual and perennial grasses native to North
America and Eurasia.

Description
Loosely tufted, stems thin or stout. Leaf blades flat. Flower panicles loose.

How to Grow
The grass described below is a woodlander and grows best in moist, fertile soil and partial to full shade. Increase by division or by seeds.

effusum 'Aureum' *p. 278*
Bowles' Golden Grass. Deciduous perennial to 18 in. (45 cm) high, with slowly creeping rhizomes and open, upright habit. Leaf blades narrow, to 12 in. (30 cm) long, soft, arching, bright yellow or yellow-green. Flowers yellow, in early summer; attractive for dried arrangements. Bright yellow color makes this plant a striking ground cover for shaded areas. Flowerheads left on plants produce abundant viable seeds; cut them to avoid this potential nuisance. Zone 5.

Miscanthus
Grass family
Gramineae

Mis-kan'thus. About 20 species of tall perennial Old World grasses, some popular ornamental grasses cultivated in the U.S.

Description
Erect, mostly clump-forming. Leaf sheaths rigid, blades with distinct white midrib and rough margins. Flowers in a flat or fan-shaped panicle with soft hairs at bases of spikelets, giving it a feathery appearance.

How to Grow
Grows best in full sun or light shade in well-cultivated, fertile garden soil that is kept moist but not soggy during growing season. Propagate in spring by dividing the woody roots, using a saw if clumps are sizable. Cut foliage down in late winter. Allow mature plants to assume full stature. Effective as specimens; taller species are useful for screening.

floridulus *p. 256*
Giant Miscanthus. Coarse-textured, to 10 ft. (3 m) high, forming clumps. Leaves pale green, elongate, to 3 ft. (90 cm) long. White flower plumes in autumn. Dramatic when properly sited, but large size limits use

in smaller gardens. Often listed as *M. sinensis giganteus.* Zone 5.

sacchariflorus p. 257
Eulalia Grass. Tufted, deciduous grass to 6 ft. (1.8 m) high, spreading by rhizomes. Leaf blades to 3 ft. (90 cm) long, 1 in. (2.5 cm) wide, turning rusty orange in autumn. Flowers silvery, decorative, produced in late summer, effective through winter. Suited to waterside plantings. May become too vigorous in light soil. Zone 5.

sinensis pp. 258, 264, 265, 272
Japanese Silver Grass. 4–8 ft. (1.2–2.4 m) high. Leaves pointed, 2–3 ft. (60–90 cm) long, 1 in. (2.5 cm) wide, arching, usually in heavy clumps. Flowers in autumn, beautiful, compound, in long terminal panicles. Species and its many varieties suitable for waterside plantings. Cultivars selected for leaf color, pattern, and inflorescence color. 'Gracillimus' (Maiden Grass), to 5 ft. (1.5 m) high, is fine-textured and of graceful, upright, arching habit; leaves buff-colored with curled tips in autumn. 'Silver Feather' is similar to the species but has showy silver plumes and blooms somewhat earlier. Excellent for backlighting effect. 'Variegatus' (Variegated Silver Grass) is of graceful, upright open habit, to 5 ft. (1.5 m) high; leaves ½ in. (13 mm) wide, with creamy stripes, buff-colored, in winter. Holds shape well through winter. 'Zebrinus' (Zebra Grass), to 7 ft. (2.1 m) high, is medium-textured and of upright, narrow form; leaves have horizontal yellow bands and turn buff-colored with rusty-orange tips in winter. All zone 5.

Molinia
Grass family
Gramineae

Mo-lin′i-a. A small genus of tufted perennial grasses native to acid heaths of Europe and parts of Asia.

Description
Small to medium-size grasses of upright arching form. Leaf blades soft, narrow, flat. Flowers in panicles.

How to Grow
Best suited to moist, acid soil in full sun,

434

but grows well in any fertile garden soil that
is not too dry or alkaline. Increase by
division.

caerulea pp. 274, 279
Moor Grass. Stiff, smooth, to 3 ft. (90 cm)
high. Leaves erect, 6–12 in. (15–30 cm)
long. Flowering panicle long, its branches
mostly erect, bearing sharp-pointed, greenish
or purplish spikelets. Two selections to 2 ft.
(60 cm) high are more widely cultivated
than the species: Var. *altissima* (Tall Purple
Moor Grass) has mounding foliage and
abundant flowering stems to 6 ft. (1.8 m)
high, bearing loose panicles of purplish
flowers in summer. Use as specimen or
background in a perennial border. 'Variegata'
(Variegated Purple Moor Grass) forms soft
mounds, with leaves striped creamy yellow.
Flowers purplish green, on stems 3 ft.
(90 cm) long. Fine specimen or edging plant
for front of a border. Zone 5.

Panicum
Grass family
Gramineae

Pan'i-kum. Panic Grass. Over 500 species of
annual or perennial grasses found in all parts
of the world, but mostly in the tropics.
Some are grown for grain or fodder, others
for ornament.

Description
Creeping or erect, varying in height and leaf
size. Flowers usually in light, feathery
clusters.

How to Grow
The species below grows best in light soil in
full sun, but will tolerate some moisture.
Easy to grow from seeds; perennial species
may also be divided in spring. Its creeping
habit suits it best for large areas.

virgatum p. 260
Switch Grass. Strong-growing, rhizomatous
perennial, 5–6 ft. (1.5–1.8 m) high. Leaves
1–2 ft. (30–60 cm) long, narrow, with
rough margins, golden-orange in autumn.
Flower clusters profuse, creating dense
buff-brown flower masses held above foliage.
Several lower-growing cultivars with red
autumn foliage exist. Can become weedy.
Zone 5.

Pennisetum
Grass family
Gramineae

Pen-i-see'tum. A genus of 80 species of chiefly tropical annual or perennial grasses, a handful grown for ornament.

Description
Stems erect. Leaf blades flat and narrow, sometimes colored. Flowers in a spikelike panicle, the spikelets with bristles beneath them; bristles sometimes plumed.

How to Grow
Grows best in fertile soil in full sun. Hardy perennial types can be increased by spring division. Annuals and perennials may be started from seeds. Dig up tender perennials and overwinter in an area not subject to hard freezes.

alopecuroides p. 262
Fountain Grass. Slender-stemmed perennial, 2–3 ft. (60–90 cm) high, hairy up to the spike. Leaves bright green. Flowering cluster cylindrical, silvery, the anthers purplish; bristles long and conspicuous. Zone 5.

setaceum p. 262
Fountain Grass. Perennial grown as an annual. Graceful, arching, to 3 ft. (90 cm) high. Leaves many, 15–20 in. (38–50 cm) long, very narrow, sometimes with margins rolled, green or variously colored. Spikes 6–10 in. (15–25 cm) long, curved or nodding, bristles of spikelets prominent. Forms with rose-purple or coppery spikes and foliage exist. Often reseeds in the garden. Zone 8.

villosum p. 263
Feathertop. Perennial grown as a half-hardy annual. To 2 ft. (60 cm) high. Leaf blades many. Spikes to 4 in. (10 cm) long, creamy-white, feathery, many bristles to 2 in. (5 cm) long. Grown primarily for its ornamental plumes. Flowerheads shatter when dried. Zone 9.

Phalaris
Grass family
Gramineae

Fal'ar-is. About 15 species of ornamental and seed-yielding grasses found in the north

temperate zone, some cultivated for their
variegated foliage.

Description
Annual or perennial, with flat, grasslike
leaves. Flower cluster terminal, a narrow
spike or panicle, its spikelets flattened.

How to Grow
The variety below tolerates a wide range of
growing conditions. Variegation may bleach
out in hot sun; growth will be lanky and
sparse in deep shade. Increase by division.

arundinacea picta p. 273
Ribbon Grass; Gardener's-Garters. Perennial,
to 3 ft. (90 cm) high. Leaves striped green
and white, .12 in. (30 cm) long, ¾ in.
(19 mm) wide. Valuable as ground cover
under difficult conditions, but in a garden it
must be restrained. Zone 4.

Phormium
Agave family
Agavaceae

For'mi-um. Two species of large perennial
herbs from New Zealand. Although not in
the Grass family, *Phormium* is strongly
vertical and can be used like ornamental
grasses.

Description
Leaves basal, very tough, long, sword-shaped.
Flowering stalk usually exceeding leaves.
Flowers red or yellow, tubular, curved.

How to Grow
Grow outdoors only in zones 8–10, in full
sun. Sow seeds in early spring in time to set
plants out that year, or increase by dividing
roots. Give *Phormium* plenty of space in
borders. Striking in clumps.

tenax pp. 273, 277
New Zealand Flax; Flax Lily. To 15 ft.
(4.5 m) high. Leaves 9 ft. (2.7 m) high,
5 in. (12.5 cm) wide, leathery, usually
red-margined, shreddy at tip. Flowers 2 in.
(5 cm) long, dull red, the cluster above the
foliage. 'Variegatum' has leaves striped with
pale yellow and white; the most striking
selections are purplish, as in 'Rubrum', or
bronze. Zone 8.

Phyllostachys
Grass family
Gramineae

Fill-o-stack'is. 30 species of Asiatic bamboos,
invasive, but several grown for ornament.

Description
Stems moderately tall, hollow, flattened or
grooved, with prominent nodes and creeping
rootstocks. Foliage delicate, light green, on
symmetrically arranged branches.

How to Grow
Bamboos grow well in rich, moist soil that
is well drained and not soggy. Shelter them
from drying winds, and in hot climates,
shade from afternoon sun. To propagate,
remove a 12-in. (30-cm) section of rhizome
just before shoot growth begins in spring;
replant 2–4 in. (5–10 cm) deep. Young
clumps also can be divided.

aurea p. 287
Golden Bamboo; Fishpole Bamboo. Running
bamboo, with stems erect, yellow, 10–20 ft.
(3–6 m) high, the upper leaf joints spread
apart, with a swollen band beneath each.
Leaves 2–4 in. (5–10 cm) long, ¾ in.
(19 mm) wide, the sheath bristly, light
green above, bluish gray beneath. Valuable
for hedges and erosion control. Zone 7.

aureosulcata p. 286
Yellow Groove Bamboo. Showy, 10–30 ft.
(3–9 m) high, quickly forming large clumps.
Stems ridged, the depression between ridges
yellow. Leaves 4–6 in. (10–15 cm) long,
smooth above, hairy at base. Mature culms
slender, olive-green, with a yellow groove.
Zone 6.

Pseudosasa
Grass family
Gramineae

Soo-doe-sa'sa. A few species of woody grasses
native to temperate e. Asia. Often classified
as *Sasa* or *Arundinaria*.

Description
Bamboos of medium height, with relatively
large leaves and persistent leaf sheaths.
Branches solitary, growing from the nodes.
Far-reaching rhizomes.

How to Grow
Culture is similar to *Phyllostachys*.

japonica p. 283
Arrow Bamboo; Metake. Stems to 15 ft.
(4.5 m) high. Leaves to 12 in. (30 cm)
long, 1½ in. (4 cm) wide, pointed, with
yellow midrib. Distinctive gray and green
pattern on undersides of leaves. Good hedge
or screen if restrained; grows well in
containers. Zone 7.

Sasa
Grass family
Gramineae

Sa'sugh. More than 150 species of woody
grasses, most native in e. Asia and Japan.

Description
Rhizomatous woody grasses of medium
height, with persistent culm sheaths and
usually solitary branches from the nodes.
Leaves relatively large, midribs conspicuous.

How to Grow
Performs best in fertile, moist soil and light
shade. Spreads rapidly under good
conditions, so restrain in the garden or
naturalize in a wild garden. Although
evergreen, foliage is frequently shabby by
winter's end; cut plants to the ground then.

palmata p. 284
Slender-stemmed, to 7 ft. (2.1 m) high,
usually less. Leaves green above, pale bluish
green beneath, to 14 in. (35 cm) long,
2½ in. (6 cm) wide, leathery. Zone 6.

veitchii p. 282
Kuma Bamboo. To 3 ft. (90 cm) high.
Canes slender, dull purple at maturity. Leaves
5–8 in. (12.5–20.0 cm) long, 2 in. (5 cm)
wide, green above, bluish gray beneath;
margins dry to parchment-color. Zone 6,
with protection.

Shibataea
Grass family
Gramineae

She-bat'e-a. Two or more Asian species of
small bamboos, related to *Phyllostachys*.

Description
Stems flattened, almost solid, slender,
grooved on one side. Stem sheaths papery.
Leaves terminal, usually solitary, petioled.

How to Grow
Performs best in rich, moist soil and light
shade. Increase by division or by removing a
rooted rhizome before spring growth.

kumasaca p. 284
Ruscus-leaved Bamboo. To 3 ft. (90 cm)
high. Leaves broad, oval, pointed, lustrous
dark green in youth, yellow-green at
maturity. Rhizomatous, but growth is
relatively compact; less likely to become
invasive than most bamboos. Cut down in
winter if foliage becomes ragged. Sometimes
listed as *Bambusa* or *Phyllostachys*. Zone 6.

Spartina
Grass family
Gramineae

Spar-tine′a. Cord Grass. About 15 species of
erect, rhizomatous, perennial grasses, widely
distributed in temperate coastal regions.

Description
Stems erect, thin, wiry. Leaf blades long and
coarse. Inflorescence a 1-sided panicle, the
individual flowers bristled.

How to Grow
Grows equally well in either freshwater or
salt marshes and in average garden soil.
Prefers full sun but will tolerate light shade.
Increase the species below by division or
seeds, the cultivar by division. Ideal for
waterside locations, where it may spread.
With average moisture, it can be restrained
enough in a garden for specimen or small
group planting.

pectinata p. 257
Prairie Cord Grass. Deciduous, of upright
open habit, to 6 ft. (1.8 m) high, usually
less in gardens. Leaf blades narrow, light
green, to 2 ft. (60 cm) long, arching, with
rough margins. Inflorescence narrow, in late
summer. Autumn color bright yellow.
Spreading roots make it useful for stabilizing
sandy soil. Often listed as *S. michauxiana*.
'Aureo-marginata' is a variegated selection,
its leaf margins striped with yellow. Zone 5.

Spodiopogon
Grass family
Gramineae

Spoe-dee-o-po'gon. Silver Spike Grass. A deciduous perennial native to the prairies of Siberia, introduced to the West via Japan.

Description
Upright, arching habit. Stems erect, leaves with prominent white midrib. Flowers in midsummer.

How to Grow
Performs best in moist or wet soil in full sun or light shade. Propagate by division or seeds. Suitable for waterside plantings.

sibericus p. 278
To 3 ft. (90 cm) high in foliage, to 5 ft. (1.5 m) high in flower. Leaves to 12 in. (30 cm) long, 1 in. (2.5 cm) wide, dark green, tinged red by midsummer, redder in autumn. Open flowering panicles to 12 in. (30 cm) long. Zone 5.

Stipa
Grass family
Gramineae

Sty'pa. Feather Grass. About 150 species of perennial grasses distributed in dry temperate regions worldwide and cultivated for their large, ornamental, feathery flowers.

Description
Leaves narrow, the margins rolled. Flowers in loose branching clusters, each spikelet bearing a long feathery bristle (awn).

How to Grow
Grows best in sun in light, well-drained, moderately fertile soil. Propagate by division of clumps or, though more difficult, by seeds. Most effective as single specimens in the middle or background of a border.

gigantea p. 258
Feather Grass. Densely tufted, with leaves to 3 ft. (90 cm) high, blades to 18 in. (45 cm) long, arching to form a mound. Panicles large, open, showy, much-branched, to 15 in. (38 cm) long, the spikelets golden with long awns in summer. Zone 5.

Appendices

Plant Chart

	Page Numbers	Zone
Ground Covers		
Achillea tomentosa	156	3
Aegopodium podagraria	119	4
Ajuga pyramidalis	116	4
Ajuga reptans	116, 208	3
Ajuga reptans 'Alba'	173	3
Ajuga reptans 'Bronze Beauty'	115	3
Ajuga reptans 'Multicolor Rainbow'	117	3
Alchemilla mollis	131	4
Andromeda polifolia	182	3
Anemone canadensis	166	4
Antennaria dioica	114, 183	4–5
Arabis species	165	5
Arctostaphylos edmundsii	94	8
Arctostaphylos 'Emerald Carpet'	80	8
Arctostaphylos hookeri	96	8
Arctostaphylos uva-ursi	98, 99	3
Arctotheca calendula	151	9
Arctotis hybrids	150	9
Arenaria montana	162	4
Arenaria verna	79, 164	3
Artemisia stellerana	130	3–4
Asarum canadense	123	4
Asarum caudatum	122	6
Asarum europaeum	123	5
Asarum shuttleworthii	122	6
Aspidistra elatior	138	8
Astilbe chinensis 'Pumila'	187	5
Baccharis pilularis	73, 109	7
Berberis verruculosa	97	6
Bergenia ciliata	135, 136	6
Bergenia cordifolia	134, 136	3

Flowers	Rapid Growth	Moderate Growth	Slow Growth	Spring	Summer	Fall	Winter	Beds/Borders	Banks/Slopes	Rock Gardens	Under Trees	Accents	Walls
■	▦	□	■	▦	□	■	▦	□	■	▦	□	■	■
■		□		▦	□	■				▦			
	▦			▦	□	■		□	■				
■		□		▦	□	■			■		□		
■	▦			▦	□	■			■		□		
■	▦			▦	□	■			■		□		
■	▦			▦	□	■			■		□		
■	▦			▦	□	■			■		□		
■		□		▦	□	■		□		▦	□		
■		□		▦	□	■	▦			▦			
■	▦			▦	□				■		□		
■	▦			▦	□	■				▦			
■		□		▦	□					▦			■
		□		▦	□	■	▦		■		□		
		□		▦	□	■	▦		■				
		□		▦	□	■	▦		■		□		
		□		▦	□	■	▦		■	▦			
■	▦			▦	□				■				
■		□		▦	□				■				
■		□		▦	□					▦			
■		□		▦	□					▦	□		
		□		▦	□	■			■	▦			
		□		▦	□					▦	□		
		□		▦	□	■	▦		■	▦	□		
		□		▦	□	■	▦		■	▦	□		
		□		▦	□	■			■	▦	□		
		□		▦	□	■	▦				□		
■		□		▦	□			□		▦	□		
		□		▦	□	■			■				
		□		▦	□	■	▦	□	■				
■		□		▦	□	■	▦	□		▦	□	■	
■		□		▦	□	■	▦	□		▦	□	■	

Ground Covers Chart

	Page Numbers	Zone
Ground Covers continued		
Bergenia crassifolia	137	3
Bruckenthalia spiculifolia	187	5
Brunnera macrophylla	132, 207	4
Calluna vulgaris 'County Wicklow'	189	5
Calluna vulgaris 'Kinlochruel'	169	5
Calluna vulgaris 'Silver Knight'	168	5
Campanula carpatica	167, 198	4
Campanula elatines garganica	200	5
Campanula portenschlagiana	204	5
Campanula poscharskyana	201	4
Ceanothus gloriosus	206	7
Ceanothus griseus horizontalis	207	7
Cerastium tomentosum	81	4
Ceratostigma plumbaginoides	199	5
Chamaemelum nobile	85	6
Chrysogonum virginianum	154	5
Convallaria majalis	138, 172	4
Cornus canadensis	112, 113, 166	2
Coronilla varia	183	4
Cotoneaster adpressus	101	5
Cotoneaster apiculatus	100	5
Cotoneaster dammeri	103	5
Cotoneaster horizontalis	100, 101	5
Daboecia cantabrica	171, 190	5
Daphne cneorum	182	5
Dianthus gratianopolitanus	84, 193	5
Disporum sessile 'Variegatum'	141	5
Duchesnea indica	110, 161	4
Epimedium alpinum	127	4
Epimedium grandiflorum	126	5
Epimedium × rubrum	126	5

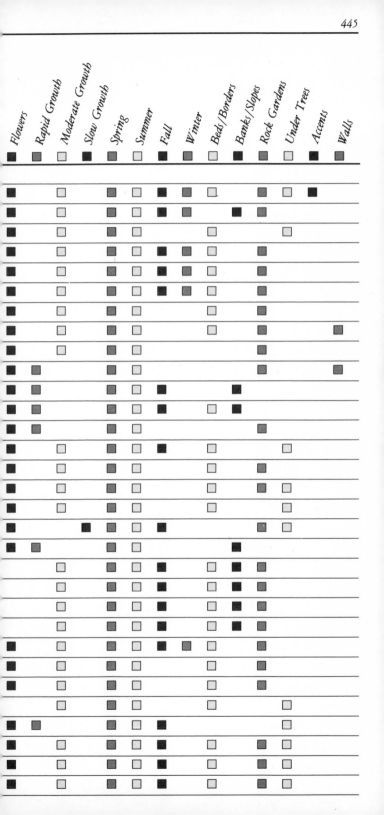

Ground Covers Chart

	Page Numbers	Zone
Ground Covers continued		
Epimedium × *versicolor*	125	5
Epimedium × *warleyense*	127	5
Epimedium × *youngianum* 'Niveum'	175	5
Erica carnea	170, 188	5
Eriophyllum lanatum	151	5
Euonymus fortunei cultivars	104, 105, 118	4
Fragaria chiloensis	113	5
Galax urceolata	133	5
Galium odoratum	82, 167	5
Gaultheria procumbens	98, 99	5
Gaultheria shallon	94, 95	6
Gaylussacia brachycera	96	5
Gazania rigens	150	9
Genista pilosa	155	6
Genista sagittalis	157	6
Geranium 'Claridge Druce'	196	4
Geranium endressii	196	4
Geranium 'Johnson's Blue'	198	4
Geranium macrorrhizum	108	5
Geranium sanguineum	197	4
Gypsophila repens	185	4
Hebe menziesii	168	8
Hedera canariensis	133	8
Helianthemum nummularium	153	6
Helianthemum nummularium cultivars	152, 194, 195	6
Hemerocallis hybrids	148, 149	3–7
Herniaria glabra	73	6
Heuchera sanguinea	130	5
Hosta hybrids and cultivars	139, 140, 141	4
Hosta lancifolia	139, 206	4
Hosta sieboldiana	134, 135	4

Flowers	Rapid Growth	Moderate Growth	Slow Growth	Spring	Summer	Fall	Winter	Beds/Borders	Banks/Slopes	Rock Gardens	Under Trees	Accents	Walls
■	▒	□	■	▒	□	■	▒	□	■	▒	□	■	▒
■		□		▒	□	■		□		▒	□		
■		□		▒	□	■		□		▒	□		
■		□		▒	□	■		□		▒	□		
■		□		▒	□	■	▒	□		▒			
■		□		▒				□		▒			
		□		▒	□	■	▒	□	■	▒	□		
		□		▒	□			□					
			■	▒	□	■		□		▒	□		
■		□		▒	□	■				▒	□		
		□		▒	□	■	▒			▒	□		
		□		▒	□	■	▒		■	▒	□		
		□		▒	□	■	▒			▒	□		
■		□		▒	□	■		□	■				
■		□		▒	□	■	▒	□	■	▒			
■	▒			▒	□	■	▒		■				
■		□		▒	□			□		▒	□		
■		□		▒				□		▒	□		
■		□		▒	□			□			□		
■		□		▒	□	■		□		▒	□		
■		□		▒	□	■		□		▒	□		
■		□		▒	□	■		□	■	▒			
■		□		▒	□	■	▒	□	■				
	▒			▒	□	■	▒		■				
■		□		▒	□					■	▒		
■		□		▒	□					■	▒		
■		□		▒	□			□	■			□	■
■		□			□	■	▒	□			▒		
■		□		▒	□			□			▒		
■		□		▒	□			□			▒	□	■
■		□			□	■		□			□	■	
■		□			□	■		□			□	■	

	Page Numbers	Zone
Ground Covers continued		
Hypericum calycinum	161	5
Iberis sempervirens	169	5
Ilex crenata	102	6
Iris cristata	205	4
Juniperus chinensis	87	5
Juniperus conferta	88, 89	6
Juniperus horizontalis	90, 91	3
Juniperus procumbens	89	5
Juniperus sabina	88	4
Lamiastrum galeobdolon	120, 121	4
Lamium maculatum	119, 120, 121	4
Lampranthus species and hybrids	152, 153, 193	9
Lantana montevidensis	181	9
Leiophyllum buxifolium	163	6
Leucothoe axillaris	92, 174	6
Liriope muscari	142	6
Liriope spicata	143	5
Lysimachia nummularia	72, 108, 158	4
Mahonia repens	92	6
Mazus reptans	104, 201	6
Microbiota decussata	86	3
Mitchella repens	105	4
Myosotis scorpioides	203	5
Nandina domestica 'Harbor Dwarf'	106	7
Nepeta 'Blue Wonder'	208	5
Oenothera tetragona	155	5
Omphalodes verna	129	5
Ophiopogon japonicus	142	7
Ophiopogon planiscapus 'Arabicus'	143	7
Opuntia humifusa	72, 160	5
Osteospermum fruticosum	192	9

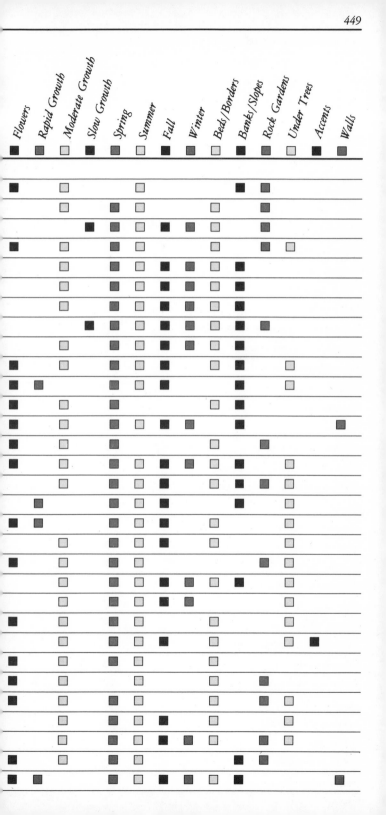

	Page Numbers	Zone
Ground Covers *continued*		
Pachysandra procumbens	112	5
Pachysandra terminalis	114, 115	5
Paxistima species	83, 97	5
Phlox divaricata	202	4
Phlox nivalis	163	6
Phlox stolonifera	203	4
Phlox subulata	162, 194, 195	4
Polygonum cuspidatum compactum	190, 191	4
Potentilla tabernaemontani	111, 154	4
Potentilla tridentata	109, 164	3
Primula × *polyantha*	146, 147	5
Primula veris	147	5
Primula vulgaris	192	5
Pulmonaria species	118, 191, 199	4
Rhododendron indicum hybrids	177, 178	6
Rhododendron kiusianum hybrids	174–179	7
Rhododendron North Tisbury hybrids	179	6
Rhododendron Robin Hill hybrids	176	6
Rhus aromatica	93	3
Robinia hispida	176	5
Rosmarinus officinalis 'Prostratus'	82	7
Rubus calycinoides	124	7
Sagina subulata	78	5
Santolina chamaecyparissus	84, 156	6
Santolina virens	85, 157	6
Sarcococca hookerana humilis	107	6
Saxifraga stolonifera	124, 173	7
Saxifraga × *urbium*	75, 184	5
Sedum anglicum	74	4
Sedum brevifolium	75	4
Sedum cauticola	74	5

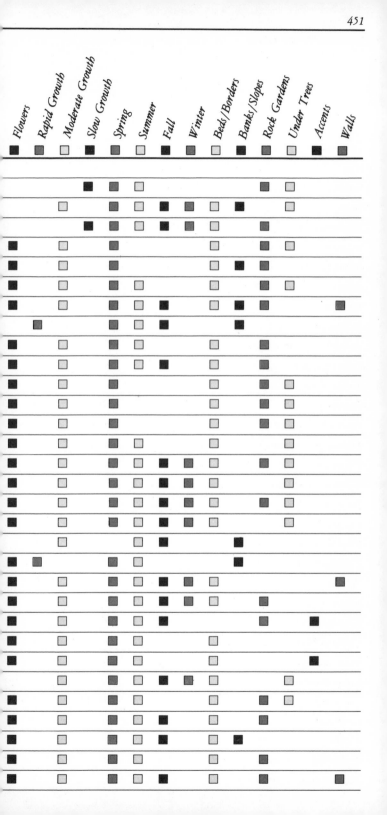

	Page Numbers	Zone
Ground Covers continued		
Sedum kamtschaticum	77, 158	4
Sedum lineare	80	5
Sedum reflexum	79	5
Sedum × *rubrotinctum*	77	8
Sedum spurium	76, 180	3
Sedum 'Weihenstephaner Gold'	76, 159	4
Skimmia reevesiana	102	7
Stachys byzantina	128, 129	5
Symphytum grandiflorum	170	5
Taxus baccata 'Repandens'	86	5
Taxus cuspidata 'Densa'	87	5
Tellima grandiflora	132	5
Teucrium chamaedrys	81, 186	5–6
Thymus pseudolanuginosus	78, 184	4
Thymus serpyllum	83, 185	4
Tiarella cordifolia	172	5
Tolmiea menziesii	131	8
Vaccinium angustifolium	95	3
Vaccinium vitis-idaea minus	103	3
Vancouveria hexandra	125	5
Verbena peruviana	180, 181	8
Veronica incana	209	4
Veronica prostrata	186, 209	4
Veronica repens	200	5
Viburnum davidii	128	8
Vinca major	107	7
Vinca minor	106, 202	5
Viola species	171, 204, 205	5–6
Waldsteinia fragarioides	111, 160	5
Waldsteinia ternata	110	4
Xanthorhiza simplicissima	93	5

Flowers	Rapid Growth	Moderate Growth	Slow Growth	Spring	Summer	Fall	Winter	Beds/Borders	Banks/Slopes	Rock Gardens	Under Trees	Accents	Walls
■	■	□	■	▦	□	■	▦	□	■	▦	□	■	▦
■		□		▦	□	■	▦	□		▦			▦
■	■			▦	□			□	■	▦			
■		□		▦	□			□		▦			
■		□		▦	□	■		□		▦			
■		□		▦	□	■	▦	□	■				
■		□		▦	□	■		□		▦			
		□		▦	□	■	▦	□			□		
■		□		▦	□	■	▦	□		▦		■	
■		□		▦	□			□			□		
			■	▦	□	■	▦	□	■		□		
		□		▦	□	■	▦	□			□	■	
■		□		▦	□			□		▦	□		
■		□		▦	□			□					
■		□		▦	□			□		▦			
■		□		▦	□			□		▦			
■		□		▦	□			□			□		
■		□		▦	□			□			□		
		□		▦	□	■		□	■	▦			
		□		▦	□	■	▦	□		▦			
■		□		▦	□			□			□		
■	▦			▦	□				■				▦
■		□		▦	□			□		▦			
■		□		▦	□			□		▦			
■		□		▦	□					▦			
■		□		▦	□	■	▦	□			□		
■	▦			▦	□	■	▦	□	■		□		
■		□		▦	□	■	▦	□	■		□		
■		□		▦	□			□			□		
■		□		▦	□	■	▦	□		▦	□		
■		□		▦	□	■	▦	□		▦	□		
■	▦			▦	□	■			■		□		

Vines	Page Numbers	Zone
Actinidia species	213, 223	5
Adlumia fungosa	212	5
Akebia quinata	221	5
Ampelopsis brevipedunculata	222	5
Antigonon leptopus	232	8
Aristolochia durior	218	5
Bignonia capreolata	227	7
Bougainvillea spectabilis	238	9
Campsis radicans	228	4
Celastrus orbiculatus	223	5
Celastrus scandens	222	3
Clematis armandii	250	7
Clematis cultivars and hybrids	240, 241, 250	5
Clematis macropetala	240	5
Clematis montana	234, 235	5
Clematis paniculata	251	5
Clematis tangutica	224	4
Clematis texensis	230, 237	5
Clematis virginiana	249	4
Clerodendrum species	231, 246	10
Clytostoma callistegioides	235	8
Cobaea scandens	243	9
Decumaria barbara	245	7
Distictis buccinatoria	229	9
Euonymus fortunei radicans	214	5
Ficus pumila	213	9
Gelsemium sempervirens	226	7
Hedera species	215, 216, 217	6–8
Humulus lupulus	220	6
Hydrangea anomala petiolaris	246	4
Ipomoea × multifida	230	Annual

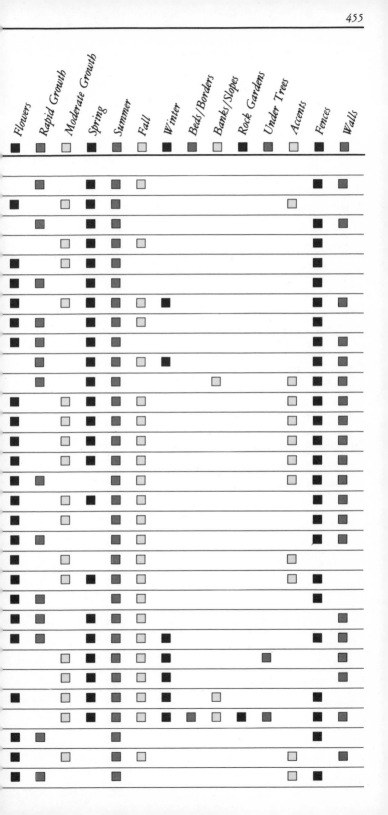

	Page Numbers	Zone
Vines continued		
Ipomoea species	231, 242, 251	8–9
Jasminum polyanthum	234	9
Kadsura japonica	214	7
Lathyrus latifolius	237	5
Lathyrus odoratus	236	Annual
Lonicera × *heckrottii*	232	4
Lonicera japonica	224	5
Lonicera periclymenum	233	5
Lonicera sempervirens	225, 233	4
Mandevilla 'Alice du Pont'	236	10
Mandevilla laxa	247	8
Menispermum canadense	219	5
Muehlenbeckia complexa	212	6
Parthenocissus henryana	220	8
Parthenocissus quinquefolia	221	4
Parthenocissus tricuspidata	219	5
Passiflora species	238, 239	7–8
Plumbago auriculata	249	9
Polygonum aubertii	244	5
Rosa climbing cultivars	239	6
Rosa species	252, 253	6–7
Schizophragma hydrangeoides	247	5
Stephanotis floribunda	248	9
Tecomaria capensis	229	9
Thunbergia alata	227	Annual
Trachelospermum jasminoides	248	9
Tropaeolum species	225, 226	Annual
Vitis coignetiae	218	5
Wisteria floribunda	242	5
Wisteria sinensis	243, 244	5
Wisteria venusta	245	5

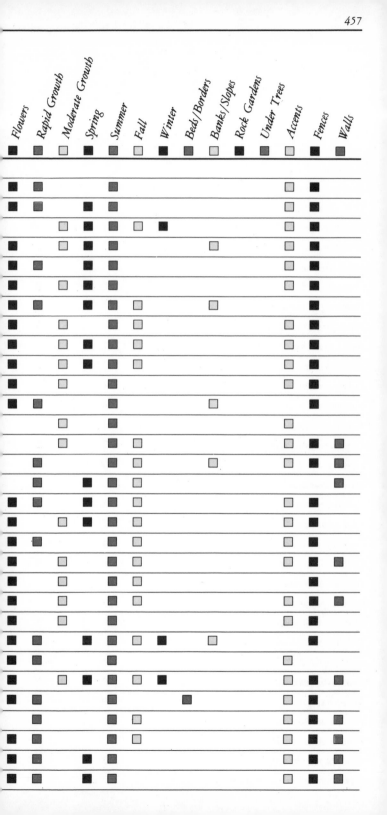

Grasses Chart

Grasses	Page Numbers	Zone
Acorus gramineus	274	6
Alopecurus pratensis	275	5
Arrhenatherum elatius bulbosum	271	5
Arundinaria pygmaea	282	7
Arundinaria viridistriata	283	7
Arundo donax	256, 286	7
Bambusa glaucescens	285	8
Bouteloua gracilis	280	5
Briza maxima	281	Annual
Briza media	280	5
Calamagrostis acutiflora stricta	261	5
Calamagrostis arundinacea brachytricha	264	5
Carex buchananii	261	6
Carex conica 'Variegata'	270	5
Carex grayi	269	3
Carex morrowii 'Aureo-variegata'	275	6
Carex pendula	268	5
Chasmanthium latifolium	281	5
Coix lacryma-jobi	285	Annual
Cortaderia selloana	263	8
Cyperus alternifolius	287	9
Cyperus papyrus	259	10
Dactylis glomerata	271	5
Deschampsia caespitosa	268	5
Elymus glaucus	266	4
Eragrostis trichodes	279	5
Erianthus ravennae	259	6
Festuca amethystina	266	4
Festuca ovina glauca	267	4
Glyceria maxima 'Variegata'	276	5
Hakonechloa macra 'Aureola'	277	5

Flowers	Seed Heads	Rapid Growth	Moderate Growth	Slow Growth	Spring	Summer	Fall	Winter	Beds/Borders	Banks/Slopes	Rock Gardens	Under Trees	Accents
■	▨	□	■	▨	□	■	▨	□	■	▨	□	■	▨
			■		□	■	▨	□	■				■
■			■		□	■	▨			▨			■
			■		□	■	▨		■	▨			■
		□			□	■				▨			■
		□			□	■							■
		□			□	■							■
			■		□	■							■
■			■		□	■	▨			▨	□		■
■			■		□	■	▨						■
■			■		□	■	▨						■
■	▨		■		□	■	▨	□	■				■
■	▨		■		□	■	▨		■				■
			■		□	■	▨	□	■				■
			■			■	▨		■		□		■
■	▨		■			■	▨				□		■
			■		□	■	▨	□	■				■
			■		□	■	▨	□	■				■
■	▨		■			■	▨	□					■
■		□				▨			■				■
■	▨		■		□	■	▨	□					■
■	▨		■		□	■	▨	□					■
■	▨		■		□	■	▨	□					▨
			■		□	■			■		□		■
■			■		□	■	▨				□		■
		□			□	■	▨			▨			■
■			■		□	■	▨		■				■
■			■		□	■	▨		■				■
			■		□	■	▨		■		□		■
			■		□	■	▨	□	■		□		■
		□			□	■							■
				▨	□	■	▨		■			■	▨

Grasses Chart

	Page Numbers	Zone
Grasses continued		
Helictotrichon sempervirens	260	4
Holcus mollis 'Albo-variegatus'	272	5
Imperata cylindrica rubra	276	5
Juncus effusus	270	5
Koeleria glauca	265	5
Luzula nivea	267	4
Luzula sylvatica	269	5
Milium effusum 'Aureum'	278	5
Miscanthus floridulus	256	5
Miscanthus sacchariflorus	257	5
Miscanthus sinensis 'Gracillimus'	264	5
Miscanthus sinensis 'Silver Feather'	258	5
Miscanthus sinensis 'Variegatus'	272	5
Miscanthus sinensis 'Zebrinus'	265	5
Molinia caerulea	274, 279	5
Panicum virgatum	260	5
Pennisetum alopecuroides	262	5
Pennisetum setaceum	262	8
Pennisetum villosum	263	9
Phalaris arundinacea picta	273	4
Phormium tenax	273, 277	8
Phyllostachys aurea	287	7
Phyllostachys aureosulcata	286	6
Pseudosasa japonica	283	7
Sasa palmata	284	6
Sasa veitchii	282	6
Shibataea kumasaca	284	6
Spartina pectinata	257	5
Spodiopogon sibericus	278	5
Stipa gigantea	258	5

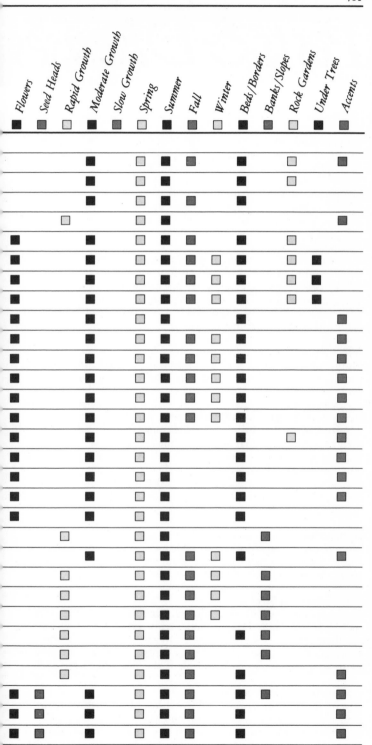

Pests & Diseases

Because plant pests and diseases are a fact of life for a gardener, it is helpful to become familiar with common pests and diseases in your area and to learn how to control them.

Symptoms of Plant Problems
The same general symptoms are associated with many diseases and pests, so some experience is needed to determine their causes.

Diseases
Both fungi and bacteria are responsible for a variety of diseases ranging from leafspots and wilts to root rot, but bacterial diseases usually make the affected plant tissues appear wetter than fungi do. Diseases caused by viruses and mycoplasma, often transmitted by aphids and leafhoppers, display such symptoms as mottled yellow or deformed leaves and stunted growth.

Insect Pests
Numerous insects attack plants. Sap-sucking insects—including aphids, leafhoppers, and scale insects—suck plant juices. The affected plant becomes yellow, stunted, and misshapen. Aphids and scale insects produce honeydew, a sticky substance that attracts ants and sooty mold fungus growth. Other pests with rasping-sucking mouthparts, such as thrips and spider mites, scrape plant tissue and then suck the juices that well up in the injured areas.
Leaf-chewers, namely beetles and caterpillars, consume plant leaves, whole or in part. Borers tunnel into shoots and stems, and their young larvae consume plant tissue, weakening the plant. Some insects, such as various grubs and maggots, feed on roots, weakening or killing the plant.

Nematodes
Microscopic roundworms called nematodes attack roots and cause stunting and poor plant growth. Some nematodes produce galls on roots and others produce them on leaves.

Environmental Stresses
Some types of plant illness result from environment-related stress, such as severe wind, drought, flooding, or extreme cold. Other problems are caused by salt toxicity, rodents, birds, nutritional deficiencies or excesses, pesticides, or damage from lawnmowers. Many of these injuries are avoidable if you take proper precautions.

Controlling Plant Problems
Always buy healthy disease- and insect-free plants that are hardy in your region, and select disease-resistant varieties when available. Check leaves and stems for dead areas or off-color and stunted tissue. Later, when you plant your ground covers, be sure to prepare the soil properly.

Routine Preventives
By cultivating the soil routinely you will expose insects and disease-causing organisms to the sun and thus lessen their chances of surviving in your garden. In the fall be sure to destroy infested or diseased plants, remove dead leaves and flowers, and clean up plant debris. Do not add diseased or infested material to the compost pile. Spray plants with water from time to time to dislodge insect pests and remove suffocating dust. Pick off the larger insects by hand. To discourage fungal leafspots and blights, always water plants in the morning and allow the leaves to dry off before nightfall. For the same reason, provide adequate air circulation around leaves and stems by spacing plants properly.

Weeds provide a home for insects and diseases, so pull them up or use herbicides. But do not apply herbicides, including "weed-and-feed" lawn preparations, too close to plantings. Herbicide injury may cause elongated, straplike, or downward-cupping leaves. Spray weed-killers when there is little air movement, but not on a very hot, dry day.

Insecticides and Fungicides
To protect plant tissue from injury due to insects and diseases, a number of insecticides and fungicides are available. However, few products control diseases due to bacteria, viruses, and mycoplasma. Pesticides are usually either "protectant" or "systemic" in nature. Protectants protect uninfected foliage from insects or disease organisms, while systemics move through the plant and provide some therapeutic or eradicant action as well as protection. Botanical insecticides such as pyrethrum and rotenone have a shorter residual effect on pests, but are considered less toxic and generally safer for the user and the environment than inorganic chemical insecticides. Biological control through the use of organisms like *Bacillus thuringiensis* (a bacterium toxic to moth and butterfly larvae) is effective and safe.

Recommended pesticides may vary to some extent from region to region. Consult your local Cooperative Extension Service or plant professional regarding the appropriate material to use. Always check the pesticide label to be sure that it is registered for use on the pest and plant with which you are dealing. Follow the label concerning safety precautions, dosage, and frequency of application.

Recognizing Pests and Diseases
Learning to recognize the insects and diseases that plague garden plants is a first step toward controlling them. The chart on the following pages describes the most common pests and diseases that attack ground covers, vines, and ornamental grasses, the damage they cause, and control measures.

Garden Pest or Disease

Aphids

Botrytis Blight

Crown Gall

Lace Bugs

Leaf-feeding Beetles

Description	Damage	Controls
Tiny green, brown, or reddish, pear-shaped, soft-bodied insects in clusters on buds, shoots, and undersides of leaves.	Suck plant juices, causing stunted or deformed blooms and leaves. Some transmit plant viruses. Secretions attract ants.	Spray with malathion or rotenone. Encourage natural predators such as ladybugs.
Gray-brown spots on plant parts. Woolly fungal growth from spots. Common in humid or wet weather. Also called gray mold.	Buds fail to open and are covered with gray fungal growth. Leaves may wither or fall.	Remove and destroy infected plant parts. Improve air circulation around plants. Spray with Botran or zineb.
Soilborne bacterial disease, forming cancerlike growths on plant stems and roots.	Rounded growths on stem near soil line. May also be present on roots and occasionally on branches.	Remove and destroy infected plants. Buy only healthy, certified disease-free plants. Plant in uninfested soil.
Numerous small, flat, square insects with transparent wings. Feed on undersides of leaves.	Infested leaves turn lighter in color, then may curl, turn brown, and drop.	Spray with malathion.
Hard-shelled, oval to oblong insects on leaves, stems, and flowers.	Chew plant parts, leaving holes. Larvae of some feed on roots.	Handpick and destroy. Spray with malathion, rotenone, or pyrethrum.

Leaf-feeding Caterpillars

Leafhoppers

Leafspots and Blights, Bacterial

Leafspots, Fungal

Nematodes

Description	Damage	Controls
Soft-bodied, wormlike crawling insects with several pairs of legs. May be smooth, hairy, or spiny. Adults are moths or butterflies.	Consume part or all of leaves. Flowers and shoots may also be eaten.	Handpick and destroy. Spray with *Bacillus thuringiensis*, pyrethrum, or malathion.
Small, greenish, wedge-shaped, soft-bodied insects on undersides of leaves. Quickly hop when disturbed.	Suck plant juices, causing discolored leaves and plants. Some transmit plant virus and mycoplasma diseases.	Spray with malathion or dust plants with diatomaceous earth.
Dark, water-soaked areas on leaves and stems.	Leaves covered with watery spots, which may merge into larger areas. Lesions may spread to stem.	Destroy severely affected plants. Avoid wetting foliage or working with wet plants.
Spots on leaves caused by fungi encouraged by humid or wet weather.	Tan, brown, or black spots on leaves. If serious, leaves may drop from plant.	Increase air circulation around plants. Remove badly diseased leaves. Spray with zineb or benomyl if serious.
Microscopic roundworms, usually associated with roots. Cause various diseases.	Stunted, off-color plants that do not respond to water or fertilizer. Minute galls may be present on roots.	Remove and destroy badly affected plants. Nematocides are available for use around valuable plants.

Garden Pest or Disease

Plant Bugs

Powdery Mildew

**Root-feeding
Larvae**

Root Rot

Scale

Description	Damage	Controls
Oblong, flattened, greenish-yellow insects, ¼–⅓ inch long. Some with black stripes. Wings held flat over abdomen.	Suck plant juices, causing spots on leaves. Some deform roots and shoots.	Spray with malathion or rotenone.
White, powdery fungal disease on aerial plant parts.	Reddish spots and powdery fungal growth. Leaves may be distorted and drop. Stems, buds, and flowers are also affected.	Remove badly infected leaves. Increase air circulation. Spray with Karathane, benomyl, or sulfur.
Small whitish grubs that feed on plant roots.	Injure roots, causing stunted, sickly, off-color plants.	Control adult leaf-feeding beetles.
Usually soilborne fungal or bacterial disease, often encouraged by waterlogged soil.	Wilted, off-color plants. Roots dark and dry or mushy, rather than firm and white.	Remove and destroy infected plants. Do not plant similar plants in the area. Improve soil drainage.
Small, waxy, soft or hard-bodied stationary insects on shoots and leaves. May be red, white, brown, black, or gray.	Suck plant juices, causing stunted, off-color plants. May cover large portion of stem.	Spray with malathion or carbaryl when crawlers are present, or use a dormant oil spray in early spring before growth begins.

Garden Pest or Disease

Slugs

 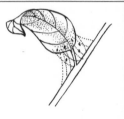

Spider Mites

Thrips

Viruses

Wilts

Description	Damage	Controls
Gray, slimy, soft-bodied mollusks without a hard outer shell. Leave slime trails on leaves; found in damp places.	Feed at night, rasping holes in leaves.	Trap slugs using stale beer in pie pans. Eliminate trash and hiding places around garden. Use bait, but keep children and pets away from it.
Tiny golden, red, or brown arachnids on undersides of leaves. Profuse fine webs seen with heavy infestations.	Scrape leaves and suck plant juices. Leaves become pale and dry. Plant may be stunted.	Spray leaves with water. Use a miticide on undersides of leaves.
Very small, slender, brown, yellow, or black insects with narrow fringed wings. Rasping-sucking mouthparts.	Scrape and suck plant tissue. Cause browning, white flecking, and gumminess. Sometimes deform flowers, buds, and leaves.	Remove infested flowers and buds. Spray with malathion, or dust with sulfur or diatomaceous earth.
Various diseases, including mosaics, that cause off-color, stunted plants. May be transmitted by aphids.	Crinkled, mottled, deformed leaves, stunted plants, poor growth.	Remove and destroy infected plants. Control the insect vector (aphids) if present. Buy only healthy plants.
Soilborne fungal diseases that cause wilting, stunting, and eventual death of plants.	Leaves turn yellow and entire plant may wilt and die. Roots may rot.	Remove infected plants. Use disease-resistant varieties.

Glossary

Acid soil
Soil with a pH value of 6.0 or lower.

Acute
Pointed.

Adpressed
Flatly pressed back.

Adventitious
Refers to roots produced on the climbing stems of some vines.

Alkaline soil
Soil with a pH value of more than 7.0.

Alternate
Arranged singly along a twig or shoot, and not in whorls or opposite pairs.

Annual
A plant whose entire life span, from sprouting to flowering and producing seeds, is encompassed in a single growing season.

Anther
The terminal part of a stamen, containing pollen in 1 or more pollen sacs.

Aril
The outer covering of a seed, sometimes pulpy.

Awn
A bristlelike appendage, especially on grasses.

Axil
The angle formed by a leafstalk and the stem from which it grows.

Axis
The central stalk of a compound leaf or flower cluster; also the main stem of a plant.

Bark
The outer covering of the trunk and branches of a tree, usually corky, papery, or leathery.

Basal leaf
A leaf at the base of a stem.

Biennial
A plant whose life span extends to 2 growing seasons, sprouting in the first growing season and then flowering, producing seed, and dying in the second.

Bisexual flower
A flower with both stamens and pistils present.

Blade
The broad, flat part of a leaf.

Bract
A modified and often scalelike leaf, usually located at the base of a flower, a fruit, or a cluster of flowers or fruits.

Bristle
A stiff, short hair on a stem or leaf.

Bud
A young and undeveloped leaf, flower, or shoot.

Bulb
A short underground stem, the swollen portion consisting mostly of fleshy, food-storing scale leaves.

Bulbil
A small bulblike structure, usually borne among the flowers or in the axil of a leaf, but never at ground level like a true bulb.

Bulblet
A small bulb produced at the periphery of a larger bulb.

Calyx
Collectively, the sepals of a flower.

Clasping
Surrounding or partly surrounding the stem, as in the base of the leaves of certain plants.

Clone
A group of plants all originating by vegetative propagation from a single plant, and therefore genetically identical to it and to one another.

Compound
Similar parts aggregated into a whole, as in a compound leaf, composed of 2 or more leaflets.

Corolla
Collectively, the petals of a flower.

Corymb
A flower cluster with a flat top, in which the individual pedicels emerge from the axis at different points, rather than at the same point as in an umbel, and blooming from the edges toward the center.

Creeping
Prostrate or trailing over the ground or over other plants.

Cross-pollination
The transfer of pollen from the flower of one plant to the pistil of another plant.

Crown
That part of a plant between the roots and the stem, usually at soil level.

Culm
A stem, especially of grasses.

Cultivar
An unvarying plant variety maintained by vegetative propagation rather than from seed.

Cutting
A piece of plant without roots; set in a rooting medium, it develops roots, and is then potted as a new plant.

Cyme
A branching flower cluster that blooms from the center toward the edges, and in which the tip of the axis always bears a flower.

Deciduous
Dropping its leaves; not evergreen.

Dioecious
Unisexual, the male and female parts in separate plants.

Dissected leaf
A deeply cut leaf, the clefts not reaching the midrib; same as a divided leaf.

Division
Propagation of a plant by separating it into 2 or more pieces, each of which has at least 1 bud and some roots.

Double-flowered
Having more than the usual number of petals, usually arranged in extra rows.

Drooping
Pendant or hanging, as in the branches and shoots of a weeping willow.

Escape
An exotic plant that has spread from cultivation and grows successfully in the wild.

Evergreen
Retaining green leaves on 1 year's growth until after the new leaves for the subsequent year have been formed.

Fertile
Bearing both stamens and pistils, and therefore able to produce seed.

Floret
One of many small flowers in a dense flower cluster, especially in the flowerheads of the daisy family.

Fruit
The fully developed ovary of a flower, containing 1 or more seeds.

Genus
A group of closely related species; plural, genera.

Germinate
To sprout (applied to seeds).

Glaucous
Covered with a waxy bloom or fine, pale powder that rubs off easily.

Half-ripened
Current year's wood from a plant still in active growth, not too soft or too hard.

Hardwood cutting
A cutting taken from a dormant plant after it has finished its yearly growth.

Heel
The base of a plant cutting or tuber used for propagation, often with some of the old stock attached.

Herbaceous perennial
A plant whose stems die back to ground level each fall, but sends out new shoots and flowers for several successive years.

Horticulture
The cultivation of plants for ornament or food.

Hose-in-hose
A tubular flower that appears to have a second flower growing from its center.

Humus
Partly or wholly decomposed vegetable matter, an important constituent of garden soil.

Hybrid
The offspring of 2 parent plants that belong to different species, subspecies, genera, or clones.

Inflorescence
A flower cluster.

Internode
A section of a stem between 2 adjacent nodes.

Invasive
Aggressively spreading from the original site of planting.

Irregular flower
A flower with petals that are not uniform in size or shape; such flowers are generally bilaterally symmetrical.

Lanceolate
Shaped like a lance; several times longer than wide, pointed at the tip and broadest near the base.

Lateral bud
A bud borne in the axil of a leaf or branch; not terminal.

Layering
A method of propagation in which a stem is induced to send out roots by surrounding it with soil.

Leaflet
One of the subdivisions of a compound leaf.

Leaf margin
The edge of a leaf.

Leaf sheath
The part of a leaf that wraps around the stem.

Loam
A humus-rich soil containing up to 25 percent clay, up to 50 percent silt, and less than 50 percent sand.

Lobe
A segment of a cleft leaf or petal.

Lobed leaf
A leaf whose margin is shallowly divided.

Midrib
The primary rib or midvein of a leaf or leaflet.

Mulch
A protective covering spread over the soil around the base of plants to retard evaporation, control temperature, or suppress weeds.

Naturalized
Established as a part of the flora in an area other than the place of origin. Also, of a planting, tended in such a way as to produce the appearance of spontaneous or "wild" growth.

Neutral soil
Soil that is neither acid nor alkaline, having a pH value of 7.0.

Node
The place on the stem where leaves or branches are attached.

Offset
A short, lateral shoot arising near the base of a plant, readily producing new roots, and useful in propagation.

Opposite
Arranged along a twig or shoot in pairs, with 1 on each side.

Ovary
The swollen base of a pistil, within which seeds develop.

Ovate
Oval, with the broader end at the base.

Palmate
Having veins or leaflets arranged like the fingers on a hand, arising from a single point. See also Pinnate.

Panicle
An open flower cluster, blooming from bottom to top, and never terminating in a flower.

Peat moss
Partly decomposed moss, rich in nutrients and with a high water retention, used as a component of garden soil.

Pedicel
The stalk of an individual flower.

Perennial
A plant whose life span extends over several growing seasons and that produces seeds in several growing seasons, rather than only 1.

Petal
One of a series of flower parts lying within the sepals and outside the stamens and pistils; often large and brightly colored.

Petiole
The stalk of a leaf.

pH
A symbol for the hydrogen ion content of the soil, and thus a means of expressing the acidity or alkalinity of the soil.

Pinnate
With leaflets arranged in 2 rows along an axis; pinnately compound.

Pistil
The female reproductive organ of a flower.

Pollen
Minute grains containing the male germ cells and produced by the stamens.

Pollinate
To transfer pollen from the anther to the stigma.

Polygamous
Bearing male and female flowers on the same plant.

Propagate
To produce new plants, either by vegetative means involving the rooting of pieces of a plant, or by sowing seeds.

Prostrate
Lying on the ground; creeping.

Raceme
A long flower cluster on which individual flowers each bloom on small stalks from a common, large, central stalk.

Ray flower
A flower at the edge of a flowerhead of the daisy family, usually bearing a conspicuous, straplike ray.

Regular flower
With petals and sepals arranged around the center, like the spokes of a wheel; always radially symmetrical.

Rhizome
A horizontal stem at or just below the surface of the ground, distinguished from a root by the presence of nodes, and often enlarged by food storage.

Rootstock
The swollen, more or less elongate stem of a perennial herb; a rhizome.

Rosette
A crowded cluster of leaves; usually basal, circular, and at ground level.

Runner
A prostrate shoot, rooting at its nodes.

Scape
A flower-stalk arising directly from the ground, without leaves.

Seed
A fertilized, ripened ovule, naked in conifers but covered with a protective coating and contained in a fruit in all other garden plants.

Self-branching
With shoots arising from every node.

Sepal
One of the outermost series of flower parts, arranged in a ring outside the petals, and usually green and leaflike.

Serrate
Having sharp teeth on the margin, pointing forward.

Sheathing base
A tubular covering around the base of a stem or around the lower part of an internode above the node; found in grasses.

Simple leaf
A leaf with an undivided blade; not compound or composed of leaflets.

Softwood
Green wood at an intermediate growth stage.

Solitary
Borne singly or alone; not in clusters.

Species
A population of plants or animals whose members are potentially able to breed with each other, and that is reproductively isolated from other populations.

Spike
An elongated flower cluster; individual flowers lack stalks.

Spine
A strong, sharp, usually woody projection from the stem or branches of a plant.

Stamen
The male reproductive organ of a flower.

Sterile
Lacking stamens or pistils, and therefore unable to produce seeds.

Stipule
A small leaflike appendage at the base of some petioles.

Stolon
A horizontal stem, just above or beneath the soil, from the tip of which a new plant arises; a runner.

Stratify
To keep seeds under cool, dark, moist conditions to encourage them to break dormancy and germinate after treatment.

Subshrub
A partly woody plant.

Subspecies
A naturally occurring geographical variant of a species.

Succulent
A plant with thick, fleshy leaves or stems that contain abundant water-storage tissue. Cacti and stonecrops are examples.

Taproot
The main, central root of a plant.

Tendril
A thin, twisting extension by which a plant grasps an object and clings for support; a modified stem, stipule, or leaf.

Terminal
Borne at the tip of a stem or shoot, rather than in the axil.

Throat
The opening between the bases of the corolla lobes of a flower, leading into the corolla tube.

Toothed
Having the margin shallowly divided into small, toothlike segments.

Tuber
A swollen, mostly underground stem that bears buds and serves as a storage site for food.

Umbel
A flower cluster in which the individual flower-stalks grow from the same point, like the ribs of an umbrella.

Unisexual flower
A flower bearing only stamens or pistils and not both.

Variegated
Marked, striped, or blotched with some color other than green.

Variety
A population of plants that differ consistently from the typical form of the species, occurring naturally in a geographical area. Also applied, incorrectly but popularly, to forms produced in cultivation.

Vegetative propagation
Propagation by means other than seed.

Whorl
A group of 3 or more leaves or shoots that emerge from a stem at a single node.

Wing
A thin, flat extension found at the margins of a seed or leafstalk or along the stem.

Photo Credits

The letter after each page number refers to the position of the color plates. A represents the picture at the top and B the picture at the bottom. Some are also in the Visual Key.

Judy Glattstein
An instructor at the New York Botanical and Brooklyn Botanic gardens.
99B, 237B

Pamela Harper
Horticultural writer, photographer, and lecturer, Pamela Harper has an extensive library of plant and garden slides.
73B, 78B, 79B, 80B, 83A, 85A, 88A, 88B, 89B, 90B, 91A, 93A, 93B, 94A, 94B, 96B, 97A, 97B, 100A, 100B, 101A, 101B, 103B, 105A, 106A, 107A, 109B, 110A, 111B, 116B, 118A, 119B, 121A, 121B, 122A, 123A, 123B, 124A, 125B, 126A, 128A, 129B, 133A, 133B, 134A, 135A, 135B, 137A, 142A, 142B, 143A, 147B, 154A, 155A, 157B, 159A, 159B, 160A, 161A, 162B, 163A, 163B, 164A, 164B, 165A, 165B, 167A, 169B, 170A, 170B, 171B, 172B, 177A, 178A, 178B, 179A, 179B, 180A, 182B, 184A, 184B, 187A, 187B, 189B, 191A, 191B, 192A, 195A, 196B, 197B, 198A, 199A, 200B, 201A, 202A, 202B, 203A, 204A, 204B, 205A, 206A, 208A, 209A, 212A, 213A, 214B, 215A, 216A, 217A, 220A, 223A, 223B, 224A, 224B, 225B, 226B, 227A, 227B, 228A, 228B, 229A, 230B, 232A, 233A, 233B, 234B, 235A, 236A, 237A, 238B, 239B, 240B, 242A, 243A, 243B, 244A, 244B, 245A, 245B, 247A, 247B, 248A, 250B, 251B, 252B, 258B, 263B, 265B, 267B, 270A, 270B, 272B, 273B, 275A, 276B, 277A, 278B, 283A, 286A

Walter H. Hodge
Author of *The Audubon Society Book of Wildflowers,* Walter Hodge has photographed plants and animals all over the world.
Cover: *Hosta* cultivar 'Jadette'.
89A, 181B, 222B, 281A, 281B, 282A, 286B, 287B

Helen Kittinger
Conservationist, lecturer, and nature photographer.
105B

John A. Lynch
A photographer specializing in gardening and wildflowers.
98B, 114B, 162A, 218A

Robert E. Lyons/PHOTO NATS
Professor of horticulture and nature photographer in Virginia.
72A, 102B, 126B, 138B, 249B

Robert F. McDuffie/PHOTO NATS
A landscape architect and professor in Virginia.
263A

Frederick McGourty
General consultant for this guide, garden writer, and nursery owner.
74A, 75A, 81B, 86B, 92B, 112B, 114A, 120A, 124B, 148A, 166B, 260A, 264A, 264B

Ornamental Horticulture Dept., Calif. Polytechnic State Univ.
285A

Richard Simon
A nature photographer working in Maryland.
115B, 127A, 155B, 257B, 259A, 268B, 269A, 278A, 279A, 282B, 284A, 284B

John J. Smith
A nature photographer published in Audubon Society guides.
95A

Joy Spurr
Writer, photographer, and owner of a photographic agency.
76B, 95B, 96A, 99A, 113B, 122B, 171A, 173A, 188A, 222A, 235B, 240A, 250A

Steven Still
Major contributor to two Taylor's guides, Steven Still is a professor of horticulture, and author of numerous articles.
70, 72B, 76A, 84A, 84B, 85B, 87B, 108B, 110B, 111A, 113A, 116A, 118B, 120B, 129A, 130A, 130B, 132A, 132B, 134A, 136A, 140B, 141B, 143B, 146A, 147A, 151B, 152B, 156A, 158A, 158B, 161B, 169A, 173B, 180B, 183B, 185A, 186A, 186B, 190B, 194A, 194B, 195B, 197A, 198B, 200A, 203B, 207A, 209B, 215B, 217B, 219A, 220B, 221A, 221B, 232B, 242B, 246A, 251A, 256A, 256B, 257A, 258A, 260B, 261B, 262A, 262B, 265A, 266B, 268A, 273A, 274B, 275B, 276A

David H. Stone/PHOTO NATS
A freelance nature and life science photographer.
149A, 149B, 160B

George Taloumis
Garden columnist for the *Boston Globe* and *Flower and Garden*.
98A, 104A, 112A, 125A, 144, 190A, 236B, 267A, 271B

Index

Numbers in boldface refer to pages on which color plates appear.

Chanticleer Staff

Publisher: Paul Steiner
Editor-in-Chief: Gudrun Buettner
Executive Editor: Susan Costello
Managing Editor: Jane Opper
Project Editor: Marian Appellof
Associate Editor: David Allen
Assistant Editor: Leslie Ann Marchal
Production: Helga Lose, Gina Stead
Art Director: Carol Nehring
Art Associate: Ayn Svoboda
Art Assistant: Cheryl Miller
Picture Library: Edward Douglas
Natural History Editor: John Farrand, Jr.
Drawings: Robin A. Jess, Sarah Pletts,
Dolores R. Santoliquido, Alan D. Singer,
Mary Jane Spring
Zone Map: Paul Singer

Design: Massimo Vignelli